The WITCH'S HOME

About the Author

Patti Wigington has been practicing as a Pagan and witch since 1987. She is the founder and high priestess of a local coven, works as an educator in the witchcraft community, blogs about magical things, and has a low-key obsession with genealogical research. In addition to a full-time job in the corporate world, Patti served as editor of the Paganism & Wicca site at LearnReligions, previously About.com, from 2007–2020. She is the author of a number of books on magical practice and serves as a board member for the Central Ohio Pagan Alliance. Patti has a BA in history from Ohio University as well as a graduate certificate in management and leadership and lives in a magical cottage in the forest with a large dog, a pair of fat, lazy cats, and an absurd collection of tarot decks. She spends her rare bits of free time putzing around in her garden, hiking local trails, dying her hair interesting colors, and performing random acts of recipe experimentation. For more on Patti and her work, please visit www.pattiwigington.com.

The WITCH'S HOME

PRACTICAL MAGIC
for Every Room

PATTI WIGINGTON

LLEWELLYN
WOODBURY, MINNESOTA

FIRST EDITION
First Printing, 2025

Book design by Christine Ha
Cover design by Kevin R. Brown

Llewellyn Publications is a registered trademark of Llewellyn Worldwide Ltd.

Library of Congress Cataloging-in-Publication Data (Pending)
ISBN: 978-0-7387-7835-8

Llewellyn Publications
A Division of Llewellyn Worldwide Ltd.
2143 Wooddale Drive
Woodbury, MN 55125-2989
www.llewellyn.com

Printed in the United States of America

Other Books by Patti Wigington

Daily Spellbook for the Good Witch

Wicca Practical Magic

The Daily Spell Journal

Herb Magic

Badass Ancestors

Witchcraft for Healing

Wicca Journal for Beginners

Candle Magic Journal and Handbook

The Witch's Complete Guide to Tarot

Libra Witch (coauthor)

Disclaimer

This book contains discussions and instructions relating to practices including the use of essential oils, incense burning, candles, various ritual items, and sex magic. The information provided herein should not be taken as medical, legal, or professional advice. The use of essential oils and incense may cause allergic reactions or be harmful if used improperly, and it is recommended to consult with a health care provider. Practices such as sex magic are intended for consenting adults and should be approached with caution and responsibility. Always ensure safety and informed consent in all practices, and consult health care professionals as needed.

Acknowledgments

No book is completed in a vacuum—it's a project that is shaped and influenced by so many people, many of whom have no idea how much they've inspired and motivated me. *The Witch's Home* wouldn't exist if it weren't for all the people who encouraged me to turn a simple ninety-minute workshop into an entire manuscript. A huge shout-out to my COPA army: Seamus and Michael from the Magical Druid, Mambo Liz of Big Liz Conjure, Heather from Violet Flame Gifts, Tiffany at WitchLab, and my dear friend, soul sister, and co-priestess LilyBeth. Additional gratitude goes to my friends in Dayton, who first appreciated this workshop so many years ago: Tam and Daile, Lisa J., and Mellissa of Familiar Books. Not only that, my entire witchy community has been invaluable to me for support, kind words, and ideas: Amy Blackthorn, Raina Starr, Debra Burris, Byron Ballard, Jason Mankey, Ivo Dominguez, Jr., Lady Brigid Eldar, and so many others. Finally, this book would never have happened if it weren't for the patience and enthusiasm of Elysia Gallo, my acquiring editor at Llewellyn, who appreciates my jokes, shares my love for genealogical lore, and always tolerates my out-of-the-blue messages saying, *Hey, so, I have this idea…*

CONTENTS

SPELLS, RITUALS, AND MAGICAL PRACTICES

INTRODUCTION

This book's origin story, which is really a pretty simple one, began many years ago when I was asked to host a workshop at a local event. What started out as me throwing a bunch of random items into a tote bag and asking attendees, *What would you do with this?* soon evolved into one of my most popular workshops. It's a session I call Household Magic, and it focuses on using mundane items around your home to do magical stuff. It's always a hit, and for ages, people have been telling me I needed to write a book about the subject. It's a fun class, half stand-up comedy and half hands-on activity, in which I invite participants to put on their witchy thinking caps. Even after presenting it dozens of times, I am continually in awe of some of the downright clever and creative ideas people come up with when they're handed a roll of duct tape, a Hot Wheels car, or a Wonder Woman holiday ornament.

Who Is *The Witch's Home* For?

This book's goal is to encourage any practitioner to think magically and mindfully—*witchfully*, if you will—about the metaphysical value of their home, the ways they can incorporate the natural energies of the space they occupy into the witchcraft they practice, and spellwork that's appropriate for any room in their home. Whether

1

you're a newbie witch or a seasoned veteran, if you want to enhance your home-based practice and drive it deeper, this book is for you. Keep in mind, *The Witch's Home* isn't intended to be a Witchcraft 101 book—there are plenty of those out there, a lot of which are really good, so I'm not going to reinvent the wheel here.

And remember—spirituality is rarely a one-size-fits-all sort of thing. While organized religion may be like a full-service sit-down restaurant, in which a server brings you a plate and you eat what's on it, spirituality is more like going to a buffet. You get to pick out the things that look interesting, take an extra helping of the stuff you really like, and disregard the dishes that have no appeal for you whatsoever. You can choose what you sample—and no one is going to bring it to you; you've got to select it for yourself.

While it's important not to use closed practices from traditions you're not involved in, or to appropriate things that don't belong to you, a lot of folk magic is designed for everyone, and *how* you practice it is uniquely personal. As a result, what you won't find in this book is me gatekeeping your practice. I have no interest in doing that because it's just not my jam—and it's something that pops up a lot in the witchcraft community, as people tell each other, *Real witches do this thing,* or *A true witch would never do that thing.* If someone is telling you your magic isn't valid because you don't own All the Tools, or that you're not serious about your practice because you have a poster from *The Craft* on your bedroom wall, or a Real Witch would *never* use a crystal they got in that spell kit from Sephora that somehow ended up at the thrift store … well, that's nonsense, and you don't need to stand for it.

Your practice is yours, and it's as unique and magical as you want it to be. Are you practicing witchcraft? Then as far as I'm concerned, you get to call yourself a witch. Are you thinking about learning to practice but just haven't gotten started yet? Great—then you're an aspiring witch. Either way, I'm excited you're here to join me as we work our way through your home.

How Did We Get Here, Anyway?

The roots of *The Witch's Home* go far deeper than just, *Hey, let's do magic with some stuff we already have*. In fact, the foundation is nigh on thirty-something years old, from days gone by, when I was a broke-ass witch. I was a newbie practitioner who first discovered magic around 1987 or thereabouts, and like many of my peers, I eventually struck out on my own. Technically, when I moved out of my parents' home, I was an adult … but I use the term very loosely because I worked a series of low-paying jobs, had a few sketchy roommates in order to afford rent, and basically lived paycheck to paycheck in dodgy places that were not exactly what I'd consider conducive to magical practice.

I didn't like it. And when I found myself, at age twenty-five, a recently separated single mom to a toddler, I liked it even less. Then at one point—and it truly was a *super* low point, after a whole lot of time on the Struggle Bus—I had an epiphany. Following a meditative encounter with the deity who would eventually become my patron goddess, I realized something incredibly valuable. I finally understood that my home—wherever it was, an apartment, a house, or crashing on a friend's couch one month when I was really strapped—had the potential to be a magical and sacred place.

I started thinking about it from a historian's perspective—I'm a history major, so I like to get my geek on when I read about ancient cultures. How did our ancestors work magic in their homes? Think about this for just a moment: The idea of going down to the local witchy shop to participate in a ritual on a Saturday afternoon—or, my goodness, attending one of the hundreds of Pagan Pride events that take place each year—is a *really* new one in the grand scheme of things. When we look at the timeline of humanity, practicing outside our house is a very new and tiny blip on the radar.

Not only that, our home is where we spend a *lot* of our time. Sure, many of us have to leave and go to work or school for a third of our day—unless you're fortunate enough to work from home— but at the end of it, we return. We come back to the place where we, hopefully, feel safe and spiritual and balanced. So that home— whatever it might consist of—needs to be a magical space that's conducive to spiritual growth.

Our ancestors—and I don't mean specifically our genetic ancestors, but simply the people who came before us and practiced magical spirituality—worked with what they had available to them. They weren't stocking up on spices at Whole Foods, but they'd have used herbs grown in their garden or foraged from the nearby woods—and the plants collected by a practitioner in a South American rainforest would have been very different than those harvested in a meadow in France or in a garden in Nigeria. They didn't shop at IKEA—but they might have made their small cottage magical by painting the walls a certain color or inscribing a protective sigil on the door in an inconspicuous spot. They upcycled old pieces of clothing, metal, and wood to create magical tools and make their space holy. Because there weren't a lot of other options.

Over the years, I've spent plenty of time cultivating my home into a magical and sacred space. I sometimes catch grief from people in the magical community because I freely admit that it's rare for me to cast a circle when doing spellwork in my home. Crazy, right?

Hear me out. If the point of casting a circle is to keep the good stuff in and the bad stuff out … well, why wouldn't I want my house to be like that *all the time?* I keep my home designated as sacred space every single day, not just when I'm doing spellwork. I go outside and refresh the boundary about once a month, but for the most part, my home exists inside a giant metaphysical safety bubble. While it may occasionally weird out the neighbors, it also serves a very valuable purpose. It creates a place where I am always safe and at peace, spiritually, emotionally, mentally, and physically.

And that makes it especially favorable for magic.

I've spent a lot of time making and creating this space, from the colors of my walls to the altar space in my living room. I've chosen magical artwork to hang in my office over the desk where I not only work a full-time job but also have written nearly a dozen books on modern witchcraft practice. My seasonal decorations are deliberately chosen for their magical purposes, and my kitchen is warm and homey, smelling of spices and welcoming to all who enter it. My outdoor space exists in a similar way—I have magical herbs growing in the garden each year, accompanied by festive flags with magical symbols, rocks I've painted and arranged just so … well, you get the idea. One of my friends calls me "a Pagan Martha Stewart," and she's not far off, although I have zero felony convictions and don't hang out with Snoop.

What You Can Expect in *The Witch's Home*

We'll look at many of the basics of home-based witchcraft; specifically, we're going to review what actually makes a space a home (plot twist: you don't have to live in a *house*, because this book is for *everyone*, no matter where they may live). We'll look at the folklore of hearth and home magic around the world (history major here, remember?) as well as how to create a sacred space you can use on a day-to-day basis. I'll share examples of protective spells, cleansing rituals, home blessings, and ways you can invite household guardians into your life and work with them in a way that's mutually beneficial. We'll also spend a little bit of time on some mundane practices you can use to keep your sacred space tidy, including some decluttering tips, and I'll share with you one of my favorite projects: the household grimoire.

From there, we'll dive into a crash course on maintaining a magical home. We'll discuss the magic of entryways, such as doors and windows, and then we'll go room by room through your home and talk about ways to make each space magical. If you don't have every room I've included in this book, that's okay—not everyone has a garage or a yard or an attic and so on. But I'd still encourage you to read those sections anyway—you might find a valuable nugget in there that can be applied to some other space you *do* have in your home. We'll spend some time looking at ways you can create sacred space in your home if you live in a smaller dwelling, like an apartment or dorm room. Finally, we'll look at ideas on where to source your stuff in a way that's affordable, accessible, and practical. Throughout the course of this book, you'll learn ways to use some of the simplest, most inexpensive things in each room of your home as you practice, with spells and rituals for love and healing, prosperity and protection, banishing and binding, and even divination.

A quick note on the use of candles, incense, and oils, which you'll see referenced in many of the pages to come. Please be sure to follow common sense safety procedures, even if they're not explicitly spelled out for you. Candles should always be placed on a safe surface—a fireproof bowl or cauldron, a dish of sand, or a designated candleholder—and you should never leave a burning candle unattended. Additionally, don't light candles near flammable items, such as next to window drapery, on a pile of paper, or close to other things that can catch fire. Incense should always be placed in a safe burner. If you use the essential oils mentioned in this book, be sure to dilute them before applying directly to your skin and perform a patch test first, as many of them can cause irritation or other reactions.

Safety tips aside, it's my hope that by the time you get to the end of *The Witch's Home*, you'll see the place where you live in a whole new light and have an entirely new mindset about how to practice. You'll be able to make your magic in your living room, bedroom, and even the bathroom with low-cost, affordable tools and components while still being an effective hands-on practitioner. Just in case you need additional ideas, though, the back section contains an appendix with some of my favorite magical household correspondences that I've curated over the years, the symbolism they can hold, and ways to incorporate them into magic. Additionally, you'll find a comprehensive bibliography of source material and recommended reading so you can pursue your practice even further.

Are you ready to get started? Good. Let's go make your home a magical place.

Chapter 1
BEFORE WE STEP INSIDE ...

I know, I know—you're all ready to read about making your home magical, and here I am, stopping you before you even set foot in the door. But the place we live is more than just some walls and a roof. It's the entirety of the space we inhabit—and that can be anything from a great big yard or a medium-sized balcony to a simple front step. Regardless of how much outdoor access you have, that area can be a treasure trove of magical activity surrounding your living space. Now, you might not have a yard of your own—not everyone does— but that doesn't mean you can't take advantage of the offerings nature has in store for you. In fact, anyone who practices magical living can benefit from time spent outside, so let's take a little time to look at that part of our environment.

The natural world provides a direct link to elemental energies— earth, air, fire, and water—which are so important to many magical practices. Immersing yourself in natural settings can help you build a deeper connection with these elements, facilitating magical workings aligned with these forces. Nature can also offer a grounding effect, helping you center yourself and reconnect with your inner sense of balance. Studies have shown that spending twenty to thirty minutes a day surrounded by the natural elements can stabilize emotions, reduce stress, and bring a sense of tranquility.[1] Being in nature—feeling the breeze on your skin, touching a plant, smelling the fragrance of the environment around you—can encourage mindfulness, enabling you to attune yourself to the spiritual energies present in your surroundings.

The natural world can also inspire creativity! Observing natural patterns, colors, and cycles can influence spellcraft, divination, or artistic expressions within magical workings. Aligning with the cycles of nature—the phases of the moon, the ever-changing seasons, or the flow of tides—will help you synchronize your magical practice with the natural world to enhance the potency of your workings. Whether you're wandering around in a remote forest, sitting on a sunny beach, or simply strolling around your city's park system, try to spend time outside regularly if you can.

Magical Decorating Outside Your Home

Decorating isn't just for indoors. There are a lot of ways you can take advantage of specialized décor to make magic outside your home. Use statues of garden gnomes, fairies, or even animal companions as guardians and protectors, or as representatives of nature spirits. Placing statues of specific deities aligns the space with their energies; leave offerings or prayers beside them to seek guidance or blessings.

Positioning specific crystals in patterns or grids in your yard, or on an outdoor balcony or step, can amplify your magical intentions. Arrange them in your garden—or in container pots—to create grids for protection, healing, or manifestation. Stones or crystals can also represent directional elements or specific energies, mark boundaries, or create sacred circles for outdoor rituals or ceremonies. I keep

....
1. Hunter, Gillespie, and Yu-Pu Chen, "Urban Nature Experiences Reduce Stress."

hematite stones at each of the four corners of my property, pushed into the soil so I don't hit them with my weed eater, as a protective measure.

Use a birdbath or fountain for offerings to nature spirits or as a place for energy cleansing. Be cautious not to add oils or herbs to the water, though—you don't want to poison your local wildlife. If you're able to put a fountain or pond fixture in place, the sound of running water can create a great ambiance for meditation or ritual work. Tabletop fountains are great for this.

Place solar lights or lanterns strategically around your outdoor space; they can guide and protect energy paths or mark specific ritual spaces for use during nighttime workings. One of my favorite things to do is hide rocks painted with runes and sigils around the yard to amplify my workings. You might also consider painting or sewing outdoor flags with your magical symbols on them. Don't forget about seasonal décor—decorating your outdoor space with seasonal symbols or ornaments can help bring your property to life at sabbats or other celebrations, marking transitions and inviting corresponding energies.

Finally, think about the value of upcycling. If you've got something in your home that is no longer needed or used—or if it's broken and unusable—ask yourself if there's a way you can incorporate it into magical outdoor décor. I've used bits of pottery and china, pieces of metal, and other items that were destined for the landfill, and instead I tidied them up with a fresh coat of paint and incorporated them into my outdoor area.

Setting Up Your Outdoor Altar

An altar is a uniquely personal space—and we'll get into more detail on them in chapter 6—but you're not limited to only having one indoors. If you've got the space, why not set one up outside? If you've got a yard, you have an expansive canvas where you can connect with the elements and the natural world. Choose a quiet corner under the canopy of your favorite tree or beside a garden to establish your sacred space. A large stone slab, tree stump, or a sturdy table can serve as your altar's base, where you can set up symbols of the elements. Use a bowl of soil or stones for earth, a flag or wind chime to symbolize air, a small cauldron or brazier to represent fire, and a dish of water. If you're able to have a permanent altar setup outdoors, it allows for the addition of larger ritual tools, statues of deities, and space for performing your magical workings.

For those functioning with limited space, such as a small balcony or a front step, the approach to setting up an altar may need to be more compact and temporary—but it should still be meaningful. A small foldable table or even a sturdy tray can act as the altar, so it will be easy to set up and dismantle as needed. Use miniature versions of elemental representations—a tiny pot of earth, perhaps a small bell to represent air, a small candle, and a compact bowl for water. This setup not only helps to conserve on space but also ensures your altar components can be quickly moved out of the way when you need to utilize the area for everyday activities.

Simple Blessings for Your Outdoor Space

I mentioned that I keep my home and yard designated as sacred space all the time. This is a simple ritual that I do once a month, typically around the full moon, to recharge the magical energy of my property.

Start by cleaning the physical space, removing any debris, and tidying up to ensure the area is as neat as possible. Once the space is physically prepared, walk the perimeter with a cleansing herb bundle made of sage, lavender, or sweetgrass, and light it. Use the smoke to cleanse the area of negative energy and create a sacred boundary. As you walk, chant or silently set your intentions for protection, peace, and prosperity within the space. The one I use is elemental focused:

> *Elements of earth, air, fire, and water, converge to bless and protect this space. Earth, ground and nurture, provide stability and strength. Air, circulate purity and wisdom here. Fire, illuminate and energize every corner. Water, flow with life and cleanse all negativity. Together, shield this place from harm and imbue it with peace, with this blessing strong and lasting. As I will, so it shall be.*

If you don't have the time to a full blessing—or if your outdoor space is smaller and something shorter is more appropriate—try one of these simple blessing incantations.

+ *Earth beneath my feet, air that moves on high, fire burning with passion, water flowing by. Earth and water, fire and air, bless this space with love and care. I bless this space and make it sacred.*

+ *This space is holy, this space is protected, this space is filled with abundance and joy.*

+ *In this place, may each corner be a sanctuary of tranquility, shielded from harm. May prosperity flourish, bringing abundance and joy to all who enter. Envelop this place in a cloak of serenity.*

Lawn Mower Sigils

I'm kind of embarrassed to admit this, but I actually *love* mowing the grass. There's something highly therapeutic about just popping in my headphones, turning on the mower, and just mindlessly pushing it through my yard for an hour or so. I don't have to think about anything at all, other than making sure I don't run over the nuggets my dog might have left behind, and it's a great opportunity to clear my head of things that are cluttering up space in my brain.

It's also a great way to make some magic by cutting symbols or sigils into your grass as you mow. I'd recommend you sketch your sigil on paper first, considering the dimensions and intricacy that can be translated onto the lawn. I've found that simple, bold designs work best for this method, especially if you have garden beds, lawn furniture, or other structures in your yard that you'll need to work around.

Wait until the grass is at a height suitable for mowing, and start cutting the lines of the sigil into the grass with your lawn mower. Be deliberate and focused while mowing, infusing the process with your intentions for the symbol's purpose. Visualize the intended outcome of the sigil as you mow each line. Concentrate on empowering the symbol with the specific energy or intention you wish to manifest. I like to do them in the spring and summer for abundance, and then my final cut of the year, in the late fall, is focused on protection throughout the winter months.

Depending on the complexity of the sigil—as well as the length and density of your lawn—you may need to make more than one pass with the mower to carve out the design. Be patient and precise, making any necessary adjustments as you go. Once the design is mowed into the grass, activate the sigil by standing in the center, focusing your energy, and visualizing the symbol radiating its intended energy into its surroundings. You can either keep it up throughout the year with regular maintenance or let the natural growth of your yard take over.

CHALK MAGIC

Chalk can be one of the most versatile tools in any witch's home. One of my hobbies includes painting, so I always have chalk on hand—it's useful for sketching out an image before I actually brush acrylic onto a canvas—and it comes in handy over and over again.

A simple stick of chalk can serve in crafting temporary or symbolic workings due to its erasable nature. One way involves drawing a sacred circle for rituals, delineating a space for spellcasting while infusing protective symbols or intentions into the circle's boundary. You can also use it for drawing sigils, symbols, or elemental representations on various surfaces like walls, sidewalks, or altars. Charge these markings with your intention as you draw them to enhance the focus of your working. Use it to create temporary labyrinths or divination diagrams. I love using it in my driveway with a pendulum for divination.

Grab a stick of chalk to inscribe protective symbols or wards on doors, windows, or thresholds to safeguard your home from negative energies or unwanted influences. It can be used to create a temporary magical calendar or lunar phase chart on a wall or floor, aiding in planning rituals or spellwork aligned with specific astrological or lunar energies.

Drawing elemental symbols or representations in outdoor spaces, aligning them with the natural elements, allows for rituals or meditations that connect deeply with earth, air, fire, and water energies. Remember that chalk is a transient medium, so it's crucial to set clear intentions and infuse your energy into the markings—but plan on seeing them fade away with the weather and time itself. I typically design my chalk workings so that once the chalk has vanished, the spell is concluded.

The Four Elements

In many modern magical belief systems, the four classical elements of earth, air, fire, and water play significant roles in how we perform rituals, the types of spells we cast, and even the orientation and positioning of our altars or magical spaces. It's a concept that has a long history and originates all the way back in the fifth century BCE with Empedocles, a pre-Socratic Greek philosopher and a prominent figure in the development of ancient Greek philosophy.

Empedocles, who lived in what is now the island of Sicily in a city called Akragas, developed a cosmological theory that everything—including the human body—in our universe is composed of four basic elements, which he referred to as *roots*: earth, air, fire, and water. This idea laid the foundation for the understanding of matter for centuries and eventually formed an essential part of ancient Greek and later Western philosophy. As far as Empedocles was concerned, these four roots were eternal and unchanging, and all substances and phenomena—basically everything under the sun and beyond—could be explained in terms of the proportions and combinations of these elements. He believed they were governed by two opposing forces: Love, or attraction, which brought the elements together to form various objects and beings, and Strife, or repulsion, which separated them, creating division and differentiation.

For today's practitioners, these same four roots—which we now refer to as elements—are often viewed symbolically and spiritually, embracing ancient symbolism to connect with nature, the self, and the Divine, rather than in a literal or scientific sense. Typically, they are believed to represent different aspects of life, nature, and the human psyche. If you break down all the different aspects of your home—and our very existence itself—into the context of the four elements, you may find yourself focusing the energies of a particular room or outdoor space on specific magical purposes and goals.

Keep in mind, these elemental associations can vary between different traditions and individual practitioners. Modern witchcraft is a pretty diverse collection of beliefs and practices that vary across cultures and regions. That being said, each element tends to have a common set of attributes in the context of today's magical belief systems:

+ **Earth** is associated with stability, grounding, and the physical world. It represents the material realm, including the body and the environment. In rituals and spells, it's often invoked for matters related to wealth, prosperity, fertility, and the security of the home. In the home, it can be linked to the kitchen or dining area, since these spaces are where food—which sustains and nourishes the body—is prepared and consumed. Earthy energies can also be incorporated into living rooms or gardens, connecting you and everyone who lives there with the natural world.

+ **Air** represents the intellect, communication, and the realm of thought. It is associated with wisdom, knowledge, and the power of the mind. Air is also linked to travel, learning, and clarity of thought. It's often invoked for matters related to education, divination, and mental pursuits. Air can be connected to home offices, libraries, or study areas where intellectual pursuits, reading, and communication take place. Decorate the study area with books, learning materials, and symbols of knowledge. Use light, airy colors and incorporate feathers, incense, or wind chimes. Keeping the space well ventilated and clutter free also helps to enhance the airy energy.

+ **Fire** symbolizes energy, passion, transformation, and purification. It represents both destruction and creation, as it can consume and transform matter. Fire is associated with courage, willpower, and drive. It's often invoked for matters related to creativity, inspiration, and personal power. Fire energy can be incorporated into the living room, the heart of the home, where family and social interactions occur, or the bedroom, a space many people associate with the spark of passion. Fire is also suitable for ritual spaces or creative spaces where inspiration is cultivated. Use warm, vibrant colors like red, orange, or deep shades of purple. Decorate with candles, artwork depicting flames or sunsets, and symbols of motivation. A fireplace or candles can serve as a literal representation of the fire element.

+ **Water** is linked to emotions, intuition, healing, and the subconscious mind. It represents the ebb and flow of life as well as cleansing and purification. Water is often associated with love, empathy, and psychic abilities. It's invoked for matters related to emotions, relationships, healing, and spiritual insight. Water can be connected with bathrooms, bedrooms, or meditation spaces where relaxation, rest, and emotional healing are prioritized. Incorporate calming colors like blue or aqua, or use mirrors or decorative bowls filled with water to represent the water element. Aquariums or indoor water features like tabletop fountains are a great way to bring water into the space. Incorporate soft fabrics, comfortable pillows, and soothing artwork.

Gardening and Planting

Gardening is pretty significant for many of us in the magical community, offering a direct connection to nature's energies and cycles, regardless of living space limitations. Gardening itself is a magical practice—it's the ultimate act of creation, taking a small seed and tending it, nurturing it, and encouraging it to grow into something big and beautiful. You can infuse each action with intention, charging your plants with magical energies or purposes.

The care and attention we give our gardens amplifies their magical potency, transforming windowsills, empty lawns, small patches of rocky soil, or balcony edges into enchanted spaces brimming with magical potential.

Gardening offers a way for us to honor seasonal cycles and celebrate nature's rhythms in our homes. We can grow things to mark the passing of seasons, aligning our magic with natural shifts. For instance, planting specific herbs associated with the sabbats or nurturing flowers symbolizing the phases of the moon allows us to engage in hands-on nature-based spirituality. Tending a garden is more than just cultivating plants—it's also about cultivating our magical practice.

Magical Garden Layouts

If you're new to gardening—or even if you're not, and you just want to try something different—think about making a themed magical garden. I've made many over the years, and all of these are adaptable to any size at all. You can either till up a big patch in your yard, or you can do a smaller scale version in a pretty decorative container to keep near a sunny window. The possibilities are limitless, with a bit of time, love, and imagination.

Moon Phase Garden

+ **New moon:** Include plants associated with new beginnings and intentions, like jasmine, daffodil, crocus, or lavender.

+ **Full moon:** Incorporate night-blooming flowers, such as moonflower, night phlox, gardenia, or white roses.

+ **Decorations:** Place moon-shaped stepping stones, the colors silver or white, and mirrors or other reflective surfaces.

+ **Crystals:** Use moonstone, selenite, lapis, amethyst, or clear quartz.

ELEMENTAL GARDEN

+ **Earth:** Plant grounding herbs like sage, thyme, or rosemary.

+ **Air:** Include aromatic plants, such as lavender or mint for mental clarity.

+ **Fire:** Choose vibrant red or orange flowers like marigolds or sunflowers.

+ **Water:** Include water-loving plants, like water lilies or lotus, or a small dish or seashell filled with clean water.

+ **Decorations:** Represent each element with themed statues or symbols.

+ **Crystals:** Use hematite for earth, amethyst for air, carnelian for fire, and aquamarine for water.

HEALING GARDEN

+ **Medicinal herbs:** Plant herbs known for healing properties like echinacea, calendula, and chamomile.

+ **Aromatic plants:** Include lavender, lemon balm, or peppermint for relaxation and stress relief.

- **Decorations:** Place a small fountain or flowing water feature for soothing energy; add an incense burner or a quiet meditation space to sit, such as a bench or stone.
- **Crystals:** Use clear quartz, rose quartz, or amethyst for healing energies.

Prosperity Garden

- **Herbs for abundance:** Plant basil, mint, or parsley, known for attracting prosperity.
- **Flowering plants:** Include vibrant flowers like marigolds, jasmine, lilies, or daisies, symbolizing wealth and success.
- **Decorations:** Add garden gnomes, a few shiny coins, or small treasure chests to evoke prosperity.
- **Crystals:** Use citrine, green aventurine, or pyrite for abundance and prosperity.

Love Goddess Garden

You can craft a garden to honor any deity at all; this guide is simply for a goddess associated with romance.

- **Flowering plants:** Plant roses, peonies, or jasmine, as they are associated with love and beauty.
- **Herbs:** Include herbs like yarrow or vervain, which are connected to love magic and enchantment.
- **Decorations:** Display statues or symbols representing Aphrodite or other love goddesses.
- **Crystals:** Use rose quartz, rhodonite, or moonstone for love and compassion.

Protection Garden

+ **Herbs for protection:** Plant rosemary, basil, or sage, as they are known for their protective properties.

+ **Thorny plants:** Include roses or hawthorn for defense against negative energy.

+ **Decorations:** Hang wind chimes or protective symbols like pentacles.

+ **Crystals:** Use black tourmaline, obsidian, or hematite for warding off negativity.

Container Gardening

For witches residing in apartments or constrained by small spaces, container gardening can become a powerful way to engage with nature's magic. Planting herbs, flowers, or small vegetables in pots or containers allows you to cultivate your own green space, infusing it with magical intent and purpose. A container garden can even serve as a miniature altar, with each plant representing an element, deity, or magical intention. By nurturing your plants—herbs, flowers, succulents, you name it—you can establish a deeper bond with the earth, even in a smaller living area.

If you've got a window, balcony, or doorstep, you can create a container garden. Choose containers that suit the available space, such as pots, window boxes, or hanging baskets. Be sure to select containers with proper drainage to prevent waterlogging. A few magical herbs in a pot—or in several—can not only brighten up your home; they'll provide handy spell components once they've grown. Decorate your pots with your favorite magical symbols. If you'd like to try your hand at planting containers with specific magical goals, consider using a few of these combinations:

+ **Prosperity:** Bergamot, coltsfoot, chamomile, comfrey, jasmine, or sweet woodruff

+ **Healing:** Angelica, carnation, chervil, chamomile, fennel, hyssop, mugwort, rue, sage, or yarrow

+ **Love:** Basil, catnip, hibiscus, lavender, lady's mantle, lemon balm, peppermint, or rosemary

+ **Protection:** Basil, coriander, feverfew, garlic, mint, sunflower, valerian, verbena, and wormwood

+ **Happiness:** Catnip, lavender, meadowsweet, or vervain

Greenhouses and Sheds

A greenhouse or shed nestled in your yard can become a potent and dedicated magical space, offering seclusion and inspiring a connection with the natural world. The greenhouse, with its abundance of natural light and controlled environment, is a perfect haven for various magical practices. Utilizing the greenhouse as a sacred space, you could cultivate magical herbs and plants, brew herbal concoctions, or perform your favorite earth- and plant-based spellwork. While I don't yet have a greenhouse of my own, I'd love to build one someday—in fact, I've been collecting old windows that I plan to upcycle into a greenhouse, which I fully intend to paint in outrageous colors and decorate with magical symbols.

A greenhouse presents an ideal setting for ritual preparation and magical crafting. The greenhouse's ambiance, filled with the aromatic scents of fresh herbs and flowers, amplifies the energy of your magical creations. It can be a space that allows for the storage and charging of magical tools, crystals, or talismans.

Even a plain storage shed can be transformed into a magical sanctuary. With careful arrangement and dedication, the shed becomes a refuge for meditation, divination, or spiritual studies. Add comfortable seating and cushions, paint the interior with soothing colors, strategically place a few of your favorite magical decorations, or hang artwork on the walls. Treat yourself to some sound therapy while you're in there, either with a portable speaker or a streaming music service from your phone. A few well-placed storage cubes can become shelving for your best-loved books on the craft. With a bit of work and energy, it can serve as an extension of your magical practice, nurturing growth and serving as a private and sacred place where your magical goals are manifested.

Gardening by Lunar Phases

For centuries, various cultures have practiced lunar gardening, revolving around the belief that the moon's phases influence plant growth and development. Historical records indicate that ancient civilizations, including the Babylonians and the Mayans, followed lunar calendars for agricultural purposes. They observed the moon's phases to determine the best times for planting, cultivating, and harvesting crops. For modern witches in the garden, this is a great way to incorporate your magical practices with the natural energy the moon provides, as each phase is associated with specific magical attributes.

In folklore, the waxing and waning of the moon correspond to two primary planting phases. During the waxing, or increasing, moon, which starts from the new moon and progresses toward the full moon, sow above-ground crops for optimal growth and yield. Accounts from medieval Europe show farmers planting grains, leafy greens, and fruits during the waxing moon. This phase is considered an ideal time for planting and nurturing plants associated with growth, abundance, and fruition. Herbs like basil, mint, sage, and lavender are often sown during this phase to encourage robust growth, enhance flavor, and promote vitality in these plants.

Conversely, the waning, or decreasing, moon, from the full moon to the new moon, is associated with below-ground growth. This phase is conducive for planting root crops, as it's thought that planting during this phase encourages strong root development and healthier underground portions of plants. Ancient agricultural practices in Asia, such as those found in traditional Chinese farming wisdom, often aligned with these beliefs, emphasizing planting root vegetables during the waning moon. From a magical perspective, the waning moon is linked to introspection, banishing, and decreasing influences. This phase is ideal for planting and harvesting below-ground crops. Plants such as garlic, onions, potatoes, and ginseng are often cultivated during this phase to strengthen their magical properties related to protection, grounding, and banishing negative energies.

Harvesting herbs during a full moon is thought to imbue them with heightened energy and potency, while harvesting during a new moon is associated with renewal and the initiation of new cycles.

Certain lunar and celestial events hold special significance in gardening folklore. For instance, the occurrence of a full moon is often seen as an auspicious time for planting and harvesting crops. Eclipses were considered potent moments in some cultures. In ancient Mesopotamia, they were regarded as omens, and farmers took precautions during these celestial events, sometimes avoiding planting or harvesting activities.

Throughout history, lunar gardening folklore has persisted and evolved across diverse cultures. While modern scientific understanding has shed light on the complexities of plant growth, you can still follow lunar planting practices to blend tradition with contemporary agricultural methods.

SACRED SOIL SPELL

To craft sacred soil to blend into your garden for a bountiful harvest, you can gather ingredients and perform a working that honors the earth's fertility and invites abundance and prosperity. You'll need:

+ Dried herbs associated with growth and abundance, such as basil, thyme, or chamomile
+ Ground crystals or gemstones symbolizing fertility and earth energy, like green aventurine or moss agate
+ Fresh, clean soil or compost
+ A clean bowl

Perform this working during the waxing moon, preferably as close to the full moon as possible, in order to harness its energy for growth and abundance. Find a quiet outdoor space where you can connect with the moon's energy or a spot near a window where you can see the moon above you. Stand quietly, allowing yourself to relax, and meditate on the power of the earth's energy. If you work with any spirits of the land, guides, or deities related to agriculture, invite them to join you. Offer gratitude for the land's abundance and ask for blessings upon the soil.

Place your soil or compost in the bowl. Add the herbs, infusing the soil with their energies, and use your finger to mix it all together, swirling gently in a clockwise direction. As you do, say, *I invite bounty from this land. I invite blessings from this land.* Sprinkle the ground crystals or gemstones into the soil, continuing to mix the contents of the bowl with your finger, and say, *This soil is sacred. This soil is blessed.*

Go to your garden—or container pots—and with your hands, lightly sprinkle the soil atop your existing plants, garden beds, or flowerpots. As you sprinkle it, say, *The harvest will be prosperous, the harvest will be abundant.* When you have distributed all of your soil, thank the spirits, deities, or energies you invoked, expressing gratitude for their presence and blessings. As you plant or tend to your garden throughout the season, visualize the sacred soil enriching the roots and fostering abundant growth.

Spirits of Land and Place

A few years ago, my niece bought a new home—and she let me know immediately that she thought there was *something* around. She just wasn't sure what it was. So, my co-priestess and I went over there one evening, wandered the house, and holy cow, did we uncover some interesting stuff! In addition to at least two disgruntled former household residents who had set up an ethereal camp in the bedroom and the cellar, there was also something attached to a massive tree in the backyard. It wasn't anything malevolent … but it also didn't feel happy. What it felt was heavy and *old*—the kind of old that seems like it's just always been there, as though it's never *not* been present. We did some divination work and discovered we'd encountered a land spirit that was very concerned the home's new owner would tear down the tree...so we counseled my niece on leaving appropriate offerings and developing a relationship with her land spirit. After all, it wasn't going anywhere.

The concept of spirits of place, or land spirits, refers to the idea that locations possess their own unique spirits or essences. These spirits are believed to embody the distinctive character, energy, and history of a particular place, influencing the environment and those who inhabit or visit it. Throughout history, various cultures and civilizations have acknowledged and revered land spirits, attributing specific qualities and significance to natural landscapes, sacred sites, and geographic locations. Because they're attached to a place, these spirits generally stay put.

Ancient Romans deeply honored the genius loci, considering them a protective deity or divine force associated with specific places. They built shrines and altars to honor their spirits, recognizing them as guardians and benefactors of the community. They believed that by appeasing and respecting these spirits, they could ensure prosperity, protection, and harmony within their homes.

In some Celtic traditions, the belief in spirits of place was intrinsic to their spiritual practices. Celtic mythology often depicted sacred groves, wells, and natural landmarks as inhabited by spirits or deities. These spirits were intimately tied to the land, embodying its energies and bestowing blessings, guidance, or warnings to those who respected their domains. Offerings and rituals were conducted at these sites to honor and connect with the spirits, seeking their favor or wisdom. Norse mythology tells of the *landvættir*, who are associated with specific places or features within the environment such as a cave, river, or mountain.

Among the Yoruba of Benin and Nigeria, Oshun, the orisha of rivers, love, fertility, and beauty, holds a significant place. She resides within the Oshun River, a sacred body of water in Nigeria. The river and its surroundings are regarded as the physical manifestation of her presence and domain. Pilgrimages and rituals are conducted at the Oshun River by devotees seeking blessings, healing, or guidance from Oshun. Offerings of honey, fruits, and other items are made to honor and appease her, and her sacred place serves as a site of worship, divination, and healing ceremonies.

Throughout history, the acknowledgment of spirits of land and place has remained prevalent in animistic and earth-centered belief systems. Today, this concept persists in many earth-based spiritual practices, where practitioners honor and work with these spirits, acknowledging their presence and role in shaping the energies and atmospheres of sacred places.

Does your home have a spirit of place, or a land spirit? Similar to a household guardian (which we'll discuss in chapter 3), a land spirit or spirit of place is unique to the location in which you live. The key difference, however, is that while a household guardian tends to focus internally, on the home and the people within it, a land spirit is typically embodied by the outdoor environment—your yard might have a stream or hillside or cave that serves as the home for your land spirit. In fact, that landscape feature might not be on your property at all but simply located nearby.

Pay attention to the surrounding natural elements, such as trees, bodies of water, or unique landscape features. These natural elements are often conduits or dwellings for spirits of place. Spend time connecting with nature in your surroundings to attune yourself to the energies present. Look for signs or synchronicities that seem to point to a spiritual presence. Offerings such as flowers, herbs, or respectful gestures made in specific areas of the land upon which you live might evoke responses or feelings of connection. Use divination tools, such as pendulums, or seek guidance from a trusted spiritual adviser or practitioner experienced in working with land spirits. They may be able to provide insights or guidance to help you understand the energies present around your home.

Discerning the presence of a spirit of land or place requires patience as well as a mindset of openness to and respect for the energies around you. Be cognizant of your intuition and experiences, as they can guide you in recognizing and honoring any spiritual presences connected to the land where you live.

LAND SPIRIT SHRINE

If you'd like to form a deeper connection to the spirits of place around you, you can set up a small outdoor shrine to honor the entities of the land. In my community, which is reclaimed coal mining land, we have very old land spirits—and there's a sense of disruption about them, likely hearkening back to the late 1800s, when this area was pillaged for coal and stripped of its resources. Around 1884, a group of workers protesting poor wages pushed burning coal carts into a nearby mine, thus ending the run of mining companies in the community. By 1936, all the coal in a thirty-six-square-mile radius had burned away. That fire still burns today, far under the ground, nearly a century and a half later. As recently as the 1990s, there were reports of steaming fissures opening in the ground in the local forests, and many of the older roads around here are slowly sinking due to mine subsidence beneath the surface.

Suffice it to say, the land spirits around these parts have seen a lot—and much of it hasn't been good, so I decided it was important to make peace with them. Hence, the origins of my land spirit shrine on the old stone retaining wall at the base of my hillside.

To set up a land spirit shrine, it's important to try to learn about the spirits around you—see the previous section on how to do that. Once you've identified them, find a quiet, serene spot on your property where you feel a strong connection to the land spirits. If you don't own your property—for instance, you're renting—that's okay. You can still set up a shrine. Just be sure to locate it in a spot where it's unlikely to be disturbed.

Begin by incorporating natural elements that resonate with the energies of the land. Consider using stones or crystals like quartz, jasper, or moss agate. If there's something unique to your area—in my case, coal—include that as well. Adding a bowl of soil or sand from the land itself can symbolize the earth element, while found birds' eggshells or ethically sourced bones represent the spirits of the air and animals respectfully. Native plants and botanicals can help forge a bond with your land spirits. Add fresh or dried herbs and wildflowers indigenous to your area as offerings and representations of the flora spirits. Adorning the shrine with branches, leaves, or bark from trees around your property further acknowledges the spirits.

You can integrate symbols and tools that hold significance in your practice. Statues or figurines of nature deities, spirits, or animals can be placed on your shrine. Lighting candles and burning incense, such as those with natural scents like pine or cedar, adds ambiance and aligns with the elements. To represent water, offer a bowl of water from a local stream—I gathered mine from the creek across the road—or collected rainwater.

Additionally, consider adding something personal, like a piece of jewelry or a handwritten note expressing gratitude or your intentions for honoring the land spirits.

Maintaining your shrine involves regular visits to refresh offerings and metaphysically cleanse the space. I leave an offering about once a week—usually a food or beverage item—with a simple invocation. You can use this one, or adjust it to fit the spirits of the land where you live:

> *Spirits of the land, guardians of the earth around me, energies of the forest and soil, I leave you this gift to thank you for the beauty of this place and as a promise that I will honor, respect, and revere this land.*

Bonfire Magic

For those of us who like to do our witchcraft outdoors, a bonfire can be a useful tool for ritual and magic. You can harness the transformative power of flames during ceremonies or rituals, utilizing the bonfire as a focal point to connect with the elements and the spiritual realm. At the heart of a gathering, a carefully tended bonfire serves as a conduit, channeling energy and intention while fostering a sacred space for practitioners. Once the flames dance and the fire crackles, it becomes a sacred medium through which spells are cast, energy is released, and rituals are amplified. You can use the bonfire's flames to burn written intentions or symbols, releasing them into the universe as offerings or manifestations of desired outcomes.

If you're fortunate enough to have like-minded friends around, a bonfire can be a focal point for communal gatherings, fostering a sense of unity and shared energy. Circled around the fire, practitioners can indulge in storytelling, chants, or guided meditations, deepening their connection to the elements and each other. As the flames leap and sway, the bonfire becomes a source of inspiration, illumination, and transformation, guiding us through magical workings and spiritual journey.

In some magical traditions, there are nine sacred woods included in a bonfire. You might want to include some—or even all—of these to take advantage of their magical properties the next time you build an outdoor fire for ritual purposes.

- **Oak:** The mighty oak symbolizes strength, wisdom, and endurance and is associated with protection and bringing in blessings.
- **Ash:** The ash represents healing, transformation, and spiritual journeys and can be used for protection and connection to the Divine.
- **Hawthorn:** Signifying cleansing and protection as well as magical self-defense, hawthorn is often utilized in rituals related to banishing, dealing with challenges, and power.
- **Holly:** The holly can be a symbol of protection, clarity, and good fortune; use it to enhance your psychic abilities, defend against negativity, and bring luck.
- **Rowan:** The rowan tree is well known for its protective properties against psychic attacks and dark forces and symbolizes strength, personal power, and vision.

- **Willow:** Associated with intuition, healing, and emotional balance, willow can be included in spells for divination, knowledge, and lunar magic.

- **Birch:** The birch tree is a symbol of rebirth and regeneration as well as protection; use birch for workings related to creativity, healing, and new beginnings.

- **Alder:** The alder represents prophecy, divination, and intuition; work with it for spells connected to making spiritual decisions and seeking guidance.

- **Hazel:** Symbolizing wisdom, knowledge, and divination, hazel is perfect for spellwork tied to dream journeys, dowsing, and even self-defense.

CONSECRATED WATER FOR BANISHING

As much as I hate to be soggy, I do love me a good rippin' thunderstorm. I like to leave a mason jar outside, collect stormwater, and then use it in banishing spells—there's something really potent about the energy in rain that's accompanied by lots of wind, thunder, and lightning. However, if you don't live in an area that gets a lot of precipitation, you can make your own banishing water using one of these simple methods.

Place a jar of water outside or in your windowsill overnight under a waning moon, particularly as it gets close to the dark moon phase, as this phase is associated with magic that eliminates things from your life.

Another option is to add sea salt or kosher salt to water while reciting incantations or prayers for banishment—even something as simple as *I send away all that does not serve me*. Stirring the water in a counterclockwise motion with a wand or the index finger of your nondominant hand aids in infusing the water with banishing properties.

Herbal infusions offer another means of consecrating water for banishing. Add banishing herbs like sage, rosemary, or rue into the water and allow the mixture to simmer gently on your stovetop. While the infusion cools, concentrate on the herbs filling the water with their inherent properties for banishment. Strain the herbs out through a piece of cheesecloth, and then store the water for future use.

Crystals known for their banishing attributes, such as obsidian or black tourmaline, can be placed around a container of water, intensifying its ability to banish negative influences. Once consecrated, water can be a powerful tool in banishing spells, rituals, or cleansing practices, effectively removing unwanted energies or influences from your life.

Disposal of Spell Components

People often ask me, *Okay, I did the spell... now what do I do with the stuff afterward?* Well, the answer to that—like so many other questions in magic—is that it really depends on what your purpose is. If you're trying to get a toxic coworker out of your life, is that energy the kind of thing you want hanging around? Likewise, if you're hoping to attract romance, that would be something you'd probably keep close by.

While not universal across all magical traditions, these are some general guidelines I've found that work best for me when it comes to disposing of the various bits and pieces of a working once I've completed it.

- To keep something close, bury it in your backyard or near your home.
- To attract something, bury or hide it close to the entrance of your home.
- To destroy its influence, burn it.
- To move it away from you, throw it in running water.
- If you are calling on spirits for intervention, hide it in a cemetery.
- To hide its point of origin, conceal it in a tree.
- If it's for protection or sweetening, keep it nearby.
- If it's for banishing or destruction, get it gone—bury it, smash it, or drop it somewhere really nasty.

It's important to note that you should be mindful of environmental considerations when you dispose of a working. For example, nonbiodegradable items, such as glass or plastic, shouldn't be placed in a waterway, buried, or left under a tree in a forest. Don't burn something that could release harmful fumes or toxins into the atmosphere. Finally, don't leave spell components as litter—be considerate of our planet and the beings that live on it.

Chapter 2
CREATING A SACRED HOME

The idea of our home being a sacred space isn't—or at least shouldn't be—a novel one. After all, it's where we spend a significant chunk of our time, and if it's not a safe, calming place, it's hard to find satisfaction, calm, and emotional well-being in our space.

When I was writing this book, I wanted to make sure the end result felt inclusive for anyone and everyone, no matter what kind of place they lived in. I have friends who live on farms with acreage, others who live in suburban neighborhoods. I've got people in my circle who live in mobile homes, many who live in apartments, and a couple of free-spirited types who are mobile and nomadic, living in camper vans or recreational vehicles. Still others don't have their own space—they're living with parents or roommates, in college dormitories, or in community shelters. Because we all bring different experiences to the table, it's important to discuss what we actually mean when we're talking about *home*.

The square footage of your home is irrelevant for the purposes of this book—that's why it's not called *The Witch's Mansion* or *The Witch's Fourth Floor Studio Apartment* or *The Witch's Great Big Llama Ranch*. But a home is so much more than just walls and a door, more than the place where you lay your head at night or where you keep your stuff. I've lived in places that never felt like home—and in others that I knew were *home* the first time I walked in the door, including the little cottage in the woods where I live today.

Home is a *feeling*. It's an energy, a vibration, an emotion. It's a place where we find sanctuary in times of strife. Home is where we feel safe, accepted, loved, and secure. It's a welcoming place of harmony and balance. Our home tells our story, not only of who we are, but of who we wish to be. Creating a sense of home isn't about designing a physical construct; it's about cultivating a sense of belonging and an emotional connection, not only for ourselves but for anyone who steps foot across our threshold. At the end of the day, while you might really love your nice granite countertops and your fancy bookcases, what the people who enter your home will remember most about it will be the way they *felt* when they were there. They'll remember the smell of the delicious meal you cooked them, the peaceful sensation of being surrounded by comforting sounds, or the sense of kindness they experienced sipping a cup of tea on your front porch as you watched the sun go down together.

For those of us who practice magical spiritual paths, our home can be one of our most powerful tools, in addition to being a place of love and refuge and protection. We can imbue it with our magic as we create a deep relationship with the physical space we're occupying. In the introduction to *The Magical Household*, Scott Cunningham and David Harrington remind us that choosing to make our home a secure and magical environment "means fashioning an escape from the all-too-physical reality of a world that has turned its back on the spiritual side of life."[2]

....
2. Cunningham and Harrington, *The Magical Household*, xv–xvi.

Your home, whether it be big or small or somewhere in between, is where you can do whatever makes you feel spiritual and serene, safe and secure, lucky and loved.

Deities of Hearth and Home

No matter what kind of magical tradition you follow or which pantheon has called you, odds are pretty good it includes deities and spirits associated with the realm of hearth and home. While you don't necessarily *have* to work with a deity or hearth spirit, if you feel like one is speaking to you—or you'd like to add a bit of divine influence to your domicile—you might want to do some further exploration with one of these gods, goddesses, or other beings from around the world, especially if your ancestors may have hailed from one of these places.

Bes (Egypt)

Bes, a beloved household god of ancient Egypt, was a deity revered for his protective and nurturing qualities. Often depicted as a dwarf with leonine features, he possessed a playful and jovial demeanor. Egyptians believed Bes safeguarded households from evil spirits, ensuring the safety of families, especially for mothers during childbirth. He was also responsible for other protective household tasks, such as killing venomous snakes that might enter and cause harm to the family. His image adorned amulets, jewelry, and household items, symbolizing happiness and safeguarding homes from danger.[3]

....
3. Jordan, "Bes."

Brigid (Ireland)

In Ireland, Brigid is a triune deity, a goddess with three separate yet related aspects. She is associated with domestic endeavors, such as healing, childbirth, poetry, and crafts, as well as divination and prophecy. Because of her connection to matters of the home, she evolved over time to take the role of a goddess of the hearth and beyond, encompassing all aspects of domestic life.[4] Her many aspects are closely tied to the well-being of the household, making her a popular goddess of the home.

Cailleach (Scotland)

The Scots Gaelic word *cailleach* means "old woman." It is also the name given to a mythical ancestral figure who represents the divine creation of the landscape itself by dropping boulders from her apron.[5] However, the Cailleach is also associated with the gathering of firewood in the middle winter; specifically on February 1, or Imbolc, she collects enough wood to make sure her home stays warm enough that she can survive until spring comes. While the Cailleach is not typically associated with domestic life in the same way that Brigid is, her presence in Scottish folklore reflects the idea that respecting the natural world, tending the land, and staying warm through the changing seasons played a central role in survival of families.

Dewi Nawang Sasih (Indonesia)

In the folklore of the Sundanese people of Indonesia, Dewi Nawang Sasih was a celestial nymph who brought rice and the ability to cook it to humankind. She offered a simple recipe to the women of

....

4. Weatherstone, *Tending Brigid's Flame*, 43.
5. Ó Crualaoich, "Continuity and Adaptation in Legends of Cailleach Bhéarra," 154.

Sudan—place a single grain of rice in a pot and boil it. She instructed them to allow the rice to divide itself over and over, eventually filling the pot. There was one important rule—Dewi Nawang Sasih insisted men were never to handle the women's cooking utensils. Once the cooked rice was abundant, there was a great feast, which went well until a king—the nymph's husband—decided he should be allowed to touch the off-limits cooking tools.[6] Annoyed by this flagrant disobedience, Dewi Nawang Sasih threw up her hands and departed, and ever since then, rice no longer swells and divides, so a significant amount of grain must be used to fill the pot.

Enekpe (Ghana)

A goddess and guardian of the family in Ewe mythology, Enekpe is deeply tied to agriculture, the earth, and abundance as well as fertility. She provides nourishment and abundance to the land and its people.[7] The Ewe people hold ceremonies and rituals to honor Enekpe, seeking her blessings for fertile soil, successful crops, and overall prosperity. Her presence ensures the well-being and sustenance of the community.

Hestia (Greece)

Hestia embodies the essence of warmth, security, and familial harmony in Greek mythology, as well as for many modern Hellenic Pagans. As the eternal flame at the center of the household, she is not just a symbol but a living presence, safeguarding the dwelling from harm and discord. Hestia blesses the place in the home where families gather, share stories, and find solace, fostering unity, hospitality, and the sacred bonds of kinship. She reminds us that

....

6. Monaghan, *Encyclopedia of Goddesses & Heroines*, 133.
7. Auset, *The Goddess Guide*, 45.

a home is more than a physical space; it is a sanctuary of love and acceptance.

Jowangshin (Korea)

In Korean shamanism, Jowangshin was a guardian of the hearth and home and was often honored in shrines by housewives. It was said that Jowangshin kept an eye on household activities and passed the news along to the heavens, so it was important for the home to be kept clean and the hearth to be maintained as a place of respect.[8]

Juno (Rome)

Like the Greek goddess Hestia, Juno was regarded as a guardian of domestic life, ensuring the well-being of the family and the sanctity of the household. Juno, in Roman mythology, was associated with marriage and childbirth and held a significant role as a protector of the home and hearth. Her presence was invoked during important life events, such as weddings and childbirth, to bring blessings and protect the home. Juno's influence extended beyond familial matters; she was also believed to safeguard the state and the well-being of the Roman people. As a hearth goddess, she symbolized the warmth, unity, and stability found within the home, emphasizing the importance of family and the bonds that held society together.

Kōjin (Japan)

In Japanese folklore, Kōjin, also known as Sanbō-Kōjin, is a deity associated with the hearth, fire, and the kitchen. Kōjin is revered as a guardian of the home, ensuring protection against fire, which was a significant concern in traditional Japanese architecture. Families often had a small household altar dedicated to Kōjin, where they

....
8. Faye, "The Pantheon."

made offerings to appease him and seek protection from fires. Kōjin is particularly important for those engaged in cooking, as he provides both culinary skills and safety in the kitchen. Over time, his role expanded to include protection against various disasters, making him a popular figure in Japanese folk beliefs associated with home and family well-being.[9]

Lamaria (Georgia)

Among the Svan people of Georgia, the goddess Lamaria is celebrated during the winter holiday season. The members of two or more families get together to host a ritual, in which a table is filled with cheeses, meat, and two cups of vodka. The oldest man and oldest woman each drink from a cup, toast the community, and then dance together, with the younger people following suit. During other periods of the year, the table is placed at the hearth, where the female members of the household offer her prayers. Lamaria is viewed as a composite goddess who evolved from earlier sources; in many ways, she is similar to other deities associated with domestic life, the hearth, and marriage.[10]

Lares and Penates (Rome)

In ancient Rome, both the Lares and Penates were honored as essential household deities, each with distinct but complementary roles in ensuring the well-being and prosperity of the family. The Lares were ancestral spirits who served as guardians of the home and symbols of familial continuity. They were typically venerated with offerings by members of the specific household; in exchange, the Lares typically provided good health for family members, protection for livestock,

....
9. Ashkenazi, *Handbook of Japanese Mythology*, 244.
10. Tuite, "'Antimarriage' in Ancient Georgian Society," 52.

or even ensured a wedding would go smoothly.[11] Meanwhile, the Penates, derived from the Latin word for pantry, were associated with safeguarding the household's food supplies and provisions, reflecting the importance of sustenance, familial bond, and the connection between past generations and the present household.

Nëna e Vatrës (Albania)

In Albania, Nëna e Vatrës is the protector of the hearth; her very name translates to "mother of the *vatër*," or fireplace, found in every home. She symbolizes the heart of the household, so families honor her by keeping the hearth well-tended and clean and ensuring there is perpetual fire and warmth in the home—to leave the hearth uncleaned will anger her. She is honored with prepared food thrown into the fire as an offering.[12]

Vesta (Rome)

Vesta, the goddess of the hearth in ancient Rome, held a central place in religion and society. As the virgin goddess of the home and family, she was honored as a guardian of the sacred flame, symbolizing the eternal fire of the hearth. Her worship focused on maintaining the heart of the household, emphasizing the importance of domestic harmony, stability, and unity. Her sacred fire represented the warmth and vitality of the home; it was believed that as long as the flame burned, Rome would endure. Priestesses, known as vestal virgins, were tasked with keeping the fire perpetually lit in her temples, and her presence was invoked during various female-focused ceremonies, especially those related to marriage and childbirth.

....

11. King, "The Organization of Roman Religious Beliefs," 306–7.
12. "Eternal Fire."

Mundane Practices to Keep Things Tidy

When I was a teenager, I thought my parents were weirdly obsessive about keeping things neat and organized. Why did it matter if I left a pile of cassettes (yes, I'm old) strewn around my bedroom or if I didn't feel like putting my laundry away and instead just left it dumped on the chair? Then I became a grown-up, and that was when I got it. I had my light bulb moment somewhere around the age of twenty-four, when I had a toddler creating a never-ending stream of onesies that needed to be washed, bottles that required a good scrubbing, and toys that had to be put away so the dog wouldn't eat them. I figured out quickly that in the midst of clutter and chaos, it's really hard to focus, so I tried to get into the habit of maintaining a reasonably tidy physical space. Fast forward a few years, to when I was trying to manage a household of two adults, three kids, and assorted pets, and I was *really* glad I raised my children to clean up after themselves.

Your spiritual space is much the same way. If it's dirty and disorganized, it's almost impossible to focus on your magic. Your spells, your rituals, your personal growth as a spiritual being will be all the more difficult because you didn't take the time to give your space a good solid physical cleaning.

Now don't get me wrong—I am absolutely aware that sometimes we just don't have the energy or mental bandwidth to tackle a cleansing, whether it's physical or spiritual. Trust me, I have been there. Not everyone has the physical ability to push a mop around, or you might not have the resources to gather all the cleaning supplies you think you need. So, here's my theory on cleaning of any type. It's a simple one: you do what you can—no more and no less.

Because if we tackle things in small increments—whatever it is we feel we can handle—it gets easier. There were days when I didn't have the time, energy, or motivation to clean the whole bathroom. So, I wiped down the sink and mirror. The next day, I cleaned the toilet. And on the third day, I took care of the bathtub. Okay, yeah, it took me three days to clean a bathroom, but that was because I only gave it about fifteen minutes each day. That was way more manageable than forty-five minutes spent all at once, which I just didn't have the bandwidth to muster up. If all you can handle is burning some incense, doing a basic blessing, and calling it a day, so be it. You do you, baby. Handle the rest when you're up to it, can afford it, and are capable.

You can do it. You can keep your physical space clean, which will make it a whole lot easier to feel connected and spiritually bonded to your home. Just like your body, a home is happier when it's in good physical condition.

Now, I'm not here to go all Marie Kondo on you and present you with a whole manifesto on how to get rid of things that don't spark joy in your life. There are plenty of other people writing about that topic who are far more qualified than I am. What I would like to do, though, is share ten simple, mundane home-management tips that work well for me. It's my hope that they'll work for you too.

1. Make your bed first thing in the morning. Seriously, before you walk out of your bedroom, pull the covers up, fluff the pillows, and tuck in the sheets. Even if your sleeping space is a temporary one—for instance, you're crashing on a friend's futon for a while—take the time to fold your blankets and sheets. Add your stuffies or whatever else brings you happiness. Because guess what? Now that your bed is made, you don't have to think about it for the rest of the day AND you've already accomplished one task!

2. Hang your clothes up immediately. I used to be terrible about this—I'd take off a top and drop it on the bench next to my closet. The next day, I'd repeat this ... and soon, by the time the weekend rolled around, I'd have half a dozen shirts, a pile of scarves, and two or three cardigans just sitting there, silently judging me. Now I put them away as soon as I take them off, as I'm changing into my jammies. I close the closet and walk away and don't have to worry about seeing them when I come back in to go to bed.

3. Keep your kitchen as clean as you can. I have a large kitchen, and it's really easy to get into the habit of just piling things on the section of counter I don't use ... but I *hate* the way it looks, so I try to avoid keeping anything there that I don't need. If space is at a premium, see what kinds of kitchen gadgets you can live without. Also, be sure to tidy up right after meals are done. I don't own a dishwasher and can't stand the idea of a pile of plates in my sink, so I try to clean as I go, and the last thing I do after eating is wash anything I've used.

4. Sort papers as soon as they appear. This goes for mail, work stuff, receipts, bills, you name it. When I check my mail, if it's junk, I don't even bring it through the door. I drop it in the recycle bin next to my trash can immediately. If it's a bill, I put it in a dedicated tray on my desk right away.

5. Purge your wardrobe as you go. Look, we all have stuff in our drawers and closets that we know we're never going to wear again. How many times have you put on a pair of pants, hated the way they looked on you, and then just

hung them right back up? I keep a large bag on the floor of my closet, and when I realize something no longer fits me—or I've decided I hate it—it goes straight in the bag. Once the bag is full, it goes in my car, and I drop it off the next time I pass the local donation station. This is so much easier than spending a whole weekend cleaning out my wardrobe.

6. Be realistic about things that are broken. I'll be the first to admit there have been times I've broken something and thought to myself, *Cool, I can fix that and use it again.* And then guess what I *never* did? Instead I'd end up with a broken thing sitting in my garage for two years, knowing damn well I was never going to touch it. And then I finally got rid of it, and it turned out I was fine without it anyway. Now, a caveat here—I realize that sometimes we can't afford to throw things away; for many of us, it's a luxury and privilege to be able to do so. But I also know that if it's something I cannot live without, I'll prioritize repairing it. The key here is to be realistic about what you have the time, energy, and interest in doing.

7. Give everything a home. It's that old adage about "a place for everything, and everything in its place." When I walk into my house, my purse and jacket go straight to the hook by the back door. My shoes come off and go right into the shoe rack in my bedroom closet. Establishing a pattern of putting things where they belong makes it easier to form the habits of organization.

8. One thing in, one thing out. I'm a self-confessed thrift store fan—I often think maybe I'm just renting my

clothing because I'll buy it for a few dollars at the thrift store, wear it until I'm bored with it, and then drop it back off for someone else to enjoy later. If I find a great deal and buy a couple of new shirts and a shawl at the local thrift shop, that means I'll be putting a few other things into my donation bag to bring back the next time.

9. Consider why you're keeping sentimental items. It's hard to let go of things we cherish, even if they don't have an inherent monetary value. Ask yourself whether you're keeping things because you really love them or because you love the memories they represent to you. I helped a friend move recently, and he and his wife were saving their son's baby clothes. Their son is *thirty years old*, but his parents were hanging on to these tiny onesies because it was so hard for them to acknowledge that their sweet bouncing baby boy was now a grown man with a family of his own.

10. Be content with "clean enough." I like a clean house, but I also know there are some tasks I don't care about much. I hate to mop—the smell of dirty mop water is like kryptonite for me—so I only mop my kitchen about once every two months. Sure, I vacuum twice a week, but the mopping can wait. For me, if my house is 80 percent clean—the pet hair is all gone, the laundry is put away, the living room looks tidy, and the bathroom smells nice—I'm happy. I don't have to impress anyone with my housekeeping skills, other than myself, so I'll accept it and call it done.

Brooms and Sweeping

Going back to the idea that a clean home makes for more efficient and effective magic, let's talk for a moment about brooms and sweeping. Certainly, if you have carpet, you may only be vacuuming, but that's a form of sweeping too. You might be sweeping your bathroom or kitchen, and even mopping. Everyone cleans floors differently, but for this section, we're going to talk about brooms specifically, because they're well known for their association with magic and witchcraft. They're one of those magical tools that passes quite well for a mundane piece of household cleaning equipment—if people don't know you're a witch, the presence of a broom won't even make them suspect it. They'll probably just think you're super tidy.

The magical broom is also known as a besom. Fun fact: Although the word *besom* can be traced back several centuries to describe a broom or other domestic tool used for sweeping, sometime around the late eighteenth to early nineteenth centuries, it became a not-very-nice term for women. Specifically, it was applied to insult women who were believed to have loose morals or questionable reputations.

Disreputable women aside, the besom is traditionally used to clean out a ceremonial space prior to ritual. Sweeping in a counterclockwise direction, or widdershins, is a great way to banish any negative energies that may be present. Often, this is done without the besom touching the floor—the besom is moved directionally as appropriate and serves to sweep energy rather than actual dust or dirt. Sweeping clockwise, or deosil, is said to bring in positive energy and is valuable in attraction magic.

Make Your Own Broom

Many witches make their own besom from an oak or ash staff, a bundle of twigs or broomcorn, and a willow binding. To make your own besom for ritual use, you'll need:

+ A length of wood for the handle, approximately 36 to 48 inches long; historically, these are made from ash, oak, or yew.

+ Thin birch branches, woody herbs, or broomcorn for the bristles

+ Heavy cording, green willow branches, or twine

+ A knife, scissors, or pruning shears to trim and shape your broom

Start with your handle—you might want to leave it natural, particularly if it's a found branch. You can also decorate it with symbols, either by painting or woodburning. Gather your twigs, broomcorn, or whatever you're using for the bristles, and trim them so they're all roughly the same length.

Hold the bristles together around the handle tightly, with the ends aligned neatly, so that you have a few inches of overlap. In other words, the bristles should come up 4 to 6 inches past the end of the handle. Use the twine, heavy cording, or willow branches to bind them into place. Start at the top and wrap the material tightly around the bundle a few times, and then tie it securely to keep the broomcorn, herbs, or twigs in place. Repeat this at the portion of bristles that sits just above the end of the handle, so that it's tightly wrapped in two spots.

Finally, use your knife, scissors, or pruning shears to trim the bristles into the shape you like—whether it's rounded, flat, or angled is entirely up to you.

Once your besom is shaped, you can ritually cleanse and purify it. You might pass it through incense smoke, sprinkle it with salt water, or perform any other cleansing ritual that resonates for you. You could take your besom outside during a full moon and charge it with energy and intention—this can include stating its purpose, such as for protection, cleansing, or prosperity. Remember that just like other items you use in spellwork or ritual, your besom can be a highly personalized and symbolic tool. Feel free to decorate it, bless it, and imbue it with your own energies to make it a unique and meaningful part of your craft. You can even create multiple brooms for different magical purposes. I have several, and they're all displayed on my living room wall under a sign that reads "Broom Parking."

Keep in mind that your magical broom should be reserved for metaphysical purposes only. Use a regular, mundane broom for actual physical cleaning. However, there can be some overlap—why not think about magical applications when you're using your mundane broom to sweep the living room floors? There are a number of different beliefs from around the world related to housekeeping and, in particular, the act of sweeping.

+ In some cultures, there's a superstition that sweeping at night is bad luck. It's believed to sweep away good fortune or invite evil spirits into the home. Sweeping during the day is considered far more auspicious.

+ Hang a broom above a doorway or fireplace to protect the home from evil spirits and prevent malevolent forces from entering. There's a story in parts of Appalachia that a broom placed across the doorstep keeps witches out; of course, the story does not specify how that works if a witch already lives in the home.

+ It's considered good luck to purchase a new broom when moving into a new home. It symbolizes a fresh start and a clean slate; in fact, superstition says you should never move an old broom to a new home. If someone you know has just found a new place to live, giving them a broom is a wonderful housewarming present. Pair it up with some salt, to inspire their space to be safe and protected, and bread so their home will never know hunger.

+ Some superstitions involve burning old broomsticks instead of just throwing them away when they've reached a point at which they're no longer usable for cleaning. This practice is believed to ward off evil spirits or negativity, and it can be done on specific occasions like the New Year.

+ It's considered rude and unlucky to sweep over someone's feet. It's believed to symbolize sweeping away their vitality and energy.

+ If you store your broom on the floor, rather than hanging it, keep the bristles pointing upward; this helps keep the luck from running out. It also, however, has a practical application. Brooms stored with the bristles on the floor will end up curving over time, which makes them less effective for sweeping.

+ If a broom falls on its own, it's sometimes seen as an omen or a sign of an upcoming visitor. The superstition varies from culture to culture.

Spiritual and Emotional Decluttering

In addition to all the mundane practices we talked about in the previous section, there are significant advantages to getting rid of the nonphysical clutter in your life—it's what I like to think of as spiritual and emotional decluttering. Now, I'm not saying every one of us should take such a minimalist approach that we get rid of every single thing we don't like—but there really are benefits to figuring out which of those things are worth your time and energy. Because plenty of them are not. It's what my mom used to call the Green Bean Issue.

When I was a kid, I hated vegetables. Thankfully, I've grown out of that, but as an eight-year-old, I was not a fan of eating plants. Lima beans, brussels sprouts, and green beans were a three-headed arch nemesis for me. I'd sit at the table for a good hour after everyone else had left, poking around at the green monstrosities on my plate; perhaps I thought by moving them around in circles I could make them vanish. Regardless, my parents tried really hard to get me to at least *try* them, but I was stubborn, and eventually I think they just gave up. Once I became an adult—one who eats a healthy selection of veggies, including brussels sprouts and green beans, although I still hate lima beans—and had a kid of my own, my mom reminded me that sometimes you have to pick your battles. She decided at some point in raising me that it wasn't worth the effort to argue with me about eating green beans when there were more important things to focus on. The Green Bean Issue.

So, when it comes to spiritual decluttering, it's a matter of paying attention to the bigger things that really don't serve you. If you can eliminate some of those, it might make dealing with the smaller unsatisfactory stuff easier.

Decluttering our spirituality by simplifying things—not just the material stuff but also our emotional responses and our relationships with others—creates a freedom to be authentic. And once you begin living as a spiritually authentic being, you'll be amazed at how much more satisfied you are with the things you chose to keep. Let's face it—we're all faced with a ton of decisions every single day. We have too many obligations, too many choices. We carry our emotional baggage and generational trauma, and when it gets super heavy, it weighs us down. We insist on staying in unhealthy relationships— and that doesn't necessarily mean abusive, although obviously, that's not only unhealthy but dangerous.

One of the best ways to figure out what you need to get clutter out of your life—you know, after you've gone through those boxes in the basement and donated those clothes from 1988 that you'll never wear again—is by self-reflection. When it comes to the emotional baggage you're lugging around with you, first, figure out what yours entails. We've all got it—maybe you suffer from anxiety, endure crippling impostor syndrome, or have spent your life being told you didn't live up to someone else's expectations. Perhaps you define yourself by the pain and trauma you experienced in the past—none of it was your fault, but it's something that shaped you. You might be someone who places unreasonable demands or expectations on yourself. Do you always need to be the best at everything—the most popular, the prettiest, the most successful—just so you can show all those people who used to shit on you that you do, in fact, have some value? Do you commit to doing things you don't really want to do because you're worried people will think less of you if you say no?

Unlike physical clutter, spiritual and emotional clutter is extremely difficult to let go of. We can't just collect the emotional clutter in trash bags and recycle it. We can't hold a garage sale, donate it, or sell it online—no one wants my anxiety disorder or my panic attacks because everyone's got plenty of clutter of their own. To release emotions that don't benefit us, they need to be expressed, but that isn't as simple as it sounds. When we're feeling fragile, it's difficult to reach out and share what's really bothering us. And many times, the paradox is emotional clutter occupies a large amount of our mental space, but at the same time, we are completely unaware of its existence. Here are a few ways you can try eliminating some of the emotional and physical stuff that's taking up extra space in your head.

- **Journaling:** Writing stuff down can be therapeutic. You might even want to keep *two* journals—one for trash, the negative things you feel and experience, and one for treasure, which is where you can chronicle positivity. Personally, I never reread the stuff I write in my trash journal. Once it's full, I burn it.

- **Meditation:** Give yourself the privilege of emptying stuff out. Imagine yourself boxing up the mental yuck that no longer serves a purpose for you. Get into a regular practice of sitting down, free from distractions, and clearing your mind of negative ideas, thought patterns, and emotions. Once they're gone, you have open space for the good stuff.

+ **Organize an emotional library:** Ask yourself, when anything happens, good or bad, *What has this experience taught me?* and *How can I improve myself from the lessons learned through this experience?* Treat an experience as an opportunity for learning and growth, whenever possible, rather than an obstacle or hindrance.

+ **Discover your true self:** There's a philosophy that everyone has three faces. The first, you show to the world. The second one is only seen by close friends and family. The third face, you never show anyone, because it is the truest reflection of who you are, so minimize your masks. Make a commitment to yourself to live authentically. Learn to accept and even like who you really are.

+ **Get rid of irrational guilt:** Allow yourself a bit of grace and understand that it's okay not to be perfect. It's all right if you didn't bake the cupcakes, or if you forgot it was trash day, or if you didn't feel like folding the laundry and just wanted to binge Netflix after you got home. Your list of completed tasks doesn't increase your value.

+ **Guard your time:** Not every pursuit in life deserves your energy. I have crafted a life I love by not saying yes to every opportunity or invitation in my inbox. I have done so by ruthlessly guarding my energy for the things that matter most to me and by learning to graciously say no to things I don't want.

+ **Be kind:** Pay it forward, compliment other people, assume the best rather than the worst. And remember that being kind is different than being *nice*. To be nice is to do the bare minimum—to be kind is intentional.

- **Take care of yourself:** An empty cup can't pour into another. Caring for ourselves is the first step in caring for others. Rest, exercise, and pursue healthy habits so you can be the best version of yourself and be fully present when you need to be.

Let's talk, for just a moment, about unhealthy relationships. They're mentally, emotionally, and spiritually draining. Some people think that it's better to have bad friendships than no friendships at all, but this can be such a destructive mindset. Remember when you were in high school and there was that Mean Girl, and you put up with her cruelty because you really wanted her to like you? And no matter what you did, she was *still* a Mean Girl. You'd think we'd outgrow this as we age, but many of us don't. In general, we really want to be liked … or at the very least, treated with compassion and kindness.

Do you keep people in your life who have hurt you, whether it's physically or emotionally? Are some of your friendships so transactional that you only have contact with the other person when they need something from you? When it comes to interpersonal connections, while it's important to consider how we feel about the other person, it's equally (or maybe even more) important to consider how they make us feel about *ourselves*. I'm a fan of quality over quantity. I have a lot of people in my life that I *like*, and who I know like me in return, and that's great. But I'm incredibly selective about how and when I spend my time, and with whom. No one gets to live rent free in my head unless they've earned the privilege.

Some relationships can't just be terminated—but you *can* set boundaries. Do you have a toxic family member or in-law who's a jerk every time you're around? You can establish guidelines, either by refusing to engage or by standing your ground. "Aunt Minerva,

I'm glad you've decided to join us for dinner, but I will not permit you to sit at my table and insult me. Pass the gravy."

Boundaries are how we train other people to treat us.

Ritual for Self-Reflection

This ritual is one I've found helpful over the years to evaluate what's going on in my life—and which of those things need to go away. I like to do this every year in January so I can look at the previous twelve months, but you can do it any time it suits you.

First, find a quiet space where you can work without interruption. Light your favorite candle and some incense—I'm partial to something tranquil and calming like sandalwood. All you need is a piece of paper and pen. Divide the paper in half, and on one half write *Positive* and the other *Negative*. Now, ask yourself these questions—and as you ask them, write the answer in the appropriate section, either Positive or Negative.

- Why was the past year important or memorable for me?
- What did I enjoy doing last year?
- Who or what is the one thing I'm most grateful for?
- What was my biggest success from last year?
- What is the mistake I learned from the most?
- What did I read, watch, or listen to that influenced me the most?

- What did I worry about the most, and how did it turn out?
- What was my biggest regret last year, and why?
- What surprised me the most last year?
- What about me changed the most?
- If I could go back to one year ago today, what advice would I give myself for the coming twelve months?

Now, look at the negative stuff on that list. Give it a good hard look and *cross it out*. Get rid of it. Draw big lines through it. *You don't need it anymore.* Tear off that half of the paper and rip it to shreds, into tiny little pieces. Burn it, bury it, or flush it down the damn toilet. As it's going out of your life, declare out loud that it no longer matters to you, that it has no more influence. Let it go.

Now, go look at what's left. It should be only the positive items from your list. Read them over thoroughly and think about the joy they brought you. Send out a thank you to the universe for allowing you to experience such positivity, and then keep that list someplace you can see it regularly. When you start questioning how things are going, reread your list to be reminded of the good in your life.

Someone once told me, "True happiness begins when you learn to enjoy the amazing abundance of what you already have," and they were right. I've learned to banish things from my life like self-doubt, self-sabotaging behavior, excuses, and a mindset of low self-worth. Instead, I invite in gratitude, confidence, mindfulness, and compassion for both myself and others.

Once you've figured out how to do that, you open up space for more blessings.

HAPPY HOME CAULDRON SPELL

If you share your home with other people, you can give the relationships a little magical boost to create a harmonious and happy living environment. Use this simple spell to strengthen the bonds you have with your family or housemates and create a sense of harmony, joy, and balance. If possible, get the other household members to join you for this one. You'll need:

+ Soil or stones from the property where you live
+ A small, tangible representation of your home (a key, a chip of paint, a bit of brick, etc.)
+ A cauldron or wide firesafe bowl
+ An item to symbolize each member of the household
+ A pinch of salt to banish negativity
+ A pinch of oregano for happiness

Place the stones or soil in the bottom of the cauldron, and add the representation of your home on top of it. Next, place the symbols of each household member in the cauldron, arranging them as close together as possible, and as you put each in the dish, speak aloud the name of the person in the household.

Sprinkle the salt over everything and say, [Names of household members], *let our home be free of strife, drama, negativity, and impatience.* Add the oregano and say, [Names of household members], *let our home be filled with joy, happiness, harmony, and love.* Raise the cauldron high and say, *This home is blessed, and I am honored to share my space with all of you.* If the people you live with are participating, pass the cauldron around in a clockwise direction and invite each of them to also speak about the home they share being blessed.

When you're finished, leave the cauldron in a centrally located or common area in the home overnight. The next day, remove any items that are not biodegradable, and sprinkle the remainder of the contents outside, near the front door.

Spellwork for Buying and Selling Your Home

Maybe you've outgrown your living space as your family has gotten larger, and it's time to move on—or perhaps your offspring have flown the coop and you're ready to downsize. Believe it or not, there are plenty of magical actions out there to help you buy or sell a home. To sell your house faster—and get the price you want—try one of these practices:

+ **Burying a statue of St. Joseph:** This tradition involves burying a small statue of St. Joseph, the patron saint of the home, upside down in the yard of a house that's for sale. It's said to expedite the sale of the property and bring luck to the process. Once the house is sold, tradition suggests digging up the statue and placing it in a prominent spot in the new home for continued blessings. While I've never been Christian or anything close to it, I did this when it was time for my family to sell our first house—and we were in contract within nine days.

+ **Painting the front door red:** In some cultures, painting the front door of a house that's for sale red is believed to attract positive energy and good luck as well as signal to potential buyers that the house is welcoming and vibrant. Red is often associated with luck and prosperity in various folklore traditions.

+ **Sweeping out negative energy:** Before showing a house to potential buyers, sweep from the back of the house to the front—it helps remove negative energy and clears the space for positivity and good luck to flow in, potentially making the house more appealing to house hunters.

+ **Baking cinnamon rolls or cookies:** If you've got a showing or open house scheduled, bake a batch of cinnamon rolls or your favorite cookies beforehand— you might even want to enchant those goodies as you place them in the oven, encouraging buyers to like your house. The aroma will linger, and people will respond positively because it makes the place smell like a welcoming home in which they want to live.

If you're in the market to buy or rent a new place, try a few of these:

+ **House hunting by moon phase:** Folklore suggests that house hunting during a waxing moon, as the moon grows in size, is more auspicious for finding a home. It's believed that the increasing lunar energy aligns with growth and new beginnings, potentially aiding in finding a suitable property.

+ **Knocking on wood:** Try knocking on wood while stating your desire or wish for a specific type of home. The action of knocking on wood brings luck and can ensure your wishes are heard and fulfilled. Why not use this practice to manifest the ideal home?

+ **Making an offering:** When you've figured out the home you really want, present it with an offering (ideally during the waxing moon phase). You can offer wine, a small piece of bread, flowers, grain, or whatever makes the most sense to you. Stand at the edge of the property, introduce yourself to it, and place your offering on the ground. As you do, express your desire to make this home your own. Be courteous and mindful of current residents—don't trespass, and don't leave litter behind.

+ **Making a vision list:** Make a list of all the things you consider a must-have in a new home. Place it on your altar, and ask your deities or guides for assistance in finding a place that matches your wish list. Leave them offerings, and be sure to show thankfulness.

+ **Attending an open house:** Is the home you're interested in available for an open house? If so, plan on going to visit it! Before you step inside, take a moment to center yourself and open your heart to the space you're about to enter. Walk through the home mindfully, taking your time and paying attention to any intuitive feelings or signs that resonate. As you do so, talk to the home—if you really love it, *tell* it! Explain to the house why you'd be the perfect person to live there. Finally, touch your fingertips to the front door as you exit, expressing gratitude and furthering your connection to the house or apartment you've just toured. If possible, take a piece of grass, a stone, or a leaf from the property before you leave so you can use it as a link in magical workings.

+ **Performing a candle manifestation:** Light a green candle to represent growth and abundance. Write down the specific attributes you're seeking in a new home on a piece of paper, and place it under the candle. Say, *Through winding streets and paths unknown, I seek a place to call my home.* Extinguish the candle, and carry the paper in your pocket when you go out exploring, looking for new places to live.

+ **Sweetening up that landlord:** If you're hoping to rent, it never hurts to be on the landlord's good side, and that starts by making a sweet first impression. In addition to showing up on time and dressing appropriately, carry a small packet or bag of sugar with you, ideally in your pocket or purse. As you enter the home, discreetly dip a couple of fingers on your right hand into the sugar. Reach out for a good firm handshake as you introduce yourself—and let the sugar manifest a bit of sweetness for your potential new landlord!

Chapter 3
PROTECTION MAGIC

O ne of the most important functions of your home is to offer
you a sense of stability, safety, and security. Thus, the topic of
protection magic is getting its very own chapter, because safeguarding
your home and the people in it from harm is one of the best ways
to take advantage of your magical skills, whether you're a beginner
or a veteran. For many of us, that starts with cleansing, blessings,
and active protective spellwork around the home. Creating a
sacred, spiritual atmosphere is the first step to making your space a
magical one.

Simple Cleansing Methods for the Home

There are a number of ways you can do a home cleansing
on a regular basis—without breaking the bank—and which
method you choose will depend on your resources, time, and
level of interest.

Smoke Cleansing

An easy practice you can incorporate daily is to burn dried
cleansing or purification herbs. As the aromatic smoke wafts

through each room, visualize it purifying the space, leaving behind a sense of tranquility and positivity. Open your windows afterward, symbolically releasing any lingering negativity into the outside world.

Sound Cleansing

Sound cleansing with tools like singing bowls, bells, or drums can be a great way to harmonize your space. The resonating tones of these instruments create vibrations that break up stagnant energy, filling your home with soothing sounds. Ring the bowls or bells or bang the drums in every room so the sound can permeate the walls and clear away any lingering negativity. You can even add chanting or singing into the mix.

Cleansing with Salt

Salt cleansing is another method that has been used across cultures for centuries. Sprinkling salt along doorways and windowsills helps absorb negative energy. As you sweep or vacuum the salt away, envision it carrying away all the unwanted energies, leaving your home spiritually refreshed.

Cleansing with Holy Water

Finally, don't discount the power of holy water. Any water that has been ritually consecrated is considered holy and sacred. Sprinkling it around your home can wash away impurities and negativity, creating a space of sanctity. You may even want to infuse the water with cleansing herbs like sage and lavender.

Home Purification Ritual

This home purification ritual is designed to cleanse your space of negative energy, which is a great way to start your protection magic practices. Approach this practice with an open heart and a positive mindset, and clear your home of any lingering yuck that might be present. You'll need:

+ A white or lavender candle, representing purity and spiritual illumination
+ Matches or a lighter
+ A tablespoon of sea salt, for its purifying properties
+ A bowl of water, representing emotional cleansing and purity
+ An empty bowl
+ Essential oils, such as lavender, frankincense, or cedarwood for a purifying aroma
+ A base or carrier oil for dilution
+ *Optional:* Your favorite relaxing music or sounds of nature to enhance the atmosphere

Find a quiet space near the center of your home. See this space as a sanctuary, free from distractions, where you can center your thoughts and energies. Place the candle on a table or your altar space, and turn on your music if you've decided to use it. Light the candle, and as the flame dances, close your eyes and take deep, cleansing breaths, allowing yourself to be filled with positive energy as you release any negativity or tension.

Place your carrier oil in the empty bowl and add a drop or two of your chosen essential oils, and swirl the bowl gently to mix and dilute your ingredients. Dip a couple of fingers into the oil and then dab them on the opposite palm. Rub your hands together and feel the soothing scent enveloping you. Blend the sea salt into the water, stirring gently with your finger. Beginning at the northern aspect of your home, walk through your home, sprinkling the water gently with your fingertips. Visualize this sacred water forming a protective boundary, allowing only positivity to enter and forcing negative vibrations to be repelled. Feel the space becoming lighter, purer, and shielded from any harmful influences.

With each step you take, gently wave your hands, letting the aroma from the oils permeate the air. Envision this scent cleansing the atmosphere, inviting in tranquility and calm. Let the fragrance wrap every corner, bringing peace and harmony to every inch of your space. As you enter each room with your bowl of salt water, say, *May this home be a space of harmony, love, and serenity. May it be protected from all negativity and filled with only the purest energy.* Feel the power of your words and intentions resonate throughout the space.

Once you've returned to your starting point, take a moment to breathe. You may wish to express your gratitude to the guardians or spirits of your home—we'll talk more about them shortly—by acknowledging their presence and assistance in purifying your space. Gently blow out the candle to mark the end of the ritual while the positivity and protection you've invoked remain, filling your home with a sense of lightness, harmony, and peace.

Household Guardian Spirits

Like so many other aspects of modern witchcraft, there's no hard-and-fast rule that you *have* to work with household guardians. But in my experience, if you can do so, it's totally worth the effort and energy you put into it. Why? Because a household guardian does exactly what its name implies—it's a being that *guards your household*. That's literally its purpose. Given the choice between existing in my home unprotected versus living here knowing there's an extra layer of security... well, I know which of the two I prefer.

Household guardian spirits, which are prevalent in folklore across cultures, protect homes and their occupants from malevolent forces. These spirits are often helpful in nature and are deeply woven into the fabric of cultural beliefs—there is such an intimate relationship between us humans and our living spaces.

In various traditions worldwide, household guardian spirits take diverse forms. Japanese folklore includes tales of the *zashikiwarashi*.[13] These mischievous spirits reside in unused rooms, bringing good fortune to the household. Similarly, in Celtic legends, brownies are small beings who perform household chores when the family is asleep, provided they are shown appreciation.

In parts of Scandinavia, the *tomte*, or *nisse*, are tiny, gnomelike creatures associated with farms. They ensure the well-being of animals and crops, but their help is contingent upon offerings and other demonstrations of respect. In Slavic folklore, the Domovyk (in some places referred to as *domovoi*) are house spirits believed to be the souls of deceased family members. They protect the living residents in return for offerings of milk and bread.[14]

---

13. Yoshimura, "To Believe *and* Not to Believe," 149–50.
14. Pamita, *Baba Yaga's Book of Witchcraft*, 32–43.

In religions of the African diaspora, ancestral spirits often play the role of household protectors. Families offer prayers and libations to honor them, seeking their guidance and protection. Similarly, in some Indigenous American cultures, various animal spirits are known to guard homes and offer spiritual guidance.

The nearly universal thread among these guardian spirits is their symbiotic relationship with humans. Families contribute respect, acknowledgment, and sometimes offerings, and in return, the spirits provide protection, fortune, and harmony within the home.

There are a variety of ways to incorporate a household guardian into your space—again, there aren't a lot of hard-and-fast rules here because everyone's circumstances and practice are different. You might consider seeing if your space already *has* an entity or spirit hanging around that could be worked with as a guardian of the home. If there's not, you can invite one in of your choosing— perhaps an ancestor spirit might be willing to help here, or you can work with the spirits of the land around your space (see chapter 1 for more on spirits of land and place).

Determining whether your home has a spirit guardian often involves paying attention to subtle signs, personal experiences, and the atmosphere within your living space. Notice the overall energy in your home. Is there a sense of calm and peace? Or do you often feel uneasy or uncomfortable in specific areas? Be aware of any unexplained sounds, movements, or unusual occurrences in your home that cannot be easily attributed to logical explanations. Trust your intuition and feelings about your home. Often, your gut feelings can provide valuable insights into the energy of your space. Pets, especially cats and dogs, are believed to be sensitive to spiritual energies. Notice if your pets exhibit unusual behavior, such as staring at specific spots or acting as if they're interacting with something unseen. If you belong to a culture or tradition with beliefs in household guardian spirits, explore the signs and rituals associated with recognizing their presence.

It's also a good idea to do a bit of mundane homework—and this will help you if you decide to create a household grimoire, which we'll talk about in chapter 4. Investigate the history of your home, especially if it's an older property. Learning about previous occupants or significant events associated with the location might provide clues. If you believe your home is likely to have a guardian spirit, create a small altar with offerings like candles, flowers, food, or incense. If there is a spirit, this small gesture is a good way to show respect and acknowledgment. My house has a clear presence inhabiting it—it's an elderly woman who lived here for six decades before passing away, and I often smell cookies baking in the evenings, letting me know she's hanging around. I always say hello to Margaret and thank her for letting me live here.

HOUSEHOLD PROTECTION OIL

Brew up a batch of protection oil and use it to anoint doorways, windows, or other entry points to your home. If possible, make this oil during the full moon. You'll need:

+ Small glass or ceramic bowl
+ ½ cup unscented carrier oil, such as jojoba or grapeseed
+ 1 teaspoon dried basil, for protection
+ 1 teaspoon dried rosemary, for purification
+ 1 teaspoon sea salt, for banishing negativity
+ Wooden or glass mixing utensil

- ◆ 1 small piece of black tourmaline, for grounding and protection
- ◆ 5 to 7 drops of essential oil; choose from protective oils like frankincense, cedarwood, bergamot, tea tree, etc.
- ◆ Cheesecloth or a fine strainer

First, cleanse your workspace. You can burn sacred herbs, sprinkle consecrated water, or use any other method you prefer to purify the area. In the small glass or ceramic bowl, mix the basil, rosemary, and sea salt.

Warm the carrier oil slightly—don't let it get too hot—and pour it over the dried herb and salt mixture. Stir gently with a wooden or glass utensil while focusing on your intention for protection, with a home that will always be safe and secure. Place the tourmaline crystal in the mixture; this stone is known for absorbing negative energy. Visualize it creating a shield around your home. Add 5 to 7 drops of your favorite protective essential oil(s) to the mixture. Essential oils like frankincense, cedarwood, juniper, or lavender are excellent choices for enhancing the protective properties of the oil. Stir gently to combine. Place the bowl under the light of the full moon for a few hours to charge it with protective energy.

After you've charged your oil, strain the mixture through a piece of cheesecloth into a dark-colored glass bottle. Squeeze out as much oil as possible from the herbs and remove the crystal. Seal the bottle tightly, and label it—be sure to include the date. Store your oil in a cool, dark place when not in use.

Protecting Your Pets

Whether your pet has feathers, fur, or fins, they're part of your family, and you love them! Pets are good for us. They comfort us when we're feeling blue, and they bring us joy and unconditional love…although my cats would probably point out I'm simply their servant who feeds them and empties the boxes in which they relieve themselves. Regardless, your pets are an integral part of your household—and if you've ever lost one, you know how devastating it can be when you suddenly have that dog- or cat- or bird-shaped hole in your heart. Keeping them safe and protected is one of many ways to show them how much you love them.

Pet Protection Ritual

Crafting a protective ritual for your beloved pet involves creating a sacred space, invoking protective energies, and imbuing items with positive intentions. You'll need several items that resonate with protective, positive energy:

- Unscented white candles
- Protective crystals, such as hematite, obsidian, or black tourmaline
- A magical link to your pet—a photo, whisker, a bit of fur, or a collar

Invite your pet to join you for this ritual, if possible. Place the magical link to your pet at the center of your altar, and arrange the candles and crystals around it, creating a safe and sacred zone. Light the candles.

Call upon your deities, household guardians, or other entities aligned with protection, guidance, and support. Clearly articulate your intention, seeking their assistance in shielding and safeguarding your pet. Hold your pet's magical link—the collar, fur, photo, or other item—and visualize it being filled with protective energy, forming a shield of safety around your pet. If your pet is with you, place one hand on them while you hold the magical link in the other, feeling the protection and love surrounding them. For pets that can't be held, such as fish, place your hand on the glass of the aquarium or tank.

Speak affirmations of protection and love for your pet, infusing the space with positive intentions. Visualize a sphere of golden light enveloping your animal friend, forming a resilient shield against any harm or negativity that may come their way. View the candle flames' energy as a light of protection, expanding the protective energies around them. When you're ready, close the ritual with gratitude, affirming the continuous protection around your pet, and extinguish the candles.

Other Ways to Protect Your Pet

If you don't have the ability to do a full ritual as just outlined, there are some other quick and easy bits of pet protection magic you can do to keep your animal companions safe.

+ Mark protective symbols on the back of your pet's tags or on the inside of their collar.
+ Keep a magical link to your pet on your altar at all times, surrounded by protective herbs and crystals.

+ Place protective crystals, stones, or shells beside or on top of tanks and aquariums.

+ Inscribe your pet's name on a small candle, such as a tealight, and dress it with a bit of protection oil. Light the candle on your altar, and allow it to burn out on its own. Take the remaining stub of the candle and keep it somewhere in your home so your pet will always feel connected to the place where you live.

Obviously, there are mundane ways to keep your pets healthy and safe in addition to magical ones. If your pet is injured, ill, or exhibiting unusual behaviors, please seek professional veterinary care immediately.

Plants Around Your Home

Adding plants to your living space can be a great way to introduce rich, versatile magical energies into your home. Gather some vases and fill them with flowers; choose them based on their symbolic meanings or magical correspondences. Try selecting roses for love, lavender for relaxation, or chamomile for tranquility. Their fragrances can also serve aromatherapy purposes, influencing mood and energy in the space. Charging flowers and plants under moonlight or pairing them with crystals can enhance their magical properties, which you can then bring back into the various rooms in your home.

Potted plants, especially those with cleansing properties like sage or rosemary, will help to continuously purify energies in a room. Growing herbs associated with specific magical properties adds depth to the space, enabling their use in rituals or spells and infusing the room with unique energies. Plants with particular shapes or colors make great decorative elements, enhancing your magical aesthetics. Finally, tending to potted plants becomes a form of plant magic—speak affirmations while caring for them or pour intentions into their soil.

Through mindful care and intention, daily actions like watering, pruning, and otherwise tending to plants infuse them with energies of growth, vitality, or healing.

Allowing the natural beauty of flowers and plants to uplift a room does more than just create a visually delightful space. They also help to make for a sacred and energetically powerful atmosphere—which is all part of crafting a magical home.

A quick note of caution: Some plants are toxic to pets. If you've got animal friends living in your home, please be sure to research whether or not a plant can be harmful to them.

Car Protection Spell

A car or any other vehicle you own can be used symbolically in spells or rituals for travel, freedom, or journeying, but you can also do workings with them directly related to safety and protection. This comes in particularly handy if you have a new, inexperienced driver in your home. I did this spell to protect my son's first car when he was a teenager because he's always been completely fearless, and I wanted to keep him as safe as possible when he wasn't at home. You'll need:

+ A toy vehicle similar in color, model, or style to the one you wish to protect
+ A black permanent marker

+ A small block of craft foam
+ A knife
+ Duct tape or heavy-duty electrical tape

Use the permanent marker to write the name of the vehicle's primary driver on the toy. As you do, visualize the vehicle being surrounded by soft protective light. Hold the toy vehicle in your hands, feeling the energy around it.

Using the knife, cut a hole in the block of craft foam and stuff the vehicle inside. Wrap the entire block with duct or heavy electrical tape. As you do this, see the safe, protective warmth of the foam enveloping the car, with the tape keeping it secure and in place. Say, *You are safe and sound as you drive around, protected in this vehicle as you travel near and far.*

Tuck the wrapped block somewhere unobtrusive in the vehicle—under a seat, in the bottom of the spare tire well, or elsewhere—and know the vehicle and its occupants will be kept safe.

Mailbox Protection Spell

When I wrote the initial outline for this book, it did *not* include a mailbox protection spell. Honestly, in thirty-plus years of practicing magic, such a thing had never even occurred to me—the number of times it popped up on my radar was exactly zero. And then, the summer I was working on the manuscript for *The Witch's Home*, my mailbox got hit by vehicles *three times* in a span of just six weeks.

The first incident was a hit-and-run driver who plowed into it so hard he knocked the post out of its hole and sent it flying across the yard—this was when I learned the previous owners of my house had never secured it in place; they'd just filled the hole with rocks and soil around the post. The box itself was pretty banged up, but I was able to reattach it to the four-by-four post; I shoved the post back in the hole and figured I'd just live with it. Two days later, a local police officer backed into it while turning around in my driveway—he knocked on the door and was appropriately apologetic. A few weeks after *that*, one of the neighbor boys ran into it with his ATV and was courteous enough to let me know, as well as get a shovel and try to fix the situation.

After the third incident, I decided something needed to happen. I didn't know *why* my mailbox had suddenly presented a big ol' target to the universe, but I was tired of fixing it. Also, after all the abuse, the door didn't close correctly, so I was constantly ending up with wet mail. So, I bought a new mailbox—it's bright red, so it really stands out—and a small bag of concrete and got to work. This was the mundane half of the solution.

I also decided some magical activity was called for and created a protection sigil to stick under the mailbox, between the box itself and the mounting bracket that sat on the post. If you're worried about someone damaging your mailbox, try this simple spell out. While you can obviously do it when replacing the box, you can also remove your existing mailbox and place the sigil beneath it.

+ **Create your sigil of protection:** A sigil is essentially a symbol. You can make one that looks like something protective—a shield, for instance—or you can make it more complex. There are a zillion different ways to create a sigil, but the way I like to do it is so easy it's ridiculous. First, I write out a word or slogan that describes my intent. In this case, it was simply *PROTECTION*. I removed the vowels, which gave me *PRTCTN*. Then I eliminated the duplicate T, leading me to *PRTCN*. Finally, I moved the letters around, blending them together to create a symbol— it was the sort of image that anyone who saw it wouldn't recognize for what it was, but *I* knew what it meant.

+ **Add the symbol to your mailbox:** There are several ways you can put the symbol on your mailbox—the key is to place it somewhere hidden, where no one knows it exists but you. You could use paint or marker if you like. If you have a wooden mailbox, you can carve it into the wood. I chose to be a little bit extra about the process. Around the same time I got the mailbox, I purchased the cutting machine mentioned in chapter 10 (because craft projects!). After I used my cutter to make a vinyl decal with my street address on it, I hopped into the machine's software program to create my sigil and print it out on leftover vinyl—it's a jaunty yellow, because I happen to love the way it looks on my bright red mailbox. Once that was done, I applied the sigil decal to the underside of the box, centered between the holds for the mounting bracket.

+ **Attach the mailbox:** Attach your mailbox to its post, or if you have a wall-mounted mailbox, hang it back up. Again, be sure the sigil isn't visible once it's in place.

+ **Wrap things up:** I always like to use a multipronged approach, so I stuck an iron nail and a hematite stone—both are associated with protection—in the soil beneath my mailbox and then said a small (and admittedly silly) incantation: *At the end of the yard right by the street, sits my mailbox, red and sweet. To protect it from drivers—a mighty feat!—I place this sigil of protection, tidy and neat.*

+ **Watch as people fail to hit your mailbox.**

Can you use this method to protect other outdoor items? Certainly! Is it a bit goofy? Sure. Is it effective? Time will tell, but so far, I've observed no fewer than four drivers and a kid on a dirt bike swerve toward it and then avert their wheels at the very last second.

Keep-Away Property Protection Spell

If you're worried about trouble from your neighbors or potential trespassers, do this spell to keep them away. If you live in an apartment or dormitory, you can still perform this working, but you'll need to adjust things a bit to work around the corners of your building. You'll need:

+ Railroad spikes
+ A large hammer

Walk around your property with the spikes and hammer, starting at the northernmost part of your yard, and move clockwise. At each corner of the yard, drive a spike into the soil. Pound it in deeply with your hammer so it's below the surface of the soil. As you swing your hammer, say, *Trespassers, beware, this place is mine. Trespassers, take care, this place is mine. Trespassers, don't you dare, this place is mine.* Once you've circled the entire property and returned to the north side, walk to the center. Extend your arms skyward and say, *This place is mine, and none shall do it harm!*

Refresh your boundary periodically if you need to, either with additional railroad spikes or with protective herbs and crystals (see the detailed list at the end of this chapter).

A brief note on railroad spikes: Please be sure to source them ethically and responsibly. Do not remove spikes being used to hold a rail in place—causing a train accident just so you could do spellwork is not responsible magic.

WIND CHIME PROTECTION SPELL

Wind chimes have a rich history in various cultures and are often associated with folklore, superstitions, and spiritual beliefs. Their gentle, melodic sounds are often used in meditation practices because the calming tones are believed to help relax the mind and enhance concentration during meditation. In many cultures, wind chimes are seen as a way of warding off evil spirits and negative energies because their sound is thought to disrupt negative energy patterns and create a harmonious atmosphere. You can find them made of just about any material—metal, bamboo, glass, or even driftwood—but I personally prefer the rich tones of metal tubes bonking into each other. You can incorporate wind chimes into this easy home protection ritual. Do this ritual during a full moon if possible. You'll need:

- A black candle and candleholder
- Matches or a lighter
- A piece of hematite or other protective stone
- A set of wind chimes; make sure you pick a set that has a sound you really love, because they're going to be banging around a lot whenever there's air movement.

Place the black candle in a holder on your altar or a table in the center of your home. Light it and take a few moments to focus on the flame as you visualize a protective energy expanding, filling, and surrounding your entire home. Pass the hematite over the candle, holding it in your dominant hand, and see the stone surrounded by a bright, shimmering light. You may wish to offer a short invocation, such as *In the twilight's hush and the moon's soft glow, I call upon energies from long ago. With elements and energy all in sync, I cast this spell, a protective link.*

Take the candle, in its holder, with you. Holding it in one hand, walk around the inside of your home, moving a clockwise direction. With the other hand, gently tap the hematite against each door and window. As you do, envision its bright light growing to create a protective bubble around your home, preventing any negativity or harm from making its way in and allowing only love and positive energy to enter.

Return to your starting point, and place the candle on the table with the hematite beside it.

Hold the wind chimes—again, with your dominant hand—and pass them over the flame. As before, you might want to speak a short invocation, like *I charge the air that fills these chimes to protect my home in uncertain times. Let only good enter this sacred space, and the negative be repelled away from this place.* Step outside, and walk around your house once more, clockwise, carrying the candle and holding the wind chimes up to each window and door. Once you've completed your circuit, extinguish the candle. Hang your wind chimes near the entrance you use the most, so they can catch the breeze and sing their protective song for you.

Place the hematite on the interior doorframe of the same entryway to function as an indoor protective charm. Whenever you hear the wind chimes sing, know your home is safeguarded and secure.

Protective Herbs and Crystals

We live in a dangerous world. Whether you're walking alone in the woods or going out for a late-night club session with friends, the fact remains that anything can happen anywhere, at any time—and it's important to take the level of safety precautions appropriate to where you live. I know people in areas who never lock their doors, and I have friends in places where the first thing you do when you enter your home is make sure the front door is latched and deadbolted behind you.

Now, I'm not going to turn this into a lengthy manifesto about all the things you need to do on a mundane level to stay safe; there are plenty of people out there who are way more qualified than me to give that advice. Furthermore, you know your neighborhood far better than I ever could, so I'm going to trust that you know what you should be doing to maximize your own safety. If you haven't read it, pick up a copy of Amy Blackthorn's book *Protection Magic*, because it's outstanding.

What I can do, however, is offer a few simple magical practices you can incorporate into your day-to-day routines for protection. It should go without saying that these should be used *in tandem* with mundane practices, not instead of them.

Protective Crystals

Crystals are a great way to feel safe and protected—plus, they're often easy to obtain, and they're generally small and portable. You can stick one in your pocket, wear it as a piece of jewelry, hide it in your purse, or even place it strategically around your home.

- **Black tourmaline:** Known for its strong protective properties, black tourmaline is excellent for dispelling negative energies. It creates a shield around the wearer, absorbing and transmuting any negativity encountered in urban environments.

- **Smoky quartz:** This crystal is adept at grounding and shielding from negative influences. It's particularly useful for transmuting negative energy into positive, fostering a sense of security in crowded or chaotic areas.

- **Amethyst:** Beyond its calming and soothing properties, amethyst offers protection against psychic attacks. Carrying this crystal can provide a sense of mental clarity and protection in bustling city environments.

- **Clear quartz:** Often considered a versatile and amplifying crystal, clear quartz is known for its ability to enhance the energies of other protective stones. Carrying it alongside other protective crystals can boost their effectiveness.

+ **Obsidian:** This volcanic glass is excellent for protection and grounding. It forms a shield against negativity and absorbs and dissipates disharmonious energies, making it beneficial for city environments.

+ **Labradorite:** Known for its mystical and protective properties, labradorite shields against negativity while enhancing intuition and perception. Carrying this stone may help in navigating city situations intuitively.

+ **Tiger's eye:** With its grounding and protective energies, tiger's eye can promote a sense of confidence and courage, helping you feel more safe and secure in urban settings.

Protective Herbs

Like crystals, herbs are generally easy to obtain, and they're portable. You can use dried or fresh ones—tuck them in your shoe or pocket, brew them into an infusion or an oil blend, or keep them in pots or jars around your home.

+ **Rosemary:** Known for its protective properties, rosemary wards off negative energies and promotes clarity of thought. A sprig or a sachet of dried rosemary offers protection in bustling urban environments.

+ **Mugwort:** A powerful protective herb, mugwort offers psychic protection and enhances intuition. Mugwort leaves can aid you in feeling shielded and offer a heightened sense of situational awareness.

+ **Basil:** Beyond its culinary uses, basil is associated with protection and purification. Carry a small bundle of basil or wear it in an amulet to create a protective barrier against negativity.

+ **Juniper:** Known for its cleansing and protective qualities, juniper wards off negative influences. The berries and needles boost a sense of security and purification in urban settings.

+ **Cinnamon:** Associated with warmth and protection, cinnamon forms a barrier against negativity. Carry a stick of cinnamon or use it in sachets to help ward off danger.

+ **Thyme:** With its purifying and protective properties, thyme dispels negative energies. Thyme, tucked in your pocket or carried in a sachet, can offer protection from those who might wish to cause you harm.

Chapter 4
MAKE A HOME GRIMOIRE

In many traditions of witchcraft, the grimoire is used as a place for practitioners to record all kinds of things related to their practice—spells, recipes, correspondences, and so on. Some people refer to this as a Book of Shadows—and a few will argue that the Book of Shadows and grimoire are two entirely different things— but I've always thought of it as a grimoire because I keep everything in one place for ease of use.

I started a home grimoire when I bought my cottage back in the summer of 2021—and really, it wasn't *meant* to be a grimoire. It just sort of turned into one organically. My original plan was to simply put together a binder of information about the house—because it needed a *lot* of things done to it. The walls on the main floor were all gloomy, dark, and covered in faux wood paneling … and I knew I couldn't live here until I did some painting. So, I grabbed a three-ring notebook and stuck all my paint swatches in it, thinking at some point in the future I'd need to double-check what colors I'd used.

In the first few weeks I was here, I kept finding small interesting bits of stuff left behind by the previous owner, who'd lived here for sixty years before her death … so I added information about those things into the book as well. Then I started discovering the abundance of wild plant life around the property and began making notes on that. When I dug my first flower bed, I found bits of broken pottery and glass as well as a few utensils. I also unearthed bricks made by a local kiln in the early 1900s. I took photos of all of these … and I'm sure you can see how this rapidly escalated into a full collection of memorabilia all connected to my little half acre.

Pretty soon I had a whole compendium of stuff comprising the history of my home. I reached out to a nice lady at the county recorder's office and obtained copies of the original deeds to the lot, going back to its first sale in 1874, when a gentleman bought the land from the local mining company for $150. I found a newspaper article from just before the Prohibition era featuring a photo of one of the house's early owners in the tavern he ran, just around the corner. In the picture, he's standing at the bar in front of the large mirror that now hangs bolted to my bedroom wall; apparently when the tavern closed, he brought the mirror home with him.

I gave my house a name—it's Cairn Brae Cottage—and ordered myself a pretty metal sign to hang out front, so there's a photo of that in the grimoire as well. I've added notes about rituals I've performed to protect my house and half acre, information about the previously mentioned long-term owner (who certainly still resides here in spirit), and more. It's brought me closer to the house and helped me make it my *home* instead of just a place I live.

Building Your Home's Grimoire

If you'd like to make a home grimoire of your own, I'd recommend getting something expandable, such as a three-ring binder. I like using mine with clear sheet protectors because there are some documents that are too long—for instance, the legal-size documents from the county deed office—to put on a traditional 8.5 × 11–inch sheet of paper. The sheet protector sleeves allow me to fold those items and still keep them in the same place as everything else. You'll also want to make sure you have blank paper for your book—you can use this to draw or sketch on, or even paste in photos, color swatches, and other nuggets of information. I'm a big fan of cardstock for its sheer durability, but you can use any kind of paper you like—a three-hole punch or protector sleeves will allow you to add it to your binder. I'd also suggest dividing your binder into sections for easier management. Let's talk about a few things you might wish to include.

A Dedication

It's a great idea to offer a dedication to your home at the opening of your grimoire. This can be something as simple as *This is the book of Morgan and Thorn's home, dedicated 2022.* Have you thought about giving your place a name? This is the ideal place to include it! Not sure what to call your house, apartment, camper, or dorm room? Well, take a look around the place—are there notable geographic or architectural features that inspire you? Does the building have any historical relevance? Is there something really unique about your place? My house is a hundred years old and sits at the front of a steep hill, and when I began digging my garden beds, I unearthed an inordinate supply of large stones, which I then stacked in little heaps around the yard. Thus, Cairn Brae Cottage was born—*cairn* is the Scottish Gaelic word for a pile of stones, and a brae is the base of a hillside. If you're really stuck, take some time to meditate, and *ask* your home what it would like to be called.

Land Records

Even if your home is newer, the land it sits on has history. In fact, that history goes back long before it was even recorded. Put in some work to learn about the timeline of the space your home occupies. If you live in North America, there are a number of apps and websites available (I recommend one called simply Native Land Digital) that will help you determine which Indigenous groups once lived in your area. Before my state was colonized, it was the home of the Adena and Hopewell cultures and later the Shawanwaki/Shawnee peoples.[15]

For more recent history, there's no better place than your county's office building. In the case of my property, I learned it was first purchased in 1874 when a local mining company decided to parcel out its land for residential sales. A gentleman by the fabulous name of Zephemiah D. Dildine bought the lot, which, at the time, was adjacent to a set of railroad tracks that ran coal from up in the hills down to the main depot here in town. Old Zephemiah kept the land for about four years, and then it went through a series of owners— one of whom built the existing house around 1921—before finally ending up in my hands. Because I took the time to do this research, I was able to learn not just the history of the property, but that of the people who have lived on it for the past century and a half.

Interior Spaces

Have you ever walked into a place and just felt like you belonged? That was my experience the day my real estate agent and I first entered the living room of my home—and looking back, it's a bit surprising I felt that way. It was a rainy day, and this house was *gloomy*. Once I closed on the sale and had the keys in my hot little hands, I knew I needed to make some significant cosmetic improvements before I moved my stuff in, so I spent an entire week cleaning, sanding, painting, removing a few ugly built-ins, and doing minor repairs.

Naturally, prior to any of that, I took *Before* photos—and these reside in my household grimoire. Additionally, I've tucked into the

....
15. "Native Land."

book the *After* photos as I worked my way through every room, and with each one is a paint card from the local home improvement store in case I ever have to answer the question, "What color IS that wall anyway?" I also took pictures of the World War II–era wallpaper, covered in battleships, that I uncovered behind the kitchen cabinets and of the crucifix found on a high shelf in the laundry room, left behind after elderly Margaret's death. I've even included a tiny swatch of floral fabric I found on the floor in a corner of the upstairs closet.

Exterior Spaces

Does your home have a big back patio, a firepit, or some other sort of gathering space? I don't have any of those—my lot was pretty much virgin soil when I bought it—but I do have an amazing front porch. It's become a de facto extension of my living room, and during the three seasons where the weather is good, I spend a lot of time out there, reading, writing, eating my dinner, drinking a glass of wine as I wave to my neighbors, and so on. It's a space I've filled with plants and artwork, and to me, it's the place that welcomes people before they've even set foot through the door. I've also turned the empty half of my yard into a beautiful garden, full of vegetables, flowers for pollinators, herbs, birdhouses, and even a few small fruit and berry plantings. Each thing I plant, every garden bed I install, each pollinator patch I till, is documented in my grimoire. Even if your outdoor space is a simple balcony with a couple of potted plants, it's *yours*. It's part of your home, so why not include it?

History of the Neighborhood or Community

Whether you're new to your neighborhood or it's the place you grew up, learning about the greater space around you can help you connect more deeply to your home. As we already discussed, you can find the land records for your home and learn about the people who lived in it, but it's also important to connect to the community at large. When was your town founded? What were some of the early industries there? Are there any interesting pieces of folklore, local legends, or important history you can learn about?

I live in an old coal mining town that became a moonshine hotbed during Prohibition, and believe me, my village celebrates both parts of its legacy equally. Many communities have local history centers—take some time to gather that information when you can to bring yourself closer to the area you inhabit.

Native Plant Species

As I became more and more immersed in my new home, exploring the dirt roads and trails that wend up into the hills around me, I discovered an incredible amount of variation in native plant life. Appalachia, where I live, is one of the most biodiverse areas in the country thanks to geography, migration patterns, climate, and microhabitats, and there's a vast selection of edible and medicinal wild plants growing in abundance. The second summer I was in my home, I selected an area of my yard that I was just going to stop mowing—it was partly because I see lawn grass as unnecessary but mostly because I wanted to find out what would happen if I simply left it alone.

For the first six weeks or so, I just got really long grass that became a favorite napping spot for my dog. After a while, though, something interesting began to happen. Plants began just sprouting up at random, growing happily in what I soon came to call my pollinator patch: asters, chicory, broomcorn, red clover, trillium, goldenrod, and mullein. The steep hillside behind my house is scattered with oaks, littering my yard with acorns in the fall. There are hickories, sugar maples, catawba, and beech trees as well as cohosh, mayapple, jack in the pulpit, and bloodroot. I threw out a handful of pawpaw seeds to see if they'll take, and hopefully, I'll get those fruits in a few years as well.

If you live in an urban area, there are still many ways you can connect with the native plants in your space—those plants are there; they're just discouraged from actively growing. Look in park spaces, along waterways, such as rivers and retention ponds, in vacant lots, and even between the cracks in the sidewalk. As I discover new species, I sketch them in my grimoire, along with some of their scientific properties (I recommend the apps PlantSnap and iNaturalist for great information), and map out their magical applications as well.

Animals and Insects

Whether you live in a heavily developed city or a rural area, there are going to be animals—it's just a fact of life. As habitats are threatened by human movement, the variation of species may dwindle, but if you pay close attention to the details in the environment around you, you'll start to notice the existence of wildlife. In my little corner of the woods, I've seen deer, foxes, bald eagles, and the occasional bobcat in addition to more common critters like groundhogs, squirrels, chipmunks, and raccoons. You might live in an area populated by black bears, moose, or even alligators.

What about insects? We often don't think about them—they're typically out of sight or, at the very least, underfoot where they're far less noticeable. But if you start looking around and paying attention, you may spot yellow orb spiders weaving a beautiful web in your garden, a luna moth flitting by, a praying mantis pollinating the flowers, fireflies lighting up the night sky, or a colony of honeybees working busily behind your home. Read up on the symbolism of the animals and insects you see and add their info to your grimoire.

Other Natural Features

What else exists in your environment? Do you live near mountains, rock formations, or a river? What about the different aspects of a nearby park or your city's designated greenspace? Get to know these spaces well. Even if they're not in your immediate backyard, try to find a way to spend some time in them, getting to know them and learning more about their historical and cultural significance. Do you feel a certain way when you visit them? Is there a feature that seems especially magical to you? How can you incorporate it into your practice?

Home-Based Rituals and Spells

Once you've begun compiling your home grimoire—and it will likely be an ongoing, ever-evolving project that could take you *years* to work on—start thinking about the spells and rituals you'll be doing that are specifically home-based. You can include workings for protection, prosperity, or abundance, a home blessing, and whatever else you can think of. As you perform each one, be sure to include the date so you can always go back later to see when you did it.

Make Your Grimoire a Permanent Fixture

Keep your home grimoire in a place of honor—one that's easily accessible to you—and as you learn more about your home and find more things to love about it, continue expanding your book so it's a living, organically growing treasure of knowledge.

Chapter 5
THE MAGIC OF DOORS, WINDOWS, AND FIREPLACES

Entryways to a home—any point that allows access—are profoundly spiritual spaces. They are thresholds between the outer world and the inner sanctum, representing a transition not only from the physical outdoors to the indoors but also from the mundane to the sacred. In a way, they are symbolic crossroads where different energies intersect—and in folklore and mythology, crossroads are places where the veil between worlds is thin, making them potent for magical and spiritual work.

Similarly, entryways are considered places where the spiritual realm meets the material world and are often intentionally designed to invite positive energies into the home. In feng shui, for instance, the arrangement of furniture and objects near the entrance is carefully considered to allow the smooth flow of Chi, or life force energy. Positive symbols, such as mirrors to reflect negativity away or potted plants to invite growth, are ideal to place near your entryways. In some cultures, the door to a home is a place for honoring ancestors. Ancestral altars or shrines can be positioned near the entrance, allowing your family to pay respects and seek guidance from your forebears, who protect the home and its inhabitants.

Front Porches and Haint Blue

Even a front porch can be a magical space. In the Lowcountry region of South Carolina and Georgia, many front porches are decorated by painting the ceiling, doors, and window frames with a color known as *haint blue*. It's a very specific shade of blue that has cultural and historical significance—the word *haint* is derived from the Gullah language, spoken by the African American communities in the area. In Gullah, a "haint" refers to a spirit or a ghost.[16] Haint blue is a pale, muted blue color, often resembling robin's-egg blue or a soft turquoise, and is traditionally believed to ward off evil spirits or haints from entering a home.

The origins of haint blue can be traced back to spiritual beliefs brought over by enslaved Africans, who combined their traditions with local Southern beliefs and practices. The color, derived from indigo, was believed to mimic water, which spirits cannot cross, thus preventing them from entering the home. Over time, the practice of painting architectural elements in haint blue became a common tradition in many Southern communities, especially in the coastal regions.

Today, haint blue is not only appreciated for its historical significance but also for its calming, soothing aesthetic. It continues to be used in architectural and interior design, particularly in the Southern United States, as a nod to tradition and folklore. However, it's important to note that even though major paint manufacturers now market and sell a color called haint blue, what makes it truly haint blue is the manner in which it's used.

....

16. Parks, "What the Color 'Haint Blue' Means to the Descendants of Enslaved Africans."

Doors

The door to your home—whether it's at the front, the back, or in that odd little spot behind the kitchen—is more than just a panel in the wall that keeps you out or lets you into a place. It's a liminal spot between the worlds, and there are some amazing bits of folklore from around the world related to doorways. After all, if the entrance to your home is a spiritual space, it stands to reason that people from every culture have ideas about what that space actually means. According to superstition:

+ The front door—or whichever door serves as your main entrance—should always be protected by a good luck charm or symbol of some sort.

+ You should wait to hug or shake hands with a guest until they've completely crossed the threshold. In Russia, it's considered bad luck to do so while they're still in the doorway because that is where the household spirits reside.

+ If you see a spider crawling up your doorframe, it means you've got an unexpected visitor coming to call soon.

+ There's an Appalachian belief that you should always leave a home through the same door by which you entered it—otherwise, you're inviting misfortune.

+ Doors should be left open when a baby is being born or if someone is about to pass away in the home. This allows the person's spirit to enter or leave the space, depending on whether they're coming or going.

Threshold Blessing

When you move into a new home, it's a great time to do an initial threshold blessing, especially if you have the opportunity to perform this before you've even moved any furniture or belongings inside. If that's not the case for you, no problem! Even if you already live in your home, this process is still effective and can be either done as a stand-alone practice or incorporated into a greater blessing and cleansing ritual. Whether the house is empty or occupied, make sure it's clean and orderly before you begin. You'll need:

+ A bowl of salt water, for purification
+ A white candle, to symbolize purity and light, and a candleholder
+ Your favorite purification incense and incense burner
+ Matches or a lighter
+ Fresh bread or grain, to represent abundance and prosperity
+ A small potted plant, for growth and vitality
+ A bell, for clearing energy
+ A small dish of honey, to symbolize sweetness and harmony

Prepare your home by standing at the threshold, just outside the door, and lighting the candle and the incense, allowing the smoke to purify the space. Set them down beside the door—a small table or flat stool is an ideal spot. Place the bowl of salt water, bread, potted plant, and dish of honey within easy reach as well. Close your eyes, take deep breaths, and visualize white light surrounding you. When you're ready, stand in the open doorway. Ring the bell (or knock on the door if you don't have a doorbell) three times to clear any lingering energies and say, *I welcome all that is positive and loving into this home. May it be a sanctuary of peace, happiness, and prosperity.*

Dip your fingers into the salt water and flick droplets around the threshold, allowing it to purify and protect the entryway. Pass the incense smoke over the threshold, visualizing it cleansing and consecrating the space. Lightly pass the bread over the flame of the candle, saying, *May this home always be filled with abundance and prosperity.*

Dribble a few drops of honey over the bread as you say, *May this home be filled with harmony, love, and joy.* Place the potted plant at the threshold and say, *May this home be blessed with growth, health, and vitality.*

Finally, seal the blessing by envisioning your entire home enveloped in a warm bubble of protection. Say, *I bless and protect this home and all who dwell within. May it be a place of love, warmth, and positive energy.*

Extinguish the candle and leave the bread outside as an offering to the spirits of the land. Keep the potted plant inside your home as a living symbol of growth and positive energy. Be sure to tend it and care for it as often as needed so it will thrive, as will your home.

Hex Signs

I'm just a short drive away from an area that has a number of Amish, Mennonite, and other people of German descent among the population. One absolutely delightful feature that appears when I travel through this part of my state is that of hex signs on homes and barns. This nifty bit of German and Swiss folklore was first brought here by the Pennsylvania Dutch.

Hex signs are symbols, each with a different meaning, painted on a circular background. Depending on what the owner wants to achieve—prosperity, luck, good health, protection, etc.—hex signs often include multiple symbols and colors arranged in a pattern.[17] Because they've become such a popular bit of Americana, they make a nice addition to the entrance of a magical home, especially if you're not trying to be obvious about your practice. Your neighbors will think you just really dig folk art and often won't have a clue about the magical meanings behind the symbols on your hex sign. Consider painting one to adorn your threshold, using magical symbols of your own or these traditional ones:

- **Stars:** Good luck, happiness, protection
- **Hearts:** Love, romance, friendship
- **Trees:** Strength, growth, longevity
- **Raindrops:** Fertility, abundance, renewal
- **Birds:** Freedom, happiness, the spirit
- **Circles:** Unity, protection, completeness

17. Donmoyer, "Hex Signs."

+ **Tulips:** Faith, hope, generosity
+ **Horseshoes:** Good fortune, protection, luck

MAKE A MAGICAL WREATH

A wreath on the door is one of the first things people see when they approach your home, and crafting one of your own using ribbons and dried herbs is a great way to invite blessings in, as well as welcome your guests. You'll need:

+ A wreath form; you can use foam, wire, grapevine, or any other base you like.

+ Ribbons in colors that represent positive attributes and blessings to you; you may want to try green for abundance, white for peace, and gold for success. See the section on color magic in chapter 12 for more ideas.

+ Sprigs of herbs known for positive magical properties; while you can use fresh ones if they're available, it's often easier to find dried ones instead. Consider lavender to symbolize harmony and peace, bay leaves for positive manifestation, rosemary for protection and purification, and sage for cleansing and wisdom.

+ Decorative items like crystals, beads, or charms that might hold special meaning for you and your family

+ Scissors

+ A hot glue gun and glue or florist wire and a pair of snippers

+ *Optional:* A small string of battery-operated fairy lights

Before you begin, sit quietly and focus on your intention. See your home filled with blessings, positivity, and harmony. Hold this in your mind and heart as you work on your wreath. Cut the ribbons into varying lengths, making sure they are long enough to tie around the wreath securely. Use the hot glue gun or florist wire to attach the ribbons to the wreath. You can create a pattern or simply place them at random—do what feels right as you're crafting.

Next, arrange the dried herbs and any additional decorations among the ribbons. Secure them with hot glue or florist wire; if you're using wire, snip it into small manageable lengths. As you attach each item, picture its magical properties infusing your wreath with blessings. Finally, add a loop at the back so you can hang it on your door. As you hang it, see the wreath inviting blessings, tranquility, and abundance into your home. Periodically touch your wreath as you enter and exit your home as a reminder of the positive energy you're welcoming inside.

Key Magic

Keys have a rich symbolic and practical significance in witchcraft and various magical traditions. They represent access to knowledge, mysteries, and hidden realms. In many belief systems, keys are seen as tools that unlock doors to the unknown, making them powerful symbols in rituals related to divination, scrying, and accessing the spirit world. They can be used in protection spells and rituals and incorporated into magic that locks away negative energies or spirits, safeguarding the home from harm. Place a key under your doormat or hang it near the entrance to ward off unwanted energies.

A form of divination known as *cleidomancy* involves using keys to gain insight. It is done by suspending a key from a thread or a chain and asking questions, much like the use of a traditional pendulum. The movement of the key is believed to provide answers from the spirit world.

You can use keys to cast circles, direct energy, or carve symbols into candles or other materials during spellwork. They are often associated with ancestral wisdom and connections. You may want to include a key on your ancestor altar as a symbol of the knowledge passed down through generations and to help invite guidance from the spirits of your ancestors in rituals.

Keys are associated with transitions and life changes. Use them in rituals to help navigate significant personal events, such as moving to a new home, starting a new job, or embarking on a spiritual journey. Finally, they make wonderful meditative focal points. By gazing at a key during meditation, you may find it easier to unlock your subconscious mind, explore your inner self, or access spiritual insights.

Knock of Opportunity Spell

Use the doors to your home as a chance to create new opportunities—and, more importantly, to recognize them when they present themselves! For this simple spell, you'll need:

+ A small piece of chalk
+ A green candle
+ Matches or a lighter

Stand outside your open front door, and light the candle. Pass it across the front of the door, moving in a circular, clockwise direction. As you do, say, *When one door closes, another one opens.* Use the chalk to draw a circle in the center of the door. Knock three times, sharply, in the middle of the circle, saying, *Opportunity knocks! Opportunity knocks! Opportunity knocks!* Gently place a fingertip in the melted wax of the candle, being careful not to burn yourself, and dab it on the exterior doorknob. Say, *I step through this door, into a realm of growth and success.*

Open the door and, still holding the candle, step inside, closing the door behind you. Draw another circle, directly in the center of the door. Place your dominant hand in the circle and say, *Opportunity is welcome! Opportunity is welcome! Opportunity is welcome!* Again, put a fingertip in the melted wax. This time, dab it on the inner doorknob. Say, *I seal my intention and will be mindful of all positive prospects.*

Allow the candle to burn out completely or extinguish it if needed. Keep an eye out for anything that will help you achieve your goals and ambitions in the future.

Windows

Like doors, windows are often seen as portals between the inside and outside worlds, bridging the gap between the mundane and the magical. In many cultures, windows are considered more than just architectural features; they are believed to possess their own unique magical properties.

A window can be a threshold for spirits, fairies, and other supernatural entities. It's said these beings can pass through windows more easily than doors, making windows a common entry point for mystical visitors. In some places, windowsills are lined with herbs or protective charms to prevent negative spirits from entering the home through this vulnerable point. Some people also place an acorn on their windowsill—it's supposed to keep lightning from striking the home.

Windows are also associated with divination and scrying, especially during the twilight hours. The soft, dim light filtering through windows at dawn and dusk can enhance psychic abilities and facilitate communication with other realms. Consider using a window as a focal point for scrying, gazing into the glass to gain insights into the future or to communicate with the spirit world.

During certain times, such as at Samhain or the Winter Solstice, windows were left open or candles were placed on sills to guide ancestral spirits back to the realm of the living. It was said departed souls could easily recognize their homes by the light in the windows. In architectural folklore, the placement and design of windows are believed to influence the energy flow within a building. Windows that face east might capture the first rays of the sun, symbolizing new beginnings and vitality, while western-facing windows can showcase the warm hues of sunset, representing endings and reflection. Many architectural traditions incorporate specific window shapes and placements to harness or deflect certain energies.

Windows also serve as witnesses to the passage of time, capturing the changing seasons, celestial events, and natural phenomena. It is sometimes said that the energy and stories of a place are imprinted on its windows. Staring out into the night through a window, you might feel an inexplicable connection to the mysteries of the universe.

Magical Window Wash

There's an old bit of folklore that says your enemies could cast the evil eye at your home by sending it through a dirty window. Although this may have been a tall tale designed to encourage people to keep their windows extra clean, it's never a bad idea to be a bit preventive! Brew up a batch of a magical window wash, and use it on the glass after you've cleaned the window inside and out. You'll need:

- A clean bowl or bucket
- ½ gallon hot water
- ¼ cup white vinegar
- Essential oils of lemon, lavender, and frankincense
- A cleansed and charged clear quartz crystal
- A clean cloth or sponge

In the bowl or bucket, combine the water and vinegar, swirling it around gently to blend. You can either use your fingers to do this or move the bowl or bucket in small circular motions. Add the essential oils—a little goes a long way, so just add a few drops at a time of each until the fragrance combination is where you want it to be. Place the quartz crystal into the water as a way of amplifying the cleansing properties of the wash.

Close your eyes, and hold your hands over the water with your palms facing down. Visualize powerful cleansing vibrations charging the water, willing away negativity, and drawing in positive clean energy. With the pointer finger of your dominant hand, slowly stir the surface of the water in a clockwise direction. You may want to offer a simple short blessing as well, such as, *I charge this water to cleanse and clear, to protect and safeguard my home, to bring harmony and joy to my space.*

Using the clean cloth or sponge, apply the wash to your windows, working your way around the inside of the house first and then the outside. Focus on each pane as you infuse it with the intention of cleansing, both physically and spiritually.

CRYSTAL LIGHT CATCHERS

You can take advantage of the natural daylight let in by your windows by making crystal light catchers that align with your magical intentions. It's an easy project to assemble, using inexpensive items from the thrift store or your craft supply box. Be aware that many crystals will fade when exposed to direct sunlight, so you should avoid hanging these in your windows if you want to preserve the integrity of your magical stones. You'll need:

+ A few of your favorite crystals for your magical purpose; try some of these to get started:
  - **Protection:** Black tourmaline, black onyx, obsidian
  - **Creativity and knowledge:** Carnelian, howlite

- **Dreamwork:** Amethyst, apatite, celestine, opal, rose quartz
- **Prosperity:** Aventurine, citrine, moss agate, sunstone, turquoise
- **Love and attraction:** Lodestone, pink agate, pink tourmaline, rose quartz, red tourmaline
- **Grounding and stability:** Agate, blue tiger's eye, granite, smoky quartz, sodalite
- **Healing:** Amethyst, bloodstone, carnelian, peridot, smoky quartz
- **Spiritual growth:** Amethyst, blue lace agate, howlite, moonstone, selenite, unakite

- Colorful glass beads; you can upcycle these from old pieces of jewelry.
- Jeweler's wire
- Pliers and scissors
- *Optional:* Charms, colorful trinkets, or small bags of dried herbs

Using the scissors, cut short lengths of wire and wrap the crystals you've chosen to use, which is easiest to do with the pliers. Be sure to leave a small loop at the top of each wrap so you can thread the crystal onto the wire.

Cut a piece of jeweler's wire—it can be any length you like, but don't go too crazy with it. I've found that 18 to 30 inches seems to be the most manageable size wire to work with. Tie a loop in one end of your wire; this is how you'll hang your light catcher.

Lay out your glass beads and crystals to figure out how you want to arrange them—you may want to sort them by color or size or just wing it and see where your creative juices lead you! Thread the beads and crystals onto the wire, leaving space between them to showcase their beauty; you can use spacer beads or simply loop the wire to create a gap. If you've decided to include charms, trinkets, or little bags of herbs, place them wherever it feels right to you—let your imagination run wild! Once your light catcher is the length you want it, and you love the placement of all your beads and crystals, tie a knot in the bottom end to keep them from sliding off the wire.

Hang your crystal creation in a spot where it can benefit from the natural lighting in your home and radiate its magical properties throughout your space.

Fireplaces and Chimneys

Fireplaces and chimneys feature as central elements in folklore around the world and are associated with warmth and protection. Like doors and windows, they are sometimes seen as thresholds, connecting the safety of the home to the wildness of the outdoors and the spirit world beyond.

The fireplace serves as a protective barrier against malevolent spirits and entities. The hearth, with its constant fire, can repel evil forces, keeping the home and its inhabitants safe. Chimneys, a passage through which smoke and spirits alike can ascend to the heavens, form a link between the earthly realm and the Divine. In some parts of Europe, it's a common practice to leave food or milk at the fireplace to appease the spirits who might live within it, ensuring their protection and blessings upon the home. It's no wonder archaeologists have found evidence of offerings left on hearths in numerous locations from a wide variety of time periods—what a sensible way to maintain this protective quality!

Fireplaces also hold a significant place in many traditions around the time of the Winter Solstice. Have you ever burned a Yule log? The Yule log, often selected with care and decorated with symbols, can bring blessings and protection to the home. As the log burns, it's customary to gather around the fireplace, telling stories and singing songs to honor the returning sun and ward off the darkness of winter. Even the imagery of Santa Claus is rooted in ancient tales of magical beings entering homes through chimneys to bring gifts or blessings.

Chimneys are also associated with divination and fortune-telling. In some places, smoke rising from the chimney was observed for omens and signs. The way the smoke billowed, the speed at which it rose, or even the sounds it made were interpreted to predict the future or communicate messages from the spirit world. The way we view fireplaces and chimneys today may well reflect our deep connection with the element of fire. The hearth is the heart of the home, embodying stability, comfort, and family.

Fire Magic

Do you have a fireplace or a firepit? How about a tabletop brazier? If so, you've got access to the power of fire magic. Even if you don't have one of these items, you can still work fire magic in a firesafe bowl or cauldron as long as you follow some common-sense safety guidelines.

Fire holds a prominent and powerful place in magical practice across diverse cultures and traditions. Its transformative and purifying nature makes it a symbol of both creation and destruction, embodying the essence of change and renewal. Fire can be harnessed for various purposes, tapping into its elemental energy to enhance spells, rituals, and ceremonies.

Use fire as a tool for purification and cleansing. The act of burning herbs, resins, or other materials for spiritual purposes is found around the world; it's a powerful way to send your intentions out into the universe. The smoke generated by burning plant and resin materials like sage, frankincense, or palo santo can clear negative energies, purify sacred spaces, and create a conducive environment for magical workings. If you haven't read Amy Blackthorn's amazing book *Sacred Smoke*, I highly recommend you pick up a copy to learn about some great incense blends you can make and burn yourself.

Fire is associated with passion, courage, and transformation. In spellcasting, it's easy to use colored candles, with each color representing specific intentions. Red candles, for instance, symbolize love and passion, while green candles represent prosperity and growth. The act of focusing on the flame during meditation or visualization can help you manifest your magical goals.

Pyromancy, the art of divination through fire, involves gazing into flames to gain insights and perceive messages from the spiritual realm. The flickering patterns and shapes in the fire are interpreted to reveal answers to questions or foretell the future. Fire scrying can be performed with various sources of fire, such as candle flames or bonfires, although it does take some practice, once you get the hang of it, you'll be able to pick up on the subtle messages in the flames.

You can use fire to consecrate tools and ceremonial spaces, acting as a bridge between the physical and spiritual realms.

It is a way to attract and honor deities, spirits, or ancestral energies, serving as a beacon to guide them into the ritual space.

Let's not forget that fire festivals and bonfires are integral parts of many Pagan and folk traditions. Celebrations for sabbats like Beltane and Samhain often involve the lighting of large communal fires around which we and our friends can gather to celebrate, perform rituals, and partake in festivities. These fires become a focal point for community energy, fostering a sense of connection and shared spiritual experience among everyone who participates.

Hearth Blessing

If you'd like to offer a blessing to your hearth, here's a simple practice you can try. Keep in mind that even if you don't have a fireplace, the hearth is so much more than that. For our ancestors, it was the place where food was prepared. If you've got a stovetop or other place where you fix hot food to eat, it can serve as a perfectly acceptable substitute during this blessing. You'll need:

+ A cauldron or fireproof bowl
+ A red candle
+ Matches or a lighter

Sit comfortably near your hearth—or stove or oven or hotplate—and place the cauldron or firesafe bowl in the center of the space, with the red candle inside it. Light the candle and focus on the flame as it flickers to life. Close your eyes, take a few deep breaths, and feel the comforting warmth of the flame surrounding you, moving beyond you and into the universe above. Say, *I call upon the power of fire, the eternal flame that warms our hearth and illuminates our home. May this passionate energy infuse our space, bringing warmth, light, and transformative power to our lives.*

Envision your hearth, the heart and center of your home, filled with warmth, and continue your blessing:

> *By the light of this sacred flame, I bless this hearth. May it be a place of love and laughter, of warmth and security. May it provide nourishment for our bodies and our souls. May the fires within this hearth always burn brightly, illuminating our path and welcoming all who enter with open arms.*

See all of the warmth and power of the flame filling your home with security, abundance, safety, harmony, and love. Visualize it expanding to envelop not only those who live in your home, but also anyone who might be welcomed as a guest. Offer a few words of gratitude and blow out the candle. As the smoke rises, visualize your blessings being carried into the universe, manifesting your intentions in the days and weeks to come.

Chapter 6
LIVING ROOM MAGIC

For many of us, the living room is where we spend the bulk of our waking hours—after all, it's called the living room because we *live* in it. It tends to hold a special place in a home, often serving as the heart of the household. Its significance goes beyond just being a space for relaxation; it's where we do all kinds of things. The living room is where families and friends gather and foster social connections. It's a place for conversations, bonding, and shared experiences, whether through casual chats or structured gatherings. Your living room might be a focal point for entertainment and recreation, where you hold movie nights, have gaming sessions, or just chill out while listening to music or your favorite podcast. It's an adaptable space and one of the first areas your guests will see when they enter your home. Your living room sends a message of hospitality, offering warm welcomes and making visitors feel cozy and comfortable.

Perhaps most importantly, this is one of the first rooms we design and decorate when we move into a new place, reflecting our style, taste, and personality. It's a canvas for expressing creativity and showcasing cherished items, from family photos and unique furniture pieces to magical collections of crystals and artwork. The living room's significance is so much more than its physical aspects—what also matters are the emotional and social connections formed there. It's a space where memories are made, traditions are upheld, and the essence of home truly comes alive.

Magical Decorating Around Your Living Room

How we decorate our living space is often a reflection of who we are as a person—so if you're living a magical life, why not include that into some of your décor? You might not be comfortable having a giant pentacle the size of a Volkswagen painted on your living room wall, but that's okay. You can still decorate in a magical way that fits your own aesthetic of what's appealing and what's ... too much.

In addition to painting your walls in magical colors (see the section Color Magic in Your Home in chapter 12), you can hang artwork, tapestries, or handcrafts that showcase who you are. If you're handy with a needle and thread, try making cross-stitched or embroidered pillows or samplers of magical symbols, phrases that are important to you, the various sabbats, or images of your deities. If you like to have a really witchy vibe, do some extra shopping for decorations at Halloween, and leave them in place throughout the seasons. Do you dig fantasy artwork, like depictions of elves and fairies? Get some attractive pictures, frame them, and hang them to display.

Deck out your tables with cauldrons, candles, bowls of crystals, live herbs in pretty pots, or statues of the gods and goddesses of your traditions. If you can find fabric in mystical, metaphysical patterns, consider displaying it on shelves or tables. This not only presents a magical flair—it also adds depth and texture to the room.

I love picking stuff up outside and then bringing it *inside*. It's a great way to connect with the changing seasons outdoors. In the fall, display bowls of gourds or glass jars filled with acorns or colorful fallen leaves. For wintertime, grab some holly or pine cones to adorn your living room. Come springtime, there will be fresh budding branches and early season greenery to gather from the ground after storms, and in the summer, you can collect flowers and produce. If there are other items you've gathered outside, make some artwork with them to display—I've got a shadowbox filled with interesting pebbles and a small stepping stone embedded with beach glass and broken pottery I picked up on a trip to Scotland.

Bring a bit of harmony and balance to your living room by placing representations of the four elements along their corresponding walls. On the north side of your room, place some crystals or a plant in a pot of clean soil to represent earth. To the east, hang feathers or flags, symbolizing air. Put candles or other fire symbols—dragons, braziers, etc.—on the south wall. A water-related item like a jar of seashells or a tabletop fountain can wrap things up on the west side of your room.

Do you paint, draw, or sketch? Are you a whiz with fiber arts? Have you learned how to make amazing woodcuts? Whatever you've created, put it on display! Remember that the act of creation is a magical one, so infuse your artwork with your intentions, and then hang your pieces up to enjoy.

Setting Up Your Living Room Altar

Do you have to have an altar? Not really. If you do have one, does it have to be displayed front and center in your living room where everyone will see it? Also, not really. But one thing I've learned over the years is that for me personally, if something is out of sight, it's often out of mind. For a while, early on in my practice, I kept my altar in my bedroom … but eventually realized that other than the seven or so hours a night I was sleeping, I rarely spent any time in there at all. So, my altar often sat overlooked until it was time for me to go to bed, and by that point in my day I just didn't have the bandwidth to think about spellwork.

I finally made the conscious, deliberate decision to place my altar in the living room instead. It wasn't big. It wasn't obtrusive … but it was *there*, and what a world of difference that made in my practice! Giving it a presence in the space I spent the bulk of my time put it right in front of me and allowed me the opportunity to do magic when I *needed* it—not just as an afterthought at the end of the day. My altar became more than just a place where I kept magical stuff, and it now serves as a symbolic and practical tool that helps me focus my energy, connect with my gods and my ancestors, and create a sacred space for my magical workings. It is a vital focal point for concentration and intention, creating a sacred atmosphere within my living space.

Each element on the altar, from candles and crystals to symbols and tools, holds symbolic meaning. These representations can vary based on personal beliefs, tradition, or the specific purpose of a ritual. You can use your altar for divination, meditation, spellcasting, and energy work. The arrangement of tools and symbols on the altar should be chosen to align with your intentions and the nature of the working—you don't need all your magical supplies on top of your altar at once. You may wish to dedicate your altar to the deities of your tradition or adapt it seasonally for the sabbats or other milestones that resonate with you. Creating and maintaining an altar is a personal practice that allows you to take ownership of your spiritual space, and you may find you're more likely to benefit from it if it's in a place you spend the bulk of your time each day. Remember that just as with many other aspects of magical living, there's no one-size-fits-all method for setting up an altar, but here are a few things you might want to keep in mind.

Before setting up your altar, clarify your intentions. What do you want to use this space for? Is it for meditation, spellwork, deity connection, or a combination of purposes? When you're looking at locations for your altar, be mindful of the other residents of your home—if you've got small children living with you, you might consider a shelf or tabletop that's out of reach of tiny hands. If your living room is also the entertainment center for your home, try to keep your altar away from gaming systems and other electronics if possible. If you're not entirely sure where to place it, read up on the principles of feng shui, which explain how and why things should be in certain parts of each room.

Cover the surface with an altar cloth—more on that in just a minute. You may want to add representations of the four elements: crystals, herbs, or stones to symbolize earth; feathers or incense for air; a candle or oil diffuser to stand in for fire; and a cup or chalice to represent water. If you work with specific deities, incorporate statues, images, or items connected to them. You'll also want to add any magical tools you use regularly—an athame or wand for directing energy, a pentacle or symbol of earth for grounding and protection, and so on.

Be sure you regularly cleanse and charge your altar tools and space. Keep it tidy and organized, as it's a reflection of your spiritual practice and intentions, and it should resonate with you. Adjust and personalize it as needed as your practice evolves and you deepen your connection with your craft and spiritual path.

Make an Altar Cloth

Creating an altar cloth of your own can be a meaningful project that enhances your sacred space and your ritual area. While there's no rule that says you *must* use one, an altar cloth does serve a couple of different purposes. It's a great way to protect your altar from any scratches or damage that can be incurred during spellwork or ritual—and if you don't think spellwork can be occasionally destructive, I can't begin to tell you how many times I've dropped sharp objects or spilled hot melty candle wax onto my altar. The cloth keeps the wood surface from looking like it's been hit by a bomb.

In addition to this very practical function, an altar cloth has the added bonus of increasing the power of my magical workings. I tend to change mine seasonally—sunflower fabric in late summer, a pumpkin or spooky motif in the fall, and bright pastel colors to welcome spring, for example. I also have some very specific altar cloths, including one decorated with goddess symbols for when I'm calling upon deities and another covered in Celtic designs for situations in which I'm doing ancestor workings.

Although having access to a sewing machine certainly helps when it comes to making your own altar cloth, it's not a requirement for the simpler versions. If you're intimidated by learning to use a sewing machine, never fear—using a needle and thread might take a bit longer, but the end result will be just as effective. In fact, some people might argue that hand-stitched items have *more* magical power.

SIMPLE ALTAR CLOTH

If you're planning on making an altar cloth, you can use any material you like! Many people believe natural fibers, such as cotton or wool, are the best choice, but use what speaks to you the most. I generally recommend evaluating things like weight and feel—I'm a weirdly tactile person and have some textures that I just find icky and can't touch them—to make sure it's something you'll love. Choose a fabric you adore and cut it to the size you need. If you like things a little neater, you can hem the edges—and even add a decorative stitch if you're feeling fancy—for a more finished look.

While you can certainly go out and buy brand new fabric for your altar cloth, there are plenty of other options. I have several altar cloths made from repurposed materials. One is fashioned from an upcycled funky boho tablecloth I found at the thrift store. Another is one I created from a pair of small curtains a former resident left behind when I moved into an apartment.

You can also use fabrics that have personal significance to you—your great-grandmother's lace tablecloth, for instance. I have a length of lightweight plaid in a tartan design from one of the Scottish clans on my dad's side of the family that I sometimes decorate my altar with. I've also used an unfinished quilt top that I acquired after the death of my mother-in-law— I'm not a quilter, and she never completed the project, but I'm honored to use that piece of fabric in my spiritual work.

If all you've got is a plain piece of fabric, that's okay too! Decorate it with embroidered stitches or use fabric paint to create designs and sigils on it. A simple piece of cloth goes a long way when it comes to your altar, and you can customize it in any way you choose.

ELEMENTAL ALTAR CLOTH

In many traditions of modern witchcraft, the four classical elements of earth, air, fire, and water are considered magically significant. If your spellwork and rituals tend to lean toward an elemental focus, you might want to make an altar cloth to represent all four of them. I've found this type of cloth tends to be better suited toward a rounded shape instead of a square or rectangle, but you can certainly adjust these instructions to fit your own altar space. First, you'll need to select four different fabrics, one symbolizing each element. You can break these down simply by color—green or brown for earth, yellow for air, orange or red for fire, and blue for water—if you like. Another option is to select patterns that have element-appropriate images on them. Your local fabric store might have some gorgeous bolts of cotton containing repeating designs of trees, clouds, flames, and waves, for instance. If you want to get really deep with your symbolism, consider elemental beings such as gnomes, sylphs or fairies, salamanders, and undines or mermaids.

You'll need about a quarter to a half yard of each fabric, depending on the desired size of your finished altar cloth. A quick pro-tip: When you're choosing fabrics, be sure to get materials that are similar in weight. I wouldn't recommend trying to stitch together a silk on one side and a heavy tapestry fabric on the other. Similarly, unless you're familiar with stitching over raised patterns, beads, or sequins, I'd suggest you avoid fabrics that contain any of those things. Personally, I'm a big fan of quilting cotton—it's reasonably affordable and is available in literally thousands of different designs and motifs.

First, cut out a quarter circle from each of your four fabrics. The easiest way to do this is by tying a piece of string to a pen. Make sure you have one square corner on your material, then hold the empty end of the string in the corner. With the string pulled taut, guide the pen along the fabric from one edge to the other, creating a quarter circle. Do this with each fabric, giving you four quarter circles that have the same radius all the way around. What happens when you connect four quarter circles? You get an entire circle!

To piece the fabric together, arrange them in pairs. Match up two adjacent quarters, such as earth and air, and stitch them along the straight edge with the right (pattern) sides together. Once you've stitched them together, unfold and press out the seam. Do this with the other two pieces as well to create two half circles. Take the two half circles and place them with the right sides together, matching up the outer edges and center seams. Stitch them together along the long straight edge and press this seam open.

Finally, press under a ¼ inch all the way around, and then fold that edge in another ¼ inch to create a smooth hem on the circle. Pin your hem in place, and then stitch the edge. You'll have a complete round altar cloth, with each of the elements represented in a quarter.

ANCESTOR WORK ALTAR CLOTH

If you do any work with your ancestors, having a special altar cloth just for that type of magic can turn a ritual into an even deeper, more powerful experience. Crafting an altar cloth to honor your ancestors is a magical endeavor you can fill with reverence and intention. To begin, gather materials that hold personal significance and symbolic value—perhaps a soft fabric like linen or cotton, a color that resonates with you, and embellishments to represent connections to your lineage. You'll need:

- Linen or cotton fabric large enough to cover your altar space
- Dried cleansing herbs, such as rosemary, mugwort, or cedar
- Embroidery thread and needles or fabric paint in symbolic colors and paintbrushes
- *Optional:* Embellishments such as family crests, ancestral symbols, or cultural motifs

Cleanse your fabric by sprinkling it gently with your dried herbs—as you do, focus your intention on clearing away any lingering energies and imbue the material with its sacred purpose. Take some time to hold the fabric in your hands, sending positive energy into it and letting the universe know this material is going to be dedicated to your ancestor work.

Next, plan out your design. You might want to decorate it with a representation of your family tree if you've done research on your kinfolk. If that seems like too heady of a project, consider symbols of ancestry that hold meaning to you—family crests, ancestral runes, cultural motifs, or colors significant to your lineage. Using embroidery thread or fabric paint, create your chosen design on the fabric—just brush the herbs aside as you do so. You can stitch or paint symbols and patterns that represent your family, incorporating meaningful colors and imagery. Remember that an ancestor altar is only for honoring those who have passed, so if you're ambitious enough to put a family tree on your altar cloth, do not include anyone who is currently living.

As you work, infuse each stitch or paint stroke with your respect and love for your ancestors. Visualize the connection between your creation and the spirits of those who came before you. If you wish to include objects, create small pockets or compartments on the cloth to hold family heirlooms or symbolic trinkets representing each branch of your lineage. Throughout the crafting process, maintain a meditative or focused state, calling upon the spirits of your ancestors to guide and bless this creation.

Once your design is complete and you feel that the cloth adequately represents your intentions and honors your lineage, place it on your altar as a tangible representation of your love and respect for your ancestors. Use it to connect with and honor your kinfolk who have crossed over, inviting their presence into your rituals and ceremonies.

Simple Blessings for Your Living Room

Since we spend the bulk of our time at home in the living room, keeping it cleansed and blessed is a great way to make it feel magical and blessed all the time, not just when work is being done at the altar. Do this easy blessing ritual to keep the space fresh and sacred. You will need:

+ A plain white candle and candleholder
+ Matches or a lighter

Begin by thoroughly cleaning the space, both physically and energetically, to remove any lingering negativity or clutter. Light a plain white candle and place it in the center of the room. Walk around the living room in a clockwise direction, ringing a bell to dispel any stagnant energies and invite positive energy. After you've circled the room, sit quietly near the candle on a cushion or comfortable chair. Close your eyes to visualize the room being filled with a warm, golden light, emanating from the candle and expanding to permeate every corner, nook, and cranny. Speak your intentions for the room aloud, such as it becoming a safe haven for family and friends, a place of relaxation and joy, or a cozy retreat for rest and rejuvenation. Finally, open your eyes and write these intentions on a piece of paper, fold it, and place it beneath the candle. You might want to include a brief affirmation, such as *This living room is free of negativity and filled with positive energy. I bless this room as a space in which joy, abundance, and love thrive.*

If you just need a quick recharge to the space, try one of these simple incantations before you engage in magical work or just on the fly as you're cleaning the room:

+ *In this common space, where moments unfold, let laughter be loud and stories be told. Comfort and joy as we come together; may this room be filled with love forever.*

+ *Let this room be a sanctuary of peace and comfort. May it be filled with laughter and warmth, a place where stress and sorrow cannot dwell. Let every corner radiate safety and relaxation, welcoming all who enter with open arms. Here, tranquility reigns supreme. This space is a blessed haven of rest and rejuvenation.*

+ *May this room be a refuge through each day and night, where love and laughter freely blend, a sanctuary of warmth and grace for all who enter.*

Seasonal Décor

One of the things I love about being a practicing witch is that we get some really cool holidays—eight of them a year—and I love to decorate for them. I don't get too out of control, because I'm super thrifty, but I've found that I can take some time before each sabbat and put out seasonally appropriate items to bring the spirit of the celebration into my living room. If your altar is the only place you get to decorate for the sabbat, keep some of these seasonal colors and themes in mind when it's time to change it up.

+ **Samhain:** Fill your home with seasonal items to mark the Witches' New Year, such as cornucopias filled with harvest foods like gourds and apples. Add pumpkins and traditional Halloween décor like ghosts, witches, bats, and black cats. Incorporate colors like black, green, purple, and orange.

+ **Yule:** When the Winter Solstice rolls around, it's time to deck your halls with boughs of green things—collect holly sprigs or fragrant pine and fir branches to display as garlands or wreaths. Yule is a festival of lights, celebrating the return of the sun, so it's the perfect time of year to bring out solar symbols, colorful candles, and sparkling string lights. Add a few bowls of nuts, berries, and fruit, and craft a Yule log with family and friends. Use red, green, white, silver, and gold for splashes of color.

+ **Imbolc:** Falling at the beginning of February in the Northern Hemisphere, Imbolc marks the midpoint between winter and spring. Fill your home with brightly lit candles, bells, and symbols of ewes and lambs. For many people, this is a sabbat associated with dairy products— why not add some cows or a decorative milk jug filled with early spring flowers? Depending on where you live, you might be seeing wintery weather, so add some snowflake decorations. Colors of the season include blue, gray, and silver. If you're using this sabbat to honor the goddess Brigid, include chalices and cauldrons, healing herbs, and her traditional colors of green and white.

+ **Ostara:** Marking the Spring Equinox, Ostara falls close to the Christian Easter celebration. Do a thorough spring cleaning, and then take advantage of holiday sales so you can deck your living room out with rabbits, carrots, and chicks. Add a few vases of bright spring flowers. Find some young willow branches, weave them into decorative baskets, and fill them with brightly colored eggs. Pick up some inexpensive wooden seasonal ornaments, paint them, and string them together as a garland. Focus on spring pastels, such as lilac and lavender, pale pink or blue, light yellow, and soft green.

+ **Beltane:** Another fire festival, Beltane (or May Day) celebrates the greening of the earth. Set out plenty of candles and flowers to honor the season. Gather some fresh greenery and make a wreath for your door or a wall garland; trim it with symbols of birds, butterflies, and bees, all of which are making their reappearance at this time of year. Fertility symbols are appropriate here as well—why not make a tabletop Maypole or string brightly colored ribbons and braids around your room? Use bold colors such as green, yellow, and purple to decorate.

+ **Midsummer:** The midsummer solstice is known as Litha in some traditions, and it's the longest day of the year. It's all about celebrating the power and energy of the sun! Open up your windows and fill your home with solar symbols—it's a great time of year to make suncatchers to hang. Fill glass jars with freshly harvested herbs from your garden, flowers, or seashells. Work with bright solar colors—yellow, gold, and orange all fit well with the theme of midsummer.

+ **Lammas:** One of the best things about modern witchcraft is that we literally have a holiday that's all about bread and grain, so get ready to do some kitchen witchery! Bake some fresh bread, wrap it up to keep it from going stale, and display it in baskets or on platters. Collect wheat stalks or other grains, and use them to create sunwheels and other symbols, or simply display them in bundles. Corn is growing this time of year, and its ears and stalks make great seasonal decorations—get some colorful varieties and showcase them around the room. Hang your late summer herbs up to dry, or place them in a vase to bring the smells of the season indoors. Add some symbols of harvest tools, such as sickles, scythes, and baskets, and draw your color inspiration from nature—use orange, light brown, green, and bold yellows.

+ **Autumn Equinox:** Sometimes called Mabon or Harvest Home, the autumnal equinox reminds us that winter will soon be on the horizon. The harvest is beginning to wind down, so gather up baskets and bowls of apples, gourds, pumpkins, and late season produce—it's even better if you can pick them yourself! Collect fallen leaves and create a colorful display as a wreath, shadow box, or framed artwork. If you have access to grapevines, weave them into wall décor or baskets. Add scarecrows, corncobs, and other symbols of the final harvest, using colors like deep red, dark brown, and burnt orange.

Board Games and Playing Cards

Does your household love a good game night? Playing board games with the people you live with—or those who spend a lot of time in your home—can help in fostering connections, learning opportunities, and bonding experiences. Gaming together creates a space for shared experiences and laughter. Beyond mere entertainment, board games encourage essential skills as players learn to express themselves, collaborate, and navigate teamwork. Whether you're into Monopoly, Risk, tabletop RPGs, or even a good old-fashioned round of Go Fish, games often involve strategy, problem-solving, collaboration, and critical thinking. Also, let's face it—games are fun!

Playing Card Divination

You can use a standard deck of playing cards for divination, which comes in handy if you don't have access to a tarot deck. Create your own associations and meanings for the cards based on your intuition, personal experiences, or cultural background. For instance, hearts might represent emotions or relationships, diamonds could signify material and financial matters, clubs might denote creativity or work, and spades could symbolize challenges, future events, or transformation. You can also explore the numerological significance of numbers (1–10) and the symbolic meanings of the suits (hearts, diamonds, clubs, spades) and face cards to derive interpretations. Pay attention to the energies each suit embodies and how they relate to your question.

In traditional cartomancy—the act of using cards for divination—there are some standard meanings. Try working from this list to get started, but if you need to change some meanings to make them more appropriate for you and your household, go for it!

- **Hearts** (Similar to Cups in Tarot)
  - **Ace:** Love, new relationships, emotional beginnings
  - **Two:** Partnership, harmony, mutual attraction

- **Three:** Celebration, social gatherings, joy
- **Four:** Stability, home, foundations in relationships
- **Five:** Loss, disappointment, emotional turmoil
- **Six:** Reconciliation, nostalgia, memories
- **Seven:** Choices in love, indecision, contemplation
- **Eight:** Emotional fulfillment, contentment
- **Nine:** Wishes granted, dreams coming true, fulfillment
- **Ten:** Harmony, family, emotional fulfillment
- **Jack:** A young person, romantic interest, flirtation
- **Queen:** Compassionate, nurturing, emotional maturity
- **King:** Wise, influential, emotionally stable

+ **Diamonds** (Similar to Pentacles/Coins in Tarot)
  - **Ace:** New beginnings in finance or material matters
  - **Two:** Balance, partnerships in business or finance
  - **Three:** Financial or work-related challenges
  - **Four:** Stability, financial security, solid foundation
  - **Five:** Financial changes, uncertainty, adjustment
  - **Six:** Generosity, sharing wealth, charity
  - **Seven:** Evaluation, assessment, reevaluation of finances
  - **Eight:** Hard work, diligence, skill development
  - **Nine:** Accomplishment, success, material gains

- **Ten:** Wealth, inheritance, financial stability
- **Jack:** A young person, hardworking, ambitious
- **Queen:** Practical, resourceful, financially astute
- **King:** Wealthy, influential, business-minded

+ **Clubs** (Similar to Wands in Tarot)

- **Ace:** New beginnings, creativity, inspiration
- **Two:** Partnership, collaboration, cooperation
- **Three:** Expansion, growth, progress
- **Four:** Stability, solid foundation, security
- **Five:** Challenges, conflicts, competition
- **Six:** Victory, success, recognition
- **Seven:** Decision-making, choices, standing firm
- **Eight:** Movement, travel, progress
- **Nine:** Achievement, completion, reaching goals
- **Ten:** Accomplishment, fulfillment, completion of a cycle
- **Jack:** A young person, ambitious, enthusiastic
- **Queen:** Warmth, vitality, leadership
- **King:** Charismatic, influential, natural leader

+ **Spades** (Similar to Swords in Tarot)

- **Ace:** Beginnings, transformation, new understanding
- **Two:** Conflict, separation, disagreement
- **Three:** Heartache, sadness, emotional pain
- **Four:** Rest, recuperation, recovery
- **Five:** Challenges, adversity, setbacks

- **Six:** Transition, moving on, leaving the past behind
- **Seven:** Deception, trickery, hidden agendas
- **Eight:** Restrictions, limitations, feeling stuck
- **Nine:** Anxiety, worry, fear
- **Ten:** Endings, loss, completion of a cycle
- **Jack:** A young person, skepticism, cunning
- **Queen:** Independent, insightful, perceptive
- **King:** Authoritative, intellectual, decisive

These interpretations can serve as a general guideline, but most people who use playing cards for divination find their intuition and personal associations play a significant role in cartomancy. Over time, you'll develop your own unique understanding and connection with the cards.

LETTER TILE ORACLE

Do you have any sort of word game that includes letter tiles, such as Scrabble? Why not use them for divination? It can be a fun and intriguing way to gain insight or guidance. You'll need:

- Scrabble tiles or any set of letter tiles
- A flat surface to shuffle and lay out the tiles

Begin by creating a quiet space where you can focus without distractions, and place the letter tiles upside down so the blank sides are facing up. Think of a question to which you need answers. Hold your question firmly in your mind, and gently shuffle the tiles around. Trust your intuition to guide the duration of the shuffle. When you feel ready, stop shuffling and draw nine tiles randomly from the pool, keeping them face down. Turn each tile over one by one, creating a sequence that's unique to your query.

As you reveal the tiles, observe their sequence, proximity, and any patterns that emerge. Trust your intuition and the associations you hold with each letter—and also be mindful of the numbers, if any, that appear with each letter! Consider their symbolic meanings, connections, and how they relate to your question or situation. Let your mind wander and explore the possible messages the letters convey. Sometimes, the act of rearranging and contemplating the letters can bring forth unexpected ideas.

You may want to write down the letters that appeared for you and carry them with you throughout the day to see if important insights are revealed to you later on.

Chapter 7
BEDROOM MAGIC

The bedroom—or any other place where we sleep at the end of a long day—should be a space of sanctuary, of rest, of calmness and tranquility. It's where we can weave our intentions, dreams, and energies into manifested results. Our bedroom provides the necessary environment for the body to recharge, heal, and prepare for the day ahead. Since quality sleep is essential for physical health and mental well-being, it's in our best interest to make the bedroom a magical sanctuary.

The bedroom serves as a personal space, offering privacy and seclusion. It can be a retreat, a haven for introspection, solitude, and personal activities. It offers a sense of emotional well-being, providing a safe and comfortable environment where we can unwind, chill out, and find solace away from the stresses of daily life. For couples or other romantic combinations, the bedroom is a space for intimacy and connection. Its private nature encourages shared emotional experiences, contributing to the strength of our relationships.

Much like the living room, the bedroom often reflects personal identity and tastes through décor and furnishings—but because our guests don't regularly spend time there, the bedroom is a place where we can truly express who we are. Your living room may reflect all the latest design trends, but your bedroom can be the place where you hang your concert posters, display your *Star Wars* collection, or paint avant-garde murals on the walls—all things that guests don't generally see. This personal expression creates a feeling of ownership, contributing to the knowledge that you are safe and comfortable within the space. Spiritually, it can be a sanctuary for practices like meditation, prayer, or spiritual reflection. It becomes a space for connecting with higher energies, facilitating self-reflection, and promoting spiritual growth. Some people focus on maintaining energetic balance in the bedroom through practices like feng shui or energy cleansing. The place where we sleep plays a central role in our holistic well-being.

Magical Decorating for Your Bedroom

The bulk of your time spent in the bedroom is probably in the bed itself, so it should be as magical as you can make it! One of the best ways to start is with the bedding—items like pillows, blankets, and sheets can become conduits for magical energies.

Choose bedding colors and patterns aligned with magical intentions. For instance, opt for calming blues, growth-related greens, patterns symbolizing protection or harmony, reds and pinks for love and romance, and so on. You can also select sheets and blankets with some amazing mystical symbols on them—one of my favorite sets of sheets is purple, covered with stars, moons, and constellations. Climbing into bed with those just makes me feel more magical—plus, they're flannel, so they're super toasty on chilly winter nights. You can also arrange pillows or fold blankets, creating a specific pattern to signify protection, balance, or energy flow within the room.

Bless and cleanse your sheets by washing them with intention, infusing the fabric with the energy of cleansing herbs like lavender or rosemary. Visualize any negative energies being washed away, leaving behind a sense of purity and freshness. Sew or embroider protective symbols, sigils, or affirmations onto pillowcases or sheet edges. These symbols act as anchors for specific intentions, such as ensuring peaceful sleep or providing protection during rest.

Charge blankets with purposeful energies during meditation or rituals. Envision them as cocoons of protection, comfort, or healing, infusing them with warmth and security. Dedicate a specific blanket for dream enhancement. Before sleep, wrap yourself in it, setting the intention to enhance dream recall, induce lucid dreaming, or receive guidance during slumber.

Create small herbal sachets filled with calming herbs like lavender, chamomile, or mugwort. Place these sachets inside pillowcases to promote relaxation, deeper sleep, or heightened dream experiences. Alternatively, tuck small crystals such as amethyst or moonstone inside pillowcases or beneath pillows to aid in relaxation, stress reduction, or dream clarity. In addition to regular laundering, periodically cleanse and renew the energies within bedding items. Utilize sound clearing, herbal sprays, or expose them to moonlight to refresh their magical qualities. Infuse your bed with intention as you make it up each morning, viewing the very act as a ritual rather than a chore.

Using fabrics, textures, and colors aligned with intentions adds depth and enhances the desired atmosphere. Intentionally arranging furniture or items can create energetic flow and harmonious vibes. Feng shui principles recommend placing the bed at a diagonal from the door, not directly opposite it, using symmetrical nightstands or lamps, and incorporating earthy elements for grounding and relaxation.

Setting Up Your Bedroom Altar

You may not have room for an altar in your bedroom—or you might not even want one! But if you've got the space and you feel like it could help strengthen the room's magical vibe, I say go for it. My bedroom is fairly small. I've got enough room for my queen-size bed and a dresser and not much else. However, I've added a narrow shelf along one wall to serve as a bedroom altar. You can also use a nightstand, a small table, or even a cedar chest.

The altar itself can include items personal and meaningful to your practice, such as elemental representations or a statue or image of a deity, spirit, or symbol that resonates with you. You may want to include herbs or flowers associated with sleep and dream magic, such as lavender, peppermint, jasmine, or rosemary, which are perfect for the bedroom. If you like the idea of your bedroom being a place of sanctuary and reflection, add a journal, tarot cards, or other divination tools on your altar, making it not only a focal point for ritual work but also a spot for private meditation and introspection.

Bedroom Blessings

I like to do a short blessing for my bedroom every time I launder my sheets, simply because it seems practical to get the whole space metaphysically tidy at the same time I'm doing a physical cleaning, but you can do it any time you like.

For an easy bedroom blessing, start by lighting a white or lavender candle to signify purity and tranquility and placing it safely on your altar. If you've opted not to have a dedicated altar space in your bedroom, the top of your dresser, nightstand, or other flat surface works just as well. Stand before the candle, close your eyes, and envision a gentle, soothing light enveloping the room. See it emanating from the candle, spreading slowly, touching every corner, and filling the space with serenity. Speak your intention out loud, focusing on keeping the bedroom a place of peace, deep reflection, and restorative rest. You might try an affirmation like:

> *In this sacred space, I invite an abundance of harmony. Here, I will replenish my spirit. Every night, this bedroom will offer me restful, healing sleep. All negativity dissipates, leaving only tranquility and comfort. This bedroom is a sanctuary, nurturing my well-being and serenity.*

Focus on the blessing for a moment, feeling the words as they infuse the room with their power. After this, place small crystals associated with calming energy, such as selenite, calcite, rose quartz, or angelite, in key places beside your bed or on windowsills. To finalize your blessing, write your intentions on a piece of paper, fold it, and place it beneath your pillow, symbolizing your commitment to maintaining these energies. Extinguish the candle, trusting that your bedroom is now a place of peace.

If you'd rather skip over the candle lighting and crystal placing, no worries! Try a few quick affirmations as you move through your bedroom on a regular basis, wash your bedding, or make your bed each day or before you go to bed at night:

+ *In this sacred space, may dreams be sweet. Here, love and peace will always meet. A place of tranquility, loving and warm, in this blessed bedroom, safe from harm.*

+ *In this room, peace and rest entwine, sanctuary is found, and serenity fills my spirit.*

+ *May this bedroom be a haven of tranquility, where peace washes over and soothes my soul. Let each night bring deep, restorative sleep and dreams filled with insight. Surround this space with an aura of calm, making it a sanctuary for rest and renewal.*

Sounds, Lighting, and Mood

Harnessing sound, lighting, and the overall mood effectively can transform the entire feel of your bedroom and help make it a more magical space. Try incorporating sound using chimes, singing bowls, or ambient music to cleanse, energize, or create specific atmospheres. Sound clears stagnant energies; ringing bells or chimes can signify the beginning or end of rituals, while soothing music induces relaxation or enhances meditation. Mantras, chants, or affirmations spoken aloud contribute to setting intentions and amplifying magical energies within the room. If you're someone who can't sleep without some white noise in the background, consider investing in an ambient sound machine—if you don't want to drop the cash for one of those, check out your favorite music streaming service and pull up playlists of falling rain, waves crashing, or other nature sounds.

Manipulating lighting can have an impact on the ambiance of the bedroom as well. Utilize candles, colored LED lights, or natural light to evoke desired moods or energies. Candlelight offers a warm, intimate glow. Different colored lights can align with intentions—soft blue for tranquility, red for passion, or green for growth.

Natural light during the day can infuse the room with vibrant energy, while dimmed lights in the evening encourage relaxation and introspection. If you like things a bit more whimsical, add a few strings of fairy lights around the room. Personally, I can't sleep in a pitch-black bedroom, so I have a small nightlight that changes colors during the night, moving from soft purple to gold to blue and green. It's dim enough that it doesn't disrupt my sleep but gives off enough of a glow that I won't trip over a cat if I get up at two in the morning to visit the bathroom.

Utilize scents through incense, essential oils, or herbal sachets to evoke specific feelings or energies. Lavender for relaxation, citrus for invigoration, or frankincense for spirituality can influence your bedroom's magical ambiance.

Candles

Candles can create a spiritually balanced atmosphere in your bedroom. Whether it's inspiring relaxation, promoting restful sleep, enhancing intimacy, or creating a tranquil space, infuse each candle lighting with your intentions.

You can also integrate candles into bedtime rituals or meditation practices. Each night before I go to bed, I light a single candle and take a few minutes to reflect on things that have happened that day—what have I learned, what was wonderful, was anything a challenge for me, and how can I do better tomorrow? Light candles during relaxation exercises or meditation sessions to deepen focus and promote tranquility within the bedroom. Incorporate them into spells or rituals aimed at enhancing the room's ambiance or fostering a peaceful atmosphere.

Utilize candles for purifying the bedroom's energy by moving a lit candle around the space, focusing on dispelling negative energies or stresses. Place candles with protective intent near entryways or windows to safeguard the room's energy. Remember to always prioritize safety when using candles in the bedroom—it's a space full of things that can catch fire easily! Ensure your candles are placed away from flammable objects, supervised while burning, and extinguished before you fall asleep or leave the room.

Sex Magic

The bedroom is a great place for exploring sex magic, which involves harnessing the potent energy of sexuality for manifesting intentions or desires. Understanding sexual energy as a blend of physical sensations, emotions, and spiritual connection is crucial. It's a force that can be directed for magical purposes once intentions are clarified.

Open, honest communication with any partner is essential; everyone involved should willingly consent to participate in sex magic and understand the intentions behind the practice. Establishing clear boundaries and mutual respect is fundamental, as consent is paramount in any magical activity, especially one as intimate as sex magic. It is completely unethical to manipulate or coerce anyone into participating.

Creating a sacred and comfortable space in the bedroom benefits everyone. You can set the scene by setting up an altar with symbolic objects representing intentions, like candles, crystals, or personal items. During sexual activity, focus on intentions and visualize the desired outcome vividly, channeling the heightened energy toward the purpose. Guide the flow of energy through breathwork and focus as you concentrate on moving the heightened energy throughout your body, aligning it with your magical intentions. Synchronizing energies and intentions with anyone involved is important for a shared manifestation or goal. For most people who practice sex magic, the spell is complete at the moment of orgasm—and ideally, anyone who's participating will get there at the same time.

Afterward, grounding energies is vital. Engaging in calming activities—even if it's just cuddling and talking—can help anchor yourself back into the present moment. Reflecting on the experience and its impact, whether through journaling or meditation, aids in processing feelings, insights, or manifestations that arise. Sex magic should always be approached with reverence and a clear understanding of the energies involved, keeping ethics and responsible use at the forefront of your practice—just like with non-magical variations of sex and intimacy.

BEDTIME RITUALS

If you've raised children—or if you can remember being a child yourself—you probably know the importance of a routine at bedtime. I've learned that for me, even as a fully formed alleged grown-up, a very specific routine helps me fall asleep each night—and if I skip it, I may flop around, tossing and turning, before I can finally drift off. Our bodies and minds respond to routine, and that's what a ritual is—it's doing things in a similar pattern every single time. Here are a few simple rituals you might want to try at bedtime to get yourself into a magical mindset before you doze off for the night.

CANDLELIGHT MEDITATION

Sit comfortably in bed with a softly lit candle nearby. Close your eyes, take deep breaths, and let the candle's gentle glow soothe your mind. Visualize releasing the day's tensions with each exhale. Focus on relaxation and letting go of any lingering stress or worries. After a few minutes, blow out the candle and slip into bed, carrying this calmness into your sleep.

Crystals for Sleep

Select calming crystals like amethyst or moonstone. Hold them in your hands or place them under your pillow, and establish an intention for restful sleep and peaceful dreams. Close your eyes and visualize the crystals enveloping you in a cocoon of tranquility, gradually easing you into a serene sleep.

Bedtime Affirmations

Sit or lie comfortably in bed and take a few deep breaths to center yourself. Repeat positive affirmations related to sleep and relaxation, such as *I am relaxed and ready for a peaceful sleep* or *I release the day and welcome rest*. Say these affirmations aloud or in your mind, letting them sink in as you drift off.

Herbal Tea Ritual

Prepare a cup of your favorite calming herbal tea like chamomile or lavender. As the tea steeps, inhale its soothing aroma. Sip the tea slowly, focusing on its warmth and tranquility. With each sip, visualize tension leaving your body, replaced by a sense of calmness. Enjoy this ritual as part of your bedtime routine to unwind and prepare for sleep.

Gratitude Journaling

Keep a bedside journal and pen. Before turning off the lights, take a moment to jot down three things you're grateful for from the day. Reflect on positive moments, small joys, or any lessons learned. This practice helps shift your focus to gratitude, fostering a peaceful state of mind before bedtime.

OTHER SIMPLE BEDTIME PRACTICES

+ Create a herbal sleep sachet with calming herbs like lavender or chamomile, and place it under your pillow or nearby for soothing scents promoting restfulness.

+ Arrange calming crystals, such as amethyst or moonstone, in a grid on your bedside table, focusing their energies for peaceful sleep while visualizing tranquility.

+ Spend a few moments before bedtime sitting under the moonlight, closing your eyes, and visualizing the moon's energy washing over you to release tensions and promote relaxation.

+ Place a few sprigs of fresh lavender in a vase on your nightstand or under your pillow to calm you as you drift off.

+ Use a selenite wand or herbal smoke stick to cleanse your energy before sleep, envisioning it clearing away accumulated stress or negative energies.

+ Create a homemade spray with lavender essential oil and water, spritzing it on your pillow and bedding for the calming aroma to enhance sleep quality.

+ Lie down comfortably, visualize roots extending into the earth, releasing excess energy, and feel a sense of peace and grounding.

‣ Journal your reflections on how the moon's phases affect your emotions and energy, aligning your intentions for restful sleep with the current lunar phase.

Dream Magic

Dream magic can take us into a mystical realm where our subconscious intertwines with the ethereal, offering opportunities for exploration and manifestation. For many practicing witches, dreams offer access to inner wisdom, healing, and divination. Through various techniques and practices, dream magic can be a powerful tool in your witchy repertoire.

Techniques like keeping dream journals beside the bed, repeating affirmations before sleep to remember your dreams, or placing crystals like amethyst under your pillows will help heighten your awareness within dreams. Lucid dreaming, where we have the ability to control our dreams, is super useful for its potential in guiding intentions, exploring inner realms, and engaging in magical workings while we sleep.

Dreams also serve as conduits for divination and prophecy. You might do dreamwork to receive messages from guides, ancestors, or the deities of your tradition. Through dream interpretation, symbols, and recurring themes, you can decode hidden meanings and insights, unraveling subconscious messages that hold guidance for waking life, offer glimpses into the unknown, and provide answers to pressing questions.

Dream magic, much like that performed during conscious, wakeful periods, does require some ethical considerations. Be sure to approach dreamwork with respect for the subconscious realm and its inhabitants. Honor boundaries, seek informed consent from dream entities, and maintain a clear distinction between dream reality and waking life. Your practices in dream magic should always uphold respect, integrity, and responsibility toward the dream realm and its inhabitants.

LUCID DREAMING

Lucid dreaming allows us to become conscious and aware within our dreams, offering a platform for exploration, manifestation, and spiritual growth. It does take some trial and error, and after you've worked at it for a bit, you'll figure out which techniques are the most successful for you. I've been doing lucid dreaming for many years, and I'd like to share what I'd consider best practices for cultivating meaningful lucid dreaming.

- **Start a dream journal:** Keep a notebook or use a smartphone app to record your dreams immediately upon waking. This habit enhances dream recall, making it easier to recognize dream patterns. Even fragments of dreams can be valuable for future knowledge. Go back later to reflect on your experiences. We'll go into more detail on this in just a moment when we discuss dream journaling.

- **Perform reality checks:** While it may sound a bit like something out of *The Matrix*, it's a good idea to ask yourself periodically throughout the day if you're dreaming. Test reality by looking at texts or clocks, trying to push a finger through your palm, or asking if your surroundings make sense. These reality checks can help you carry this habit into your dreams.

- **Set clear intentions:** Before bedtime, affirm your intention to become aware within your dreams. Repeatedly tell yourself, *I will be aware that I'm dreaming* or *I will recognize my dreams tonight.* Visualize yourself becoming lucid as you drift off to sleep.

- **Stay safe:** Give yourself permission, as you fall asleep, to exit out of any dream that makes you feel frightened, anxious, or unsafe. Just like in our waking environment, you're allowed to leave places or situations that cause you to be uncomfortable, with no excuses or justification needed.

- **Relax before bed:** Engage in relaxation practices before bed, such as meditation or deep breathing. A relaxed mind increases your chances of accessing the dream world.

- **Stabilize the dream:** Upon realizing you're dreaming, focus on stabilizing the dream. Rub your hands together or concentrate on your surroundings to maintain clarity and prevent the dream from fading.

- **Respect dream characters:** Interact respectfully with dream characters or entities you might encounter. Seek consent and practice kindness within the dream realm.

Cultivating lucid dreaming involves consistent practice, patience, and a willingness to explore the subconscious realm. You'll eventually develop the ability to become conscious within your dreams, unlocking a realm of limitless possibilities.

Herbal Dream Sachet

When I first began paying attention to the messages my dreams offered, I learned that aromatherapy is a particularly effective way for me to fall asleep, rest well, and be able to recall my dreams upon waking. I also, at the time, had a cat that would eat pretty much any dried plant material at all, so I would wake up to bare stalks of chewed-up herbs (especially if I was using catnip) on my nightstand. The solution was to stitch up an herbal dream sachet that I then tucked into my pillow, thus preventing said cat from stealing the whole thing and running off with it. That particular cat has long since departed, but I still love falling asleep to the fragrance of an herbal sachet.

Crafting a sachet for restful sleep and positive dreaming helps harness the calming and dream-enhancing attributes of the herbs inside. If you handcraft one with intention, it can serve as a potent aid in promoting a tranquil night's sleep and encouraging vivid and positive dream experiences. This is a simple and easy craft project you can make with just a few minutes of your time. You'll need:

- Soft fabric in a color or pattern you find relaxing
- Needle and thread
- Cotton batting or Polyfill for stuffing
- 1 teaspoon each of two or three dried herbs associated with sleep and dreaming, such as catnip, chamomile, lavender, mugwort, or yarrow
- A small bowl

✦ A small crystal associated with sleep and dreaming, such as amethyst, smoky quartz, moonstone, or selenite

Cut the fabric into a pair of squares—they don't have to be huge, and in fact, smaller seems to be better. Aim for a size that comfortably fits in your palm while allowing ample room for the herb mixture. Place the two pieces right side together, and stitch around three of the edges. As you sew, visualize yourself falling into restful sleep and experiencing positive things in your dreams. When you get to the end of the third side, stop sewing, but don't cut off the thread. Turn the fabric right side out and set it aside.

Combine your dried herbs in the bowl. Mix them thoroughly with your fingers in a clockwise motion to ensure an even distribution of the blend. Fill the fabric halfway with your stuffing material, add the crystal, and then place a few pinches of your herb blend inside. Stuff it the rest of the way so it's full. Stitch the open side shut, and secure it tightly so none of the herbs can escape. Hold the finished sachet in your hands, focusing on your intentions for restful sleep and positive dreams. Visualize your desired outcomes, infusing the sachet with these intentions.

Place the sachet under your pillow, near your bed, or on a bedside table before bedtime—be sure to position it where you'll benefit from its calming aroma while sleeping. Over time, the herbs may lose potency, so consider replacing or refreshing the sachet by adding fresh herbs or crafting a new one to continue benefiting from its properties.

Keep a Dream Journal

Once you start working with dream magic and journaling your experiences, you may find it helpful to look for recurring themes. Two of the most common errors we make as humans are looking for patterns where there are none and refusing to see patterns when they do exist. By writing things down first thing in the morning, you can return to your dream journal later to see what symbols and images appear regularly.

Keeping a dream journal involves capturing the details, emotions, and symbols of your dreams immediately upon waking. The key is to record your dreams promptly, as they tend to fade rapidly from memory once we get up, use the bathroom, fix coffee, feed the dog, and so on. Keep your dream journal or a notebook and pen within easy reach of your bed to ensure quick access upon waking.

Immediately upon waking, jot down any fragments, emotions, colors, people, places, or events you remember from your dreams. Even brief keywords or phrases can trigger vivid memories of the dream later in the day when you have time to expand upon them. The goal is to capture as much detail as possible, no matter how small or seemingly insignificant, as these details often reveal hidden meanings or contribute to understanding dream patterns.

When writing in your journal, record the dreams in the present tense, describing them as if they are currently happening. This technique can immerse you back into the dream scenario, aiding in better recollection of the sequence of events and emotions experienced during the dream. Focus on how you felt during the dream. Were you happy, anxious, excited, or confused? These emotions can provide valuable insights into the underlying themes or messages within the dream. Did you travel anywhere in your dream? Was it a familiar place or somewhere you've never been? Were there other people in your dream, and did you speak with them? What did they say—and what did you say to them?

I'd recommend organizing your dream entries by date—I also like to include things like day of the week, moon phase, and how many hours of sleep I got that night. This helps in tracking patterns, identifying recurring symbols or themes, and making connections between different dreams. Periodically review your dream journal to analyze these patterns and reflect on the connections between your dreams and waking life.

Be patient with the process of dream journaling. Dream recall improves with practice. Embrace the journey of self-discovery and exploration that your dream journal offers, knowing that each recorded dream holds the potential for deeper understanding and personal growth. While each person's dreams are unique and informed by personal experiences, there are often some common themes found in dreams. Here are just a few you might run into along the way.

+ Flying often represents freedom, liberation, or the ability to rise above challenges.

+ Water reflects emotions, the subconscious mind, or a sense of fluidity in life.

+ Teeth symbolize confidence and power—but if you dream about them falling out, it could mean insecurity or anxiety.

- Being chased represents avoiding an issue, fear, or feeling pursued by an unresolved situation.

- Falling signifies a loss of control, insecurity, or fear of failure.

- Different animals convey various meanings, such as owls for wisdom, butterflies representing transformation, or wolves symbolizing instinct.

- Nudity often indicates vulnerability, authenticity, or a fear of exposure and judgment.

- Being lost indicates a feeling of directionless, uncertainty, or lacking guidance in life.

- Death symbolizes change, transformation, or the end of something, not necessarily literal death.

- Vehicles represent life's journey, progress, or control over one's path.

- School or exams can reflect self-evaluation, learning, or pressure to perform in waking life. If you dream of failing a test, it could indicate self-doubt, fear of inadequacy, or a need for validation.

- Doors and gates signify possibilities, new beginnings, or opportunities for change.

- Money reflects self-worth, success, security, or issues related to finances.

- Being late symbolizes anxiety about missed opportunities, pressure, or feeling unprepared in life.

For a far more thorough and comprehensive breakdown, I highly recommend *The Element Encyclopedia of 20,000 Dreams* by Theresa Cheung.

Kids' Bedrooms

We've talked in detail about different aspects of your bedroom, but you may have younger people living in your house—if you've got kids in your home, their bedrooms can be just as magical as yours! Particularly if you're raising children in a magical tradition, it's a great idea to make their sleeping space a calming sanctuary that's also a place for play, learning, and contemplation. No matter how enchanting your décor may be, keep in mind basic age-appropriate safety tips—don't hang anything that could present a strangulation risk, and avoid small items that could present a hazard if your child is still at the age where things get inserted into noses, mouths, or ears.

Adorn the ceiling with glow-in-the-dark stars, transforming it into a celestial night sky for bedtime wonder and learning about constellations or zodiac symbols. Hang tapestries or artwork depicting mythical creatures, fairy tales, or nature scenes to spark imagination and storytelling. Incorporate elemental themes like a corner for earthy activities, a small "water" area, or wind chimes for air representation, encouraging curiosity about nature's elements. To include fire, avoid candles, and use fire-related images instead.

Interactive learning spaces within your kiddo's room can inspire both curiosity and education. Create a cozy nook filled with magical storybooks, cushions, and a blanket for a comfy reading space. Install colorful and interactive maps for geography lessons, including maps of mythical lands or magical realms to spark curiosity. Introduce a miniature indoor herb garden where children can learn about plants and their magical properties—be sure to use only nontoxic plants.

Magical tools and props can add a touch of enchantment to the space. Include musical instruments like a small xylophone or a set of bells for sound exploration. Set up a treasure chest filled with crystals, dried flowers, shells, or other natural items for sensory play and imaginative adventures.

Celestial and elemental nightlights can create a calming and magical ambiance. Use nightlights shaped like moons, stars, or clouds to softly illuminate the room, instilling a sense of comfort and enhancing bedtime rituals. Introduce nightlights corresponding to the elements to add a mystical touch to the room.

Set up a dedicated crafting area with supplies for creating wands, magical artwork, or simple "potions" using safe, child-friendly materials. Rotate seasonal decorations or create themed displays for celebrations like equinoxes or solstices. By blending education and creativity, your child's bedroom can be a space where your little one can explore, learn, and let their imagination soar in a safe and nurturing environment.

Children's Altar

You may have a household altar in a commonly shared space in your home, but kids often have vastly different ideas of what's important or magical than grown-ups do. You can help your child set up their very own altar in their bedroom to encourage their exploration of spirituality in a safe and imaginative way. Again, be sure to follow age-appropriate safety guidelines—you know your child best.

Begin by selecting a safe and accessible area in the room where the child feels comfortable and can freely interact with the altar. It might be a shelf, a small table, or a dedicated corner that they can easily access and engage with. Include age-appropriate magical objects and symbols that resonate with your kiddo's interests. This can include crystals, feathers, small figurines, seashells, or special rocks collected during nature walks. Encourage your child to add their personal touch to the altar, such as drawings, crafts, or sentimental items, fostering a sense of ownership and connection to their spiritual space.

Kids need to feel safe in their space, so ask them what items represent protection to them. If your child wants to add dinosaurs, dolls, race cars, or a handful of broken crayons to the altar, so be it—let them do so. It's *their* magical space.

You can add representations of the four elements in a way that's easily understandable for children. For instance, try a small dish of soil or a stone, a feather or a small bell, a fire-related image or statue, and a small bowl of water. If your kid expresses interest in magical tools of their own—which they likely will, especially after seeing these items on your household altar—help them come up with child-safe versions of wands, athames, or divination tools.

Encourage a simple daily ritual or reflection at the altar. It could be a moment of gratitude, making a wish, or a few minutes of quiet contemplation where your child can express their thoughts and feelings—this can be a great part of the nightly bedtime routine. Consider your child's altar space as a place to engage in open conversations about their beliefs, experiences, and observations.

Allow the altar to evolve over time according to your child's interests and spiritual growth. Encourage them to rearrange or add items as their understanding and connection to spirituality develops.

Chapter 8
BATHROOM MAGIC

Although we often don't like to talk about the bathroom and the things that go on in there, we can't avoid the fact that it's a pretty important room in your home. Whether you have just one or you've got five, the bathroom is an essential space in daily life. My home only has one, which is fine for my needs since I live alone, but when I was raising a family, I lived in a house that had two full bathrooms and a half bath. Each of the rooms had its own very distinct personality—one was fun and silly for the kids, one was calm and relaxing for me, and the half was mostly just utilitarian and served a dual purpose as a laundry room.

Obviously, the bathroom is where we engage in essential activities like bathing, grooming, and using the toilet. But it can also offer a private sanctuary for personal care routines, allowing us to unwind and relax. Whether through a warm shower or a tranquil bath, it provides moments of solitude and relaxation amid daily hustle. It's often a perfect spot for engaging in meditation or having reflective moments in a serene environment. When my kids were really young, and still at the age where I had very little free time or peace and quiet, the bathroom was the one place I knew I could escape to and not be bothered … at least for a little while.

Magical Decorating for Your Bathroom

There are plenty of ways to infuse a bit of magic into the bathroom! Utilize essential oils or incense known for their mystical and soothing properties. Scents like lavender, frankincense, or sandalwood can evoke a sense of tranquility and enchantment, creating an ambiance of magic and relaxation.

Incorporate symbolic elements representing the elements within the bathroom décor. Display crystals near the sink or windowsill, hang wind chimes for gentle melodies, place a small bowl of water infused with flower petals or crystals, and introduce plants to bring in the essence of nature. If your shower has a curtain rod, look at some of the many commercially available magically themed shower curtains. I tend to rotate mine seasonally, and they're covered in witchy symbols, fantasy elements, and nature images.

Introduce candles strategically around the bathroom to harness their mystical glow. Choose colors aligned with your intentions, such as white for purification, blue for tranquility, or purple for spiritual connection. Display mystical symbols or sigils that resonate with your practice. Whether runes, pentacles, or sacred geometric shapes, place them discreetly around the bathroom as subtle reminders of your magical journey.

Place natural elements like sea salt or Himalayan salt in small bowls to purify energy and promote a sense of grounding. You might want to include seashells, stones, or other items collected from nature as decorative elements. Keep a dish of fragrant soaps infused with lavender, chamomile, rose petals, or other herbs known for their relaxing and mystical properties available for washing up.

SETTING UP YOUR BATHROOM ALTAR

In general, most practitioners—myself included—don't recommend using the bathroom as a place for an altar. However, the one exception is often for a healing altar. That's because the bathroom can be a place of rejuvenation and blessed solitude at the end of a long day. If you've ever slid into a warm, relaxing bath after a terrible shift at work, you know what I'm talking about. There's nothing like it in the world.

My previous home had an absolutely enormous clawfoot tub in the upstairs bathroom. It didn't have a shower attachment, so my teenagers completely avoided it—which meant the tub was all mine, to use at my leisure. It was such a bright, sunny space that I soon realized a small shelf on the wall above the bathtub was the perfect spot for a healing altar. At the end of a rough day, I could fill the tub with warm water, add some oils, light a candle, turn on some soft music, and just let my troubles slide down the drain while I focused on self-care.

To create a healing altar of your own in the bathroom, be sure to choose an area that's not going to get splashed or damp—no one wants wet herbs molding away. Windowsills work well, as do shelves, or if you have enough counter space, consider using a small tray that you can move around as needed.

Incorporate natural elements such as small crystals, seashells, or a bowl of salt to represent the earth element, which can help connect you to nature and grounding energies. Include any ritual tools that resonate with you, such as a small bowl for consecrated water, a feather to represent air, or a bell for cleansing and setting intentions. Select crystals known for their healing properties; I like clear quartz for purification, rose quartz for self-love and compassion, amethyst for relaxation, and citrine for positivity and energy. Place them directly on your altar or arrange them in a bowl.

Add dried or fresh herbs like lavender, chamomile, or eucalyptus for their calming and healing scents—if you've got the ability to do so, small pots of live herbs are a wonderful addition to your space. Alternatively, use essential oils in a diffuser to fill the space with healing aromas. Include candles for their soothing ambiance and energy. I'd recommend using unscented or naturally scented candles to avoid overpowering other fragrances in the room. Light them during your healing rituals or meditation—there's something truly decadent and powerful about bathing by candlelight.

Make space on your altar to place written healing affirmations or intentions. These could focus on self-care, wellness, or specific areas you want to heal in your life, whether they be physical, spiritual, or emotional. Personalize your altar with items and symbols that resonate with your healing journey.

Simple Blessings for Your Bathroom

To bless your bathroom and turn it into a sanctuary of cleansing and renewal, start by doing a good deep clean to remove any physical grime and dirt. This will form a fresh foundation for a metaphysical blessing. After cleaning, light a blue candle, which is associated with healing and will help you align with the water energies of the room. Place the candle on the bathroom counter, and let it act as a beacon of light, guiding positive vibrations into the space. Add a few crystals like clear quartz or aquamarine around the bathroom to boost the energies of purification and relaxation. If you like, add a few drops of essential oil like lavender or eucalyptus to a diffuser to fill the air with calming, cleansing scents.

Draw a small amount of water in the sink or bathtub and dip your fingertips in it. As you touch the water, you might want to offer a short affirmation, expressing your intentions for harmony and healing within your bathroom, such as:

Let this water be a force of purity, cleansing all negativity from this space. May the light fill the room, creating a sanctuary of calm and renewal, where each moment spent is a step toward healing and peace. With this blessing, I invoke serenity.

Remove the plug from the sink or tub, and envision the water absorbing any negativity, washing it away down the drain, then extinguish the candle.

If you'd rather not spend much time in the bathroom and would prefer a quick blessing you can offer on the fly, try one of these:

+ *Here, where water flows and cleanses, let serenity fill each drop that dispenses. Refresh my body in this sacred space, in this tranquil healing place.*

+ *In this bathroom, I release away all stress and negativity. May this space be filled with tranquility and offer calm for my body, mind, and soul.*

+ *As without, so within, as I clean my body, so do I refresh my spirit.*

The Magic of the Bathtub and Shower

With a bit of creative thinking, you can incorporate your tub and shower into a number of different magical applications! Before showering, visualize the water washing away any negative energy or stress. Add a few drops of essential oils or herbs known for purification, such as eucalyptus, rosemary, or sage, to a washcloth, or use herbal soaps.

If you've got a tub, create bath rituals by infusing the water with intentions and magical ingredients. Use bath salts, herbs, or essential oils that correspond to whatever you wish to manifest. Focus on your intentions while soaking in the water to amplify the magical effect. Utilize the relaxed state achieved during bathing for visualization or meditation practices. Close your eyes, focus on your breath, and visualize your intentions manifesting. Envision the water cleansing and energizing your body, mind, and spirit.

Try harnessing the energy of the moon by taking baths or showers under different lunar phases. During a full moon, infuse the water with moon-charged crystals or place them nearby to absorb the lunar energy. I actually love to use my shower as a private space for spellwork or affirmations. Speak or silently repeat positive affirmations aligned with your intentions while washing, and then envision the steam carrying those magical goals out into the universe for manifestation. Alternatively, you can visualize symbols, sigils, or words disappearing down the drain as you finish to release things that no longer serve you.

If your living situation doesn't include a private, personal shower or tub—for instance, you're in a dorm or sleeping on a friend's couch—that's okay! Anything that can be done with a shower or tub can also be adapted for use with just a sink or even a bowl of clean water.

Bath Bombs, Oils, and Soaps

Creating bath bombs, oils, or soaps for use in the bathtub or shower is a great way to bring some magic into the bathroom—plus, you'll smell great in the process! Turn your bathing experience into a sacred and magical ritual, amplifying intentions, cleansing energies, and connecting with elemental forces for personal growth and manifestation.

MAKE AN HERBAL BATH BOMB

I love the feeling of a really enchanting bath bomb, but many of the recipes out there for homemade ones seem to call for a *lot* of ingredients, most of which I don't have on hand. I've figured out through a lot of trial and error that many of those ingredients—such as colorants—are strictly cosmetic and don't matter in the grand scheme of things. The herbal bath bombs I make—and often give as a gifts to magically inclined friends—are pretty basic and plain, but they get the job done. Be sure to consider any skin or fragrance sensitivities you might have before making a bath bomb or any other item to add to your bath water. You'll need:

- 1 cup baking soda
- ½ cup citric acid
- ½ cup corn starch
- 2 tablespoons coconut or jojoba oil
- Essential oil of your choice; try rose for love, lavender for relaxation, eucalyptus for healing, or peppermint for energy.

+ Two mixing bowls and a whisk
+ A silicone mold

Place the dry ingredients in a bowl and whisk them together until fully blended—I actually like to run mine through a flour sifter first to eliminate clumps. In a second bowl, blend the coconut or jojoba oil with the essential oil—use as many drops as you like, but start slowly and add to it, because you can't subtract essential oils if you put too much in. Slowly pour the oil mixture into the dry mixture, mixing as you go. If it seems overly dry, you can add a few extra drops of coconut or jojoba oil, but be careful not to add too much. While blending the ingredients, infuse them with your intentions. Visualize the purpose of the bath bomb—whether it's for relaxation, healing, manifestation, or spiritual cleansing.

Place your mixture into the silicone mold and mash it down so it's heavily compacted. Leave it in place for several hours—I usually let mine sit overnight—and then remove from the mold. Let the bath bombs dry completely before storing them in an airtight container. Label them with their magical intent, and you're ready to drop them into your tub!

MAGICAL BATH OILS

Because my one bathroom only has a walk-in shower/tub combo unit that takes forever to fill with water, I've become a big fan of bath oils I can use directly on my skin while showering. It makes my skin feel soft and smell amazing, plus

I can fill my shower routine with extra magical manifestation. To make a simple magical bath oil, you'll need:

+ Unscented carrier oil such as coconut, almond, jojoba, safflower, or grapeseed
+ A clean glass bottle or jar with a lid
+ Essential oils aligned with your intention; try lavender, lemon, eucalyptus, sandalwood or other skin-safe oils.

Pour 2 to 4 ounces of your carrier oil into a clean glass bottle or jar. Add 10 to 15 drops of essential oil per 2 ounces of carrier oil. Focus on your intention while adding each oil, visualizing its properties contributing to the magical outcome. Gently stir or shake the mixture to thoroughly combine the oils—I like to give mine a good swirling.

Perform a patch test on a small area of your skin to ensure you have no allergic reactions. If the blend is too potent, dilute it further with more carrier oil. Charge the oil by holding the bottle, infusing it with your intentions and concentrating on the purpose of the blend. Seal the bottle tightly and label it with the blend's purpose, ingredients, and creation date. Store it in a cool, dark place to maintain its potency. Add a few drops of your oil to bathwater or apply it to your skin after bathing to take advantage of its magical vibrations.

Magical Soaps

Have you ever thought about making your own soap? Soapmaking has a long history, dating back to around 2500 BC in ancient Sumer, where a concoction of fats blended with ashes created the earliest known form of soap.[18] Around 1500 BC, the Egyptians developed soap-like substances using animal and vegetable oils combined with alkaline salts. Soapmaking techniques spread across civilizations, including the Greeks and Romans, who used soaps for personal hygiene, and by the Middle Ages, it was a thriving industry in Europe. The process evolved over time, incorporating various oils, lye, and scents, and by the eighteenth century, advancements in chemistry further refined soap production, leading to the modern soap formulations and manufacturing techniques we use today.[19]

There are several different methods to making soap, and the most common involve using lye as an ingredient. You can certainly learn how to do this—with proper safety precautions—but the technique I'm going to share with you is one I learned how to do as a Girl Scout, a million years ago. It's easy, it's fun, and I can avoid injuring myself with splashing lye. You'll need:

+ Unscented soap bars
+ A cheese grater
+ A bowl

....
18. Cassidy, "Who Invented Soap?"
19. "Soaps & Detergents History."

+ Dried herbs or essential oils corresponding to your magical purpose, ground to a powder in your mortar and pestle

+ Double boiler or a makeshift one, such as a heatproof bowl over a pot of simmering water

+ Large spoon for stirring

+ Soap molds or a shallow tray, lined with parchment paper or greased with oil

+ *Optional:* Additional oils like coconut, olive, or almond for extra moisturization

Start by grating the unscented soap bars into the bowl using the cheese grater. This increases the surface area of the soap, which helps it to melt evenly. You'll need about 2 cups of grated soap for this recipe. Ready the double boiler or create one by placing a heatproof bowl over a pot of simmering water. Add the grated soap to the top of the double boiler or the bowl and allow it to melt slowly. Stir occasionally to ensure even melting.

After the soap base has melted completely, add your dried herbs or essential oils. For dried herbs, about 1 to 2 tablespoons per cup of grated soap is a good ratio. If you're using essential oils, start with a few drops and then adjust based on your desired scent strength. Stir the melted soap thoroughly to evenly distribute the herbs or essential oils. Be sure they are well blended into the soap mixture.

Once mixed, swiftly pour the soap mixture into your prepared molds or tray. Silicone molds work well for shaping smaller single bars, but if you use a shallow tray, you can cut the solidified soap into desired shapes after it's completely cooled.

Allow the soap to solidify at room temperature. This usually takes several hours or even overnight, depending on the thickness of the soap and the room temperature. Once it's completely solid, gently remove your soap from the molds, or cut them from a larger block if you poured them into a tray. Let your soaps cure for a few weeks in a well-ventilated area to increase hardness and longevity. Once all the bars have cured completely, individually wrap them in paper for storage. Use them in ritual showers or baths as you choose.

Here are some of my favorite herbal soap combinations:

+ Pine, peppermint, and sage for protection
+ Basil, bay, and lemon verbena to banish negativity
+ Jasmine, catnip, and rose petals for love
+ Chamomile, nutmeg, and vervain for prosperity
+ Mugwort, orris root, and yarrow for divination enhancement

If you want to learn in more detail about how to make magical soaps using lye and other ingredients, check out *Soapmaking: A Magickal Guide* by Alicia Grosso.

Herbal Ritual Bath

I love a good long cleansing soak prior to working significant rituals. When I first began practicing, a long time ago in a galaxy far away, I got into the habit of taking a ritual bath before every single working. Although I now reserve it only for special occasions, there's definitely something empowering and sacred about a herbal bath prior to spiritual activities. For an herbal ritual bath, you'll need:

+ Equal parts dried lavender, mugwort, rosemary, peppermint, and juniper (or any other herbs associated with purification that you prefer)
+ Small pouch or muslin cloth
+ 3 white candles
+ Matches or a lighter
+ Amethyst, clear quartz, and selenite crystals
+ *Optional:* Epsom salts, bath salts, or bath oil

Start by preparing a serene environment in the bathroom. Clean the space and ensure it's free of disturbances. Turn on some music or nature sounds if it helps you create a calming, sacred atmosphere.

Place your herbs inside the pouch or muslin cloth. As you do, visualize the healing properties of each infusing the bathwater with soothing and rejuvenating energies. Securely tie the pouch to prevent the herbs from escaping, and hang it over the faucet. Fill the bathtub with warm water, letting the water course over your bag of herbs. If you'd like to add salts or oils for additional relaxation or healing properties, now is a good time to do it.

Position the candles around the bathtub and light them one by one. Focus on their tranquil flames, setting your intention for healing and relaxation. Arrange the crystals nearby or around the bathtub, visualizing their energies amplifying the space's healing properties. If you only have one of each crystal, place one beside each candle; when you've got multiples, consider positioning them into a crystal grid.

Stand beside the filled bathtub and take several deep breaths, centering yourself. Close your eyes and visualize a comforting, purifying light surrounding you. Slowly immerse yourself into the bath, feeling the warm water enveloping you. Embrace the sensation and aroma of the herbs, allowing their energies to wash over you. Visualize any tension, stress, or negativity melting away, replaced by a sense of calmness, peace, and renewal.

Relax in the bath for as long as desired, utilizing the time for meditation, self-reflection, or simply enjoying the healing effects of the herbs and crystals. When you're ready to conclude, visualize any remaining tension or negativity being washed away as you drain the bathwater.

Extinguish the candles one by one, allowing yourself to feel gratitude for the energies they provided. Allow the crystals to continue emanating their energy in the bathroom or cleanse them afterward. Remember to hydrate yourself after the bath, and then, when you're ready, move on to your spiritual space for your ritual work.

Bath Crayon Sigils

When my children were small, one of their favorite tub time activities was the use of bath crayons. By the time they were all nice and clean and smelling fresh, there was all kinds of artwork on the tiles around the bathtub—flowers, hearts, random letters of the alphabet, animals. You name it, they drew it. Well, kids don't have a monopoly on fun or creativity, so why not use bath crayons yourself, and do a bit of sigil magic?

First, be sure to clarify your intention and purpose—what is it you hope to achieve? What do you wish to manifest? It can be a concrete goal, a feeling, or just a concept you'd like to focus on. Take some time to meditate on this, and allow your mind to drift a bit. Focus on the substance of your goal—don't worry about specific words or phrases. Allow an abstract symbol or image to form in your mind that represents your intention. This could be a geometric shape, a flowing design, a pattern, or any symbol that feels connected to your desire. Hold on to that image in your mind, and then turn on the water, letting your shower get good and steamy.

Get in the shower, and use bath crayons to draw or create the symbol that you visualized on the shower wall, glass doors, or tiles. Let your intuition guide your hand—and keep going as long as you feel you need to. Add or remove elements until it feels like a powerful representation of your magical goal. Focus on making it a distinct and meaningful symbol for *you*, empowering it with your purpose as you draw.

When you've finished drawing your sigil, proceed with your shower routine as usual while focusing on the image. As the water washes over it, visualize the energy of the sigil activating and mingling with the steam, carrying your intentions into the universe. At the end of your shower, you can either gently rinse away the sigil or leave it in place to gain strength—just trust your intuition, and believe the magic has been set in motion.

Beauty Magic

Since the bathroom is the place where many of us get ready to start our day—washing our faces, brushing our hair, peering into the mirror as we apply makeup—it's a great place to work on beauty magic. There's a lot to be said for beauty magic, and often, it ties in closely with workings related to love and romance. That's not because you need to have a "conventionally pretty" look to be worthy of love—quite the contrary. When I say it ties into love magic, it's because spells related to romance and attraction can often be focused on self-love, which in turn can make us more confident in ourselves. Confidence, poise, and self-esteem can go a long way in making ourselves more attractive to other people if that's what we so desire.

As I've gotten older, I've spent less time worrying about my physical appearance—I wear makeup only on special occasions, and my standard hairstyle rotates between a super practical ponytail and "Bellatrix Lestrange Just Got Out of Bed." I've stopped caring so much about the opinions other people might have of my looks and instead have spent years working on my opinion of myself. My partner thinks I'm beautiful, my friends love my style, and strangers compliment me on completely random aspects of my vibe when I'm out in public; possibly the best response I've ever gotten was from a girl about ten years old in the grocery store, who looked at me and screamed, *HEY RED-HEADED LADY, I LOVE YOUR ENERGY.*

Frankly, I love it too, and I think I'm pretty damn awesome.

And that, at its crux, is the end result of the beauty magic we're going to discuss in this section. The goal is not to look like something you aren't—I'll never be built like a runway model, and I'm cool with that—but instead to enhance your natural positive qualities and give you confidence in yourself.

Enchanting Cosmetics and Personal Care Items

As I mentioned, I rarely use makeup, but my one weakness is a bold red lipstick. I have six or seven tubes of it, all in varying shades, and I wear it because it makes me feel sassy and strong and powerful. When I feel an especially strong need to walk in and take over a situation, I use one of my two personal favorites, which I refer to as my Lipsticks of Awesomeness. They make me feel like a total badass the minute I apply either of them (if you're wondering, they are Besame's *Victory Red 1941* and *Ruby Woo* by MAC). By enchanting your cosmetics or other personal care items—lotion, aftershave, shampoo, etc.—you can give yourself a little bit of an extra self-esteem boost any time you need it. You'll need:

- A tube of your favorite lipstick or other personal care product
- A small piece of rose quartz
- A pink candle
- Matches or a lighter
- A pen and paper

Find a quiet and comfortable space where you won't be disturbed and light the candle; an ideal spot for it is the counter if you're working in the bathroom or on your altar or a tabletop if you're in a different room of your home. Hold the rose quartz in the palms of your hands, and feel the vibrations of love and beauty emanating from it. As you do, close your eyes, and in your mind, create your confidence mantra. It can be something as simple as *I am radiant and attractive* or my favorite, which is *I am awesome, amazing, and excellent.*

Place the rose quartz in front of the candle, and pick up your lipstick, shampoo, cologne, or whatever you're about to enchant. Hold it over the crystal, and tell your lipstick what its job is—*This is my lipstick of radiance* or *I hold my cologne of confidence.* Visualize the energy from the candle and crystal filling your chosen item with whatever attribute you have now given it, and see yourself effortlessly projecting confidence and self-assuredness anytime you use this particular product.

Extinguish the candle, and whenever you want to feel completely amazing and empowered, use the personal care item you've just enchanted.

Mirror, Mirror, On the Wall

You might not have mirrors in every single room of your home, but most people have one hanging in their bathroom. Mirrors have long been seen as a magical tool, and there are a number of ways you can take advantage of your mirrors—whether it's in the bathroom or not—and use them in ritual and spellwork. A mirror reflects not only images but also energy—and because of that, they can also repel the unwanted.

MIRROR BEAUTY MAGIC

Why not take advantage of your bathroom mirror in your beauty rituals and spells? Mirror magic can be a potent tool for beauty spells, as mirrors are often associated with reflection, self-perception, and amplification of energy. Here are a few things to try:

+ Stand in front of your mirror and speak positive affirmations about your beauty and confidence— *I am fabulous, I love my great skin, my hair looks terrific today!* Repeat these affirmations daily to reinforce positive self-perception.

+ Cleanse your energy and enhance your beauty by using a consecrated mirror. Pass the mirror through incense smoke, sprinkle it with salt water, or use a cleansing herb while visualizing any negativity and self-doubt being removed.

+ Surround your mirror with items that represent self-love and beauty, such as rose quartz, dried flowers, or candles. Meditate in front of it, visualizing self-love and confidence flowing into you through the reflection.

+ Create a sigil that represents your desired beauty outcome, like confidence, radiance, or self-acceptance. Draw or inscribe this sigil on your bathroom mirror using a washable marker or with your finger in the steam from your shower. Charge the sigil with your intention and visualize its manifestation.

Remember that when working on beauty magic, it's best to approach your spellwork with positivity, self-love, and a clear intention. Always work within your comfort zone, and try to avoid obsessing over physical appearance.

Magical Mirror Lore

Since mirrors have been around for ages—pretty much since the time people realized they liked looking at themselves—there are plenty of ways to use them in magic, far beyond beauty spells. Consider using your mirror for scrying—you can either use a handheld mirror or one hanging on your wall. Ground yourself through meditation or deep breathing, and light a few candles for ambient lighting without causing reflections in the mirror. Stand or sit comfortably in front of your mirror and allow your gaze to soften, focusing on a point just short of the glass. Observe any images or symbols that appear, letting them unfold naturally without immediate analysis. Afterward, ground yourself again and record your experiences and visions in a journal for later evaluation.

You can also use a mirror in spellwork that returns a hex or curse back to its sender while at the same time avoiding harm to yourself or any collateral damage to others. For this, you'll want a small mirror not attached to your wall (a cosmetic compact works nicely for this) as well as something that represents the person who sent negative magic your way or a representation of the curse itself. Place the representation of the person or the curse on top of the mirror, face down, so it's reflected back upon itself. Add a black candle on top of it. Light the candle, and visualize that negative energy being bounced back to its original source. If you like, you can add a short incantation, such as *May this curse no longer bind; its way back home it shall find.*

Use your mirror as a tool for introspection and spiritual self-reflection. Have a conversation with your mirror self. Include affirmations of self-love and strength as well as questions designed to uncover hidden truths about the choices you've made or where you hope to go in the future. Allow your mirror self to speak to you in your heart and mind—imagine you're having this conversation with your best friend, and reflect upon the answers you receive. Be sure to express gratitude for any insight or guidance offered.

To cleanse a mirror used for magical purposes, you can use an herbal mirror wash. One of my favorite ways to do this is to brew up an infusion of purifying herbs—my go-to blend includes mugwort, rosemary, lavender, and sage—and mix it with a few cups of vinegar. I spritz it on my mirror using a mister bottle, let it air dry for a few minutes, and then gently wipe down any residual spots before they can set.

Mirrors and Luck

We've all heard it dozens of times—*if you break a mirror, that's seven years of bad luck!* That's a doozy, right there. I'm busy and don't have time for seven years of misfortune. I used to think this was something parents told their children to encourage caution when handling a breakable mirror, but it turns out it goes back a long time. In 1832, Alfred Lord Tennyson, wrote about the jinx of a broken mirror in "The Lady of Shalott":

> *The mirror crack'd from side to side;*
> *"The curse is come upon me," cried The Lady of Shalott.*[20]

Fortunately, if your mirror has "crack'd from side to side," there are a couple of folk remedies you can use to alleviate seven years of disaster coming your way.

The first method involves cleanup, which you'll have to do anyway if you've got shards of broken mirror all over the place. Simply sweep the pieces up into a cardboard box or wrap them in heavy paper, being careful not to cut yourself, and bury them

....

20. Tennyson, "The Lady of Shalott."

somewhere outdoors. Be sure to do this someplace you can retrieve them later; after a full moon cycle has passed, dig them back up (remember that mirror pieces aren't biodegradable) and dispose of them as you normally would broken glass. Folklore suggests you should do this during the light of a full moon, but you can get rid of them as soon as its convenient. The second way to eliminate the seven-year-long catastrophe is to throw salt over your left shoulder, which is well known as a counter-charm to help break free of misfortune … but you'll still need to clean up your broken mirror.

The Mighty Toilet Paper of Banishing

In the introduction to this book, if you can remember that far back, I mentioned my Household Magic workshop. In it, I always make sure to tell people about this toilet paper banishing spell. It's one I've used for ages, and it's ridiculously stupid in its simplicity. I love it because (a) it really only requires two components and (b) it's incredibly effective.

When I share this spell, I've found that workshop attendees fall into two distinct camps. The first group looks at me with obvious horror—after all, what kind of disgusting witchcraft involves an adventure in the bathroom? The second group … well, they're generally making a list in their heads of the people they want to banish. But regardless of which party they're in, people from all walks of life have come up to me weeks or months later to tell me they couldn't believe how well this one worked for them.

In fact, it's so effective that honestly, I'd recommend only using it on someone you *really* don't want in your life. If there's even a remote chance you'd like to reconnect with the person in the future, I'd probably avoid this one. It's a bit of a scorched earth strategy. Reserve it for people who are really on your … ahem … shit list.

The first thing you're going to need—as you most likely guessed from the title—is some toilet paper. Don't use that flimsy see-through stuff like they have in the bathroom at your local gas station, which is so weak you can practically read a newspaper through it. Go get the good toilet paper—the two-ply superstrength kind. After all, you deserve nice things. Your second tool is something every witch should have handy at all times—a black permanent marker. If you don't have one, go buy or borrow one, because they're fantastic. Remember that black is associated with banishing.

Pull a length of squares off the roll of your fancy toilet paper. It can be any number you like, but I like to use nine. This is partly because nine is a magical number—three times three—but also because nine squares is just about the right length for what I'm about to do to this toilet paper. Obviously, your mileage may vary.

Using your black Sharpie, write the name of the person you wish to banish on each square. You can use their real name—first, last, both, or even a nickname. If you're not certain of the person's full name, write something descriptive like *That jerk in the payroll department*. The universe knows who they are.

Now that you've got their name written on all your squares, it's time to use the restroom. And friends, this is not the kind of restroom trip you make when you've slurped down a gallon of diet soda and your bladder is full. No, I'm talking about the kind of bathroom experience you have after you went on a late-night chalupa bender with extra Taco Bell hot sauce. You know *exactly* what I mean. We've all been there. So, go ahead, use the bathroom—think about your target person the whole time, and make it as celebratory as possible. Once you've finished doing your business, grab that length of toilet paper, wad or fold it up as you normally do, and wipe yourself with it. Drop your soiled toilet paper into the bowl, don't look back, and flush that person right on out of your life.

And this should be a no-brainer, but be sure to wash your hands when you're done. Hygiene is your friend.

Chapter 9
KITCHEN MAGIC

For so many of us, the kitchen feels like the most magical place in our home. It's partly because the concept of "kitchen witchcraft" has gained in popularity recently. Personally, I love the idea of calling it *domestic witchcraft*, because that rather implies the existence of its opposite, which would be *feral* or *untamed* or *wild witchcraft*. I'm pretty sure I know which side of that spectrum I fall upon. Regardless, we'll stick to "kitchen witchcraft" for the purposes of this discussion.

But the other part of it is that the kitchen is symbolic of the hearth fires of old—long before we had microwaves and gas ovens and air fryers, cooking was done over a simple fire. Creating a meal was not just for sustenance and for survival; it was also for familial bonding, forging a sense of community, and boosting the spirit. Preparing food and sharing it with those we care about allows us to express our feelings and offer (and receive) hospitality. Food is often part of a ritualized experience, either in the way we make it or the way in which it's consumed. There's an ancient connection between food and magic, and as a result, the place where we prepare, serve, and eat the dishes we make becomes a space of reverence. The more magic we do in the kitchen, the more sacred it becomes.

Kitchen witchcraft focuses on the practical and magical use of everyday items found in—you guessed it—the kitchen. Cooking and baking become sacred acts, in which we can infuse our culinary creations with intention, energy, and magical purpose. Preparing a meal can be a ritual in itself. Each ingredient is chosen not just for its flavor but also for its magical properties.

Many kitchen witches are experts at herb magic, utilizing culinary plants for magical purposes. They create herbal blends, teas, infusions, and potions for various intentions, such as healing, protection, love, and divination. These magical concoctions can be used in rituals or consumed for their specific magical properties. From soothing teas to homemade salves, kitchen witches use their knowledge of herbs and plants to promote health and well-being within their households.

You can even elevate your kitchen magic by honoring the changing seasons and cycles of nature with your meals. Try incorporating seasonal ingredients into your magical cooking. Each sabbat and its associated foods carry specific energies you can harness in your magical workings.

Your Kitchen Layout: The Triangle Theory

Odds are good that when you moved into your home, you didn't get to design the kitchen—if you did, you're very fortunate! Certainly, many of us have lived in places where we absolutely *hated* the layout of the kitchen—it was weirdly set up, designed in a way that just didn't make sense, the fridge was around a strange corner, or whatever. Most likely, the way your kitchen sits right now is the way it's always going to be—most of us can't just relocate a stove or sink to the opposite side of the room if we don't like its placement.

That said, you may be able to make your kitchen run more efficiently once you get an idea of how the triangle theory works. Sometimes called the kitchen work triangle, this is a design principle used in kitchen layouts to create an efficient and functional workspace. The concept is based on the idea of creating a clear path and efficient workflow between the three main work areas in a kitchen: the sink, the stove, and the refrigerator. These three points form a triangle, hence the name. The goal of the kitchen work triangle is to minimize unnecessary movement and maximize convenience for the person working in the kitchen.

To make the kitchen work triangle effective, designers consider a few different factors. There's the length of the triangle, in which the total distance of the three sides of the triangle (sink to stove, stove to refrigerator, and refrigerator to sink) should ideally be between 12 and 26 feet. This ensures the triangle is neither too cramped nor too spread out, allowing for efficient movement. Second, designers look at setting up clear, unobstructed paths between the triangle points. They typically avoid placing large appliances, cabinets, or islands in the triangle's path to prevent obstacles and ensure smooth movement. Finally, it's also crucial to consider the layout in the context of other kitchen activities. For example, if a kitchen includes a food preparation area, a designer might look at its proximity to the sink and storage areas for ingredients. By adhering to the triangle theory, kitchen designers create layouts that optimize efficiency and functionality to make a user-friendly kitchen space.

If your kitchen is set up this way, great! I'm a little jealous, honestly. But if it's not, and you feel like your kitchen witchcraft is suffering a bit, there are a few ways you can make your kitchen more efficient—without relocating all your major appliances.

First, consider organizing your kitchen into zones based on functions. Create designated areas for food preparation, cooking, cleaning, and storage. Group related items and tools together in each zone to minimize movement within the kitchen—such as keeping all your herb preparation materials in one place instead of scattered about. If you've got the space, you can introduce specialized workstations within your kitchen layout. Having dedicated areas for specific tasks reduces clutter and saves time.

Invest in smart storage solutions to maximize your kitchen's efficiency. Utilize pull-out shelves, lazy Susans, and drawer organizers to make items more accessible. Consider using vertical space with tall cabinets or open shelves for storing items that are not frequently used. Ensure that each key area in your kitchen is well lit. If your kitchen has a dining area, think about using furniture pieces that serve dual functions. For example, a dining table with shelves underneath can provide additional storage space. Proper task lighting, especially over the countertop, stove, sink, and food prep areas, can help improve not only efficiency but safety.

Analyze your daily kitchen routine and arrange items based on frequency of use. Place frequently used items in easily accessible cabinets and drawers if you have the room. I keep both my toaster and my coffee maker in a cabinet directly under the counter—because I only use my toaster a couple of times a week, and I make coffee in the mornings but then the pot just sits there, unused, the rest of the day. Once I'm done with my coffee maker, I wash it and tuck it away. Store pots and pans near the stove and cooking utensils close to the food preparation area.

Finally, take some time periodically to review your kitchen items and declutter. Donate or discard items you don't use to free up space and reduce kitchen junk. An organized kitchen is an efficient kitchen—and that makes for far more efficient witchcraft!

Magical Decorating For Your Kitchen

Turning your kitchen into a magical space involves a lot more than just practical décor—it's more about weaving magic into as many elements as possible so that the space doesn't just *look* magical but *feels* magical. Now, I know everyone has different ideas of what they like and what they don't—we're all unique individuals with unique tastes. That means some of the suggestions I'm about to make might seem way over-the-top to you, or you might feel like they clash with your more minimalist approach, or you don't have the space or the resources to make them happen. That's okay! Just like when you visit a buffet table, as we discussed way back in the introduction, take what you think you'll enjoy, and leave the rest for someone else.

Do you have a spot where you can hang herbs to dry? Display bundles of herbs like rosemary, thyme, lavender, and sage from your ceiling (if it's high enough) or on hooks along your walls. This doesn't just add a rustic touch—it also offers the benefits of the herbs' magical properties, such as purification and protection. Adding a touch of greenery with houseplants or a small indoor herb garden also brings life and vitality to the kitchen—have pots of aloe, rosemary, and sage growing on a glass shelf across the window over the sink.

If you feel like you need more lighting in your kitchen, fairy lights strung in unexpected places, like around windows or along shelves, add a twinkling whimsical vibe. Try incorporating natural materials such as wood, stone, and clay. Wooden bowls, small stone statues, or terracotta pots can help ground your kitchen space and connect it to earthy energies.

What about color? I realize many people—particularly those in newer homes—have kitchens that are white or gray, both of which have a classic, timeless feel. But if you don't love them, why not choose colors that evoke a sense of magic and wonder for you? Deep blues and greens can create a serene backdrop, while rich purples and burgundies add a luxurious, mystical aura. You might paint or wallpaper an accent wall, use colored tiles for a backsplash, or select appliances and cookware in colors that bring you joy. I love a cottagecore feel, so I've covered one wall in mushroom-patterned paper and painted my boring 1980s cabinets a calming, sage-green color. It makes me feel content and magical, and when I have friends over, that kitchen is where the bulk of my guests want to hang out.

You can incorporate symbols and patterns that hold either traditional or personal magical meanings for you—a pentacle, a triple spiral, Celtic knotwork, or whatever resonates with you. You're not restricted to just wall art with these either! What about dish towels, pottery, or trivets featuring these designs?

Finally, don't rule out the kitchen as a place to showcase some of your magical collections. If you've got shelf space, think about displaying decorative jars full of your favorite crystals. Do you make your own kitchen crafts, such as carved spoons or crocheted hot pads? Add them to your décor! Add those little fairy statues you've been trying to find a spot for. Select a wall for magical artwork or other items—I've hung my collection of copper jelly molds on the wall above my kitchen table, which seems like the perfect spot since copper is associated with both love and communication. I also have my mortar and pestle sets—I think there are seven or eight of them?—neatly lined up along a stretch of counter near where I hang my herbs. Your kitchen space can be functional, beautiful, and magical all at the same time.

Setting Up Your Kitchen Altar

A kitchen altar can serve as a focal point for your magical work. If you've got the room for it, setting up a small kitchen altar is a great way to infuse the cooking and culinary activities of your home with magical intention and spiritual energy. Select a corner of your kitchen, a countertop, or a small table where you can set up your altar. Be sure to choose a place where you feel comfortable and, ideally, won't be disturbed during your magical workings. If you're short on counter space, you might want to construct a portable altar on a tea tray or box that you can move around when you need the additional room to work.

Gather items that hold personal and magical significance to you, such as crystals, herbs, spices, small figurines or charms, symbols of the elements (such as a small bowl of salt or a dish of water), and any kitchen tools or decorations that resonate with your practice. I'm a big fan of wooden spoons myself—while I don't like using them in meal prep, I love the way they look when they're woodburned, so I have a few that are inscribed with magical symbols hanging over my kitchen altar corner.

Do you have kitchen-related family heirlooms? I've got a well-loved set of my grandmother's Blue Willow dishes that she brought with her when she emigrated from England to North America in the 1950s. It's so beautiful, and it reminds me of her, so I often use one of the dishes on my altar as a way to honor her as I celebrate my magic in the kitchen.

Many books and articles on kitchen witchcraft suggest the addition of candles to the altar, and you can absolutely include those if you wish. BUT. Here's the thing with candles—you'll want to make sure you only use unscented ones on your kitchen altar, especially if they're burning while you're cooking. Otherwise, your food will take on the fragrance of the candle burning in the space. Now, if you're baking a pie and you have a pumpkin-scented candle going, okay. That's one thing—but that pumpkin fragrance isn't going to be quite as nice when it's infused into your chicken dinner. All I'm saying is, use some common sense here when it comes to candles in the kitchen, because I once had a lilac candle burning in my kitchen and my lunch ended up tasting like a can of air freshener.

Your kitchen altar can also be a perfect place to make offerings to your household spirits, ancestor deities, or other guardians of the space. I work regularly with my ancestors and like to leave them wine, whisky, and baked goods, so the kitchen altar is ideal for that task. In addition to food and drink, you can place a small bowl of salt, representing earth, or a bowl of water on your altar. For seasonal celebrations, think about adding fresh fruits, grains, or other items that hold significance to you. You can also decorate your altar based upon upcoming festivals, sabbats, or moon phases. For example, during autumn, you might include fall foods, like apples and gourds, or autumn-themed dish towels, teacups, and trivets. Your spring altar might include eggs, milk, or fresh seasonal produce along with a set of pretty spring salt and pepper shakers. Be creative as you think about what logically fits with the natural cycles and energies around you.

It's a good idea to establish a daily ritual for your kitchen altar. It could be as simple as taking a moment to focus your intentions before you begin cooking or baking, or even expressing gratitude for the ingredients and the nourishment they provide. Your kitchen altar is a personal and sacred space, so go ahead and customize it based on the needs of your own practice and the resources you have available to you.

Simple Blessings for Your Magical Kitchen

Like any magical space, your kitchen deserves blessings of its own. You can do a simple blessing with a short incantation each time you prepare a meal, or you can perform a more detailed one as part of your regular magical cleansing routine.

Start by giving your kitchen a good thorough physical cleaning—wipe down countertops, sweep the floor, put away the dishes, and so on. Invite your household guardians or the deities of your tradition to join you, asking for their presence and blessings, and present them with an offering, ideally of something you've cooked or prepared in the kitchen itself. Anoint key areas, such as the stove and sink, with consecrated water to bless and protect them. Offer a brief prayer for health, abundance, and happiness in your kitchen. Conclude by thanking your guardians or deities and ground the blessing by enjoying a small meal or snack in the newly sanctified space.

Or, if you're in a rush and just trying to get a meal on the table, try one of these simple incantations:

+ *In this kitchen, let laughter mix with spice; our meals full of love and everything nice. Nourish hearts and bodies as we eat; blessings on this kitchen, content and sweet.*

+ *In this kitchen, let the spirit of hospitality flourish, where every dish prepared and every cup poured brings joy and warmth to those who gather here. May it be a sanctuary of laughter, conversation, and shared meals, enriching the lives of all who enter.*

✦ *Bless this hearth with joy and light, where warmth glows every day and night.*

✦ *May the elements grace this kitchen—earth, ground it in abundance; air, fill it with creativity; fire, ignite passion for cooking; and water, flow through every meal prepared here.*

Food Preparation as a Magical Action

Whether you identify specifically as a kitchen witch or you're simply a witch whose home has a kitchen, you can turn simple food prep into a sacred, spiritual practice in which you fill your dishes with magical energy. Consciously set intentions for your meals, focusing on their purpose, which can be anything from health to love to abundance for your family. Be mindful as you select ingredients, considering their magical properties. Herbs like basil for prosperity, cinnamon for warmth, or garlic for healing can align with your intentions, infusing every bite with specific energies.

Embrace the elements in your cooking—fire, water, earth, and air. Acknowledge these elements' significance and incorporate them into your culinary practice. Create symbolism with ingredients, arranging them in ways that represent your magical goals. Shape dough or garnishes to symbolize luck, love, or abundance. While you're preparing food, pay attention to textures, aromas, and sensations—how do they make you feel?

Before serving, express gratitude for the meal, its ingredients, and the energies put into its preparation. Speak a blessing or affirmation over the food, infusing it with positive energy. Simple kitchen witchcraft practices allow you to manifest magic in not just your own life but the lives of the people who join you at your table.

Stirring and Blending

Stirring and blending during food prep can become a potent magical act. When you stir ingredients, infuse your motions with intention. Stir clockwise to invite positive energies, such as love, abundance, or healing. Stir counterclockwise to banish negativity or unwanted energies. Visualize your desired outcome manifesting as you stir.

You can recite chants, affirmations, or incantations while stirring. Choose words that resonate with your magical goals; let the rhythm of your words sync with the movement of your stirring, amplifying the magical energy in the dish. When blending ingredients, visualize the ingredients merging harmoniously to create a unified energy. See the flavors and energies mingling and amplifying each other, creating a harmonious and potent outcome.

Charge your stirring utensils, like spoons or spatulas, with specific purposes. Hold the utensil in your hands, focus on your intention, and visualize the energy transferring into the tool—and then eventually to the food itself as you stir it.

Sigil Magic in the Kitchen

We've already talked a little bit about sigil magic, and it's one of my favorite methods of spell delivery. I like creating symbols that represent my magical goals, and once you've designed one, you can repeat it anywhere you wish. Sigil magic is deeply personal, and the power lies in your intent and belief. Once you've created your sigil, you can use it in a number of different ways around the kitchen.

+ Draw your sigils on labels of herbs, spices, or jars containing ingredients used frequently in your kitchen. This permeates the ingredients with your desired energy each time they are used in cooking.

+ Inscribe sigils on wooden spoons, cutting boards, or any other kitchen tools. They can be symbols of protection, harmony, or amplification of positive energies for your family.

+ Add them to the outside or bottom of containers used to store water or cooking liquids. Charge the containers with the sigil's intention, infusing the liquid with that specific energy for use in cooking or drinks.

+ Use oil or butter to inscribe the sigils on parchment paper and place them on your baking sheets or on the stovetop underneath the ingredients you're adding. If you're making food with condiments, such as a sandwich or burger, use ketchup, mustard, or mayonnaise to draw your sigil directly on the food.

+ Create a specific sigil representing your kitchen's overall intention—such as promoting nourishment, love, or positivity within the space. Charge it during a ritual and hang it in the kitchen as a constant source of focused magical energy.

+ Design a sigil to represent the desired outcome of a dish, such as comfort, healing, or joy. Draw it on recipe cards or near recipes in cookbooks to empower the cooking process.

+ Use sigils for cleansing or protecting the kitchen space from negativity and chalk them on doors, windowsills, or near the entrance to the kitchen to create a shield against unwanted energies.

Magical Kitchen Tools

Ever noticed how the kitchen is like a secret laboratory for everyday magic? I'm all about using regular kitchen tools for a bit of enchantment. Think about it—your spoons, knives, and pots aren't just for cooking; they're magical tools in disguise. With a pinch of intention and a sprinkle of creativity, we can infuse our meals with good vibes or set intentions while we chop veggies, fill a mug, or beat an egg. Let's look at ways we can use mundane kitchen tools to add some magic into our daily cooking adventures.

Mugs, Cups, Bowls, and Utensils

Utensils are a huge part of a kitchen witch's arsenal, each possessing its own unique magic that's just waiting to be unlocked. Picture this: as you stir a bubbling pot of soup or stew, you infuse your thoughts and desires into the motion, turning the act of stirring into a spell in itself. Spoons are a great way to dole out intentions. Use them to portion ingredients with purpose, assigning specific meanings or energies to each scoop. A pinch of love, a dash of abundance— each spoonful becomes a ritual of its own in building the flavors of your spell or meal. Knives are fantastic for cutting ties or severing unwanted energies. When chopping ingredients, visualize releasing negativity or cutting away obstacles, transforming the mundane act of slicing veggies into a powerful act of magical release. Forks are perfect for blending together your intentions and mixing energies.

Mugs and bowls hold the potential for crafting potions and elixirs. Whether it's a morning brew or an evening herbal concoction, infuse your favorite mug with intentions of comfort or vitality. And those trusty mixing bowls? They're perfect for blending together ingredients while blending energies, uniting different elements to create a harmonious whole.

Your whisk, with its rhythmic motions, can be used to whip up energy and intentions, infusing a batter or mixture with your desired outcomes. With every twirl, see yourself stirring positivity and manifestation into your creations. Each of these utensils serves as a conduit for the energy and intention you infuse into your culinary concoctions.

Mortar and Pestle

The mortar and pestle set is a fundamental kitchen tool that has been used for centuries around the world. It consists of a small bowl, the mortar, and the pestle, which is a club-shaped grinding tool. I have a bit of an obsession with these and have about a dozen of them scattered around my house—no two are alike, and I have them in stone, wood, and ceramic, among other materials. You can even find them made of metal. This ancient culinary instrument is not only practical for grinding and pulverizing herbs, spices, and other ingredients but also can hold significant symbolism in kitchen witchcraft.

For some practitioners, the mortar and pestle represent the union of the elements of earth and fire. Think about it for a moment: the solid, grounded nature of the mortar embodies earth, while the repetitive grinding motion with the pestle generates heat and energy, symbolizing fire. This comes in handy if you want to work closely with natural elements to infuse your culinary creations with magical intent and energy.

- **Herb and spice preparation:** The primary purpose of the mortar and pestle in kitchen witchcraft is grinding herbs and spices; if you do this with intention, it can enhance their magical properties. You can also use the mortar and pestle to combine herbs, resins, and spices for specific spells, rituals, tinctures, sachets, powders, or salves and ointments.

- **Charging and empowering ingredients:** As you use a mortar and pestle to grind your herbs, you can also charge your ingredients with specific magical goals, infusing the mixture with your energy to manifest your desires.

- **Preparing offerings:** Offerings can be prepared and ground using a mortar and pestle as a way to honor deities, spirits, or ancestors before placing them on your altar or offering plate.

Pots and Kettles

We all know about cauldrons, but what if you don't have one handy? Never fear! Pots and kettles, which you probably already own, are incredibly versatile tools, carrying a wealth of symbolic and practical magic. They can be vessels for transformation, making them ideal for brewing potions, infusions, and concoctions that harness specific energies. You may want to consecrate a special kettle for brewing up your magical teas, utilizing different herbs, spices, and intentions to create blends that promote healing, relaxation, or energy alignment (be sure to read later in this chapter for some of my favorite herbal tea blends). Stirring these mixtures clockwise or counterclockwise can correspond to drawing in or banishing certain energies respectively, adding an extra layer of intention to the process. The very act of heating water in a kettle can represent the activation of energy, which makes it perfect for rituals focusing on manifestation or change. Additionally, the steam rising from the pot can carry your intentions out into the universe, similar to the use of sacred smoke or incense.

Beyond their magical symbolism, pots and kettles have practical uses when it comes to the craft. They can be a substitute cauldron during ceremonies, representing the element of water or fire depending on how you use them. You can inscribe symbols or sigils onto the bottom of your pots to infuse your cooking with particular energies or intentions, making meal preparation even more of a magical act. Also, consider the metal composition of pots and kettles when you incorporate them into spells—copper, for instance, is associated with amplification and communication, while iron is linked to protection. I've got my late grandmother's old cast iron Wagner skillets, and let me tell you, those things get used on the regular! Repurposing old pots or heirloom kettles can fill them with personal and ancestral energies, enhancing their magical potency within your practice.

Mixer Blessing

Many years ago, my mom bought me a stand mixer that I absolutely love. It's not something I'd have ever been able to afford myself back then, so she ordered it for me as a birthday gift, and it's perfect. My stand mixer is a lovely purple, with a massive bowl, and I actually named it when I first set it up— her name is Hildegard, after Hildegard of Bingen. She sits on my counter, happily waiting for me to throw dough into her bowl for making cookies, biscuits, cakes, and darn near anything else I can think of. Because I wanted to get many years of use out of her (my mom's mixer is nearly as old as I am), I did a short blessing ritual before I took her on her inaugural run.

Note that while this blessing is written with a mixer in mind, you can do it with any appliance you've got in your kitchen or adapt it for items in other rooms in your home. You'll need:

+ Your stand mixer
+ A clean cloth
+ Herb-infused water
+ Decorative ribbon or string
+ Music or your favorite kitchen dance tune
+ *Optional*: Crystals or charms

Begin by cleaning your stand mixer thoroughly—give it a good scrubbing! Wipe it down with a clean cloth, cleansing any lingering energies as well as any stray bits of dough or dust that might be stuck on there. Play your favorite upbeat tune in the background to set a fun and lively atmosphere. Spritz a bit of herb-infused water on your cloth for a final wipe down. As you do, visualize happy, positive vibrations filling your stand mixer.

Place your mixer in the center of your kitchen, and let yourself dance—sing along with your tunes if you want to! Allow your movements to be playful and lighthearted; let them permeate the space and the mixer itself with your joyous energy. Imagine the mixer coming to life and joining in the dance with you.

It's time to offer words of blessing and empowerment to your stand mixer—be as poetic or as whimsical as you like. Personally, I tend to lean a bit toward the quirky, so the blessing I offered to my mixer was a simple, rather silly one:

Hildegard, Hildegard, purple and bold, mix up delicious treasures untold! Cookies and bread, biscuits and cakes, all turn out perfect with no mistakes. Sugar, milk, eggs, and flour, mixing is your superpower!

Adorn your mixer with a decorative ribbon or string as a reminder of its magical status—if you like, attach small crystals or charms, each representing a unique kitchen magic quality, like precision, creativity, or efficiency. Just be sure to remove these before using it to mix up food!

Dance or celebrate one last time, acknowledging the joyful bond you've established. Seal the blessings by immediately using your stand mixer to whip up your favorite recipe, infusing your creation with the magical energy you've bestowed upon it.

Magical Food Correspondences

When it comes to kitchen witchery in the home, we often think about the obvious stuff—herbs and spices. But there are so many other magical ways you can use different types of food, from cheese to fruit to the treats in your liquor cabinet.

Eggs

Eggs are symbols of fertility, new beginnings, and transformation. Use them in spells related to personal growth, creativity, and protection. Include eggs on your altar during the Spring Equinox as you celebrate the warming of the earth. You can also grind up eggshells into powder and use it to form a protective barrier around your home or in a ritual to release negative energies. In some folk magic traditions, this is done via an egg cleansing—rub a raw egg gently over the body or around the space, visualizing it absorbing and neutralizing any negative energy. Afterward, crack the egg into a bowl of water and observe the shape it takes, which can provide insights into the type of energy that was removed. Create protective talismans by decorating eggs with symbols, sigils, or meaningful patterns using natural dyes or markers.

Milk and Cheese

Got milk? It represents nurturing, motherhood, and sustenance. It can be used in spells to promote emotional healing, enhance psychic abilities, and attract positive energies. Drip a few drops of milk into a bowl of water for a bit of divination, and observe the shapes and patterns it forms. Use your intuitive abilities to interpret these shapes and gain insights into your questions or concerns. This method is particularly useful for gaining clarity on emotional or subconscious matters. Pouring a few drops of milk into a bowl or chalice as an offering can be a simple yet powerful ritual—and if you don't do dairy, don't worry. I tend to use plant-based milk myself, and I've found the results don't vary much from when I use animal-based milk.

Do you love cheese? It's one of those items I have in my refrigerator just about constantly! Cheese embodies transformation and preservation and also can symbolize indulgence—after all, we feel pretty well stuffed after devouring a cheese plate. Use cheese for workings related to personal growth, the wisdom that comes with age, and protection. You can even present it as an offering to deities associated with agriculture and abundance. Share your favorite cheese with loved ones during rituals focused on strengthening relationships. Prepare a platter with a variety of cheeses—you can even cut them into magical shapes like circles, which represent coins and abundance, or hearts, which symbolize love. As you indulge in this delicious offering, visualize the bonds of friendship and love growing stronger.

Bread and Grains

Bread can be a symbol of sustenance, life, and community. It's associated with the Lammas sabbat and can be included in rituals or spells to promote unity and harmony within families or groups. Sharing bread can strengthen bonds and invite abundance. If you're able to bake bread yourself, that's wonderful! Use a few pieces as an offering to your deities or household guardians—and if you don't bake, store-bought is fine as well. Have you ever thought about using bread crumbs for divination? After you've finished a meal, focus on a question or intention as you break apart a piece of bread. Observe the pattern and arrangement of the crumbs left on your plate, and see if they can offer insights or answers to your questions through their unique shapes and symbols.

For an easy home blessing, bake a loaf of your favorite bread. As you mix and blend the dough, envision it filling with harmony and happiness. Bake it in a clean oven, and as you begin to smell the fresh aroma, visualize that rich bready fragrance carrying joy and blessings throughout your home. Once it's done baking and has cooled enough to eat, share a piece with every member of your household.

Corn embodies prosperity and nourishment, making it a potent ingredient for spells and rituals focused on abundance and sustenance. Cornmeal, corn flour, or whole corn kernels can be employed in recipes and rituals to attract prosperity and abundance into the home. Incorporating corn into dishes during rituals or cooking sessions infuses meals with energies of fertility and growth.

Add it into bread or stews to draw prosperity from the bountiful blessings of the earth. Even corn husks, with their pliability, become handy tools in kitchen witchery—use them to wrap and bind ingredients, seal intentions, or even create small pouches (like a tamale) for magical blends.

A staple food in many cultures, rice represents nourishment, fertility, and protection, so it's great for spells to promote health, security, and prosperity. Scatter rice around your home or use it in sachets for protective purposes to absorb negative energies. Place a bowl of uncooked rice on your altar, visualizing it multiplying and bringing prosperity into your life. Mix rice with herbs and spices associated with wealth, such as cinnamon and basil, and use the mixture as a charm or sprinkle it around your home for prosperity. Rice can be included in spells and rituals aimed at promoting healthy, happy relationships. Cook a pot of rice, infuse it with an intention of love and harmony, and share it with your favorite people. You can also create rice charms or sachets with love-drawing herbs like rose petals and carry them to attract romantic love or strengthen existing relationships.

Honey

If you need a bit of cooperation, sweetness, or collective effort, try using honey or even a full honeycomb if it's available to you. It's perfect for spells to foster teamwork, enhance social connections, and attract positive collaborations. It is also associated with the energy of the sun, so it's perfect for a midsummer altar. Use it in money spells to attract abundance and wealth; anoint green candles with honey and roll them in herbs associated with prosperity, such as basil or bay leaves. Light the candles, focusing on your financial goals and envisioning yourself surrounded by prosperity. Honey is believed to enhance psychic abilities and intuition as well as our connection to the Divine. Mix honey into your favorite tea blend to aid in divination, dreamwork, or meditation.

Fruits

Fruits such as apples, oranges, and grapes are associated with abundance, vitality, and fertility. Different fruits can be used in spells for specific intentions—apples for healing and love, lemons for cleansing, oranges for happiness—and as offerings to your deities. Infuse your cooking with magical intent by incorporating fruits into your recipes, or create jams, sauces, or desserts using fruits that correspond with your magical goals. Try baking a blueberry pie for peace and tranquility or whipping up a citrus-infused drink for energy and vitality. As you prepare and consume your treat, focus on the intention you wish to manifest, filling the food with your magical energy. For a bit of love divination, peel an apple in a single long piece, and let the peel fall to the floor. If it forms a letter or shape, that could be an indication as to the identity of a future lover.

Wine, Mead, and Other Alcohol

Alcohol, such as wine, has a long history of being used in religious and spiritual ceremonies. It represents celebration, communion, and the Divine. Use it in rituals to honor deities, mark special occasions, and enhance ritual consciousness. Red wine is often associated with grounding and passion, while white wine is linked to purification and clarity. I like to keep a dram of whiskey or a cup of mead as an offering on my ancestor altar—most of my family is Scottish and Scandinavian—but if there's a particular beverage that speaks to you, give it a try. You can use alcohol as a cleanser or purifier of your magical tools or infuse a bottle of vodka or rum with magical herbs to create a potent elixir for spellwork.

If you're not a drinker, don't worry—nonalcoholic beverages are a perfectly acceptable substitute in many cases. Try sparkling grape juice or apple cider instead for offerings and consecrated water for cleansing magical tools.

Fish

Fish are creatures of water and can represent wisdom, intuition, adaptability, and hidden knowledge. Prepare a fish dish to use in spells related to emotional healing, divination, and exploring the depths of the subconscious mind. In some communities, fish represent abundance—cook one up if you want to attract wealth and prosperity—as well as transformation. Meditate as you eat a fish dinner, imagining yourself as adaptable and flexible as a fish swimming along through the currents of life. Let it help you navigate change and challenges more smoothly.

Magical Herbs in the Kitchen

Your magical herb collection can come in handy when it comes to mealtime—just be mindful that any herbs you cook with are indeed safe for human consumption! Add some of these to your recipes to fill your food with delicious witchy goodness.

- **Protection:** Rosemary, basil, sage, thyme, garlic
- **Love and romance:** Lavender, chamomile, cinnamon, cardamom
- **Prosperity and abundance:** Basil, cinnamon, bay leaf, mint, ginger
- **Healing:** Echinacea, peppermint, calendula, lemon balm, turmeric
- **Purification and cleansing:** Sage, hyssop, lemon verbena

- **Creativity:** Peppermint, thyme, basil
- **Harmony and peace:** Lavender, chamomile, rosemary
- **Energy and vitality:** Ginseng, ginger, cayenne pepper, cinnamon

Protective Black Salt

To add an extra level of protection to your home, you can mix up a batch of black salt, well known for its ability to keep negativity and danger out of your space. You'll need:

- A clean bowl
- Sea salt, either coarse or fine
- Charcoal or ashes from burned herbs
- Dried protective herbs—rosemary, sage, basil, or bay leaves, for example
- Mortar and pestle or a grinder
- A jar with a lid

Begin in a dedicated space within your kitchen, ensuring it's cleansed and free from distractions. Grind the protective herbs into a fine powder using your mortar and pestle. Combine the powdered herbs with the sea salt in a bowl—a good ratio is approximately 1 part herbs to 3 or 4 parts salt. Add the charcoal or ashes to the mixture—I like to end up with about half salt and half charcoal, but you can use whatever proportions feel right for you.

Blend the ingredients thoroughly, either using your hands or a spoon. While mixing, envision a shield forming around the salt, filling it with strong protective energy. Set the bowl in a place where it can soak up natural energy, whether from moonlight or sunlight, for a few hours—just make sure it's in a place where it won't get damp. You might even want to place a protective crystal in the salt to amplify the energy of the salt.

Once the salt mixture has charged, store it in a jar with a lid for safekeeping. Use it in rituals, sprinkle it around your home, or incorporate it into spells and other workings, following your intuition on when and how to utilize its protective properties. Please note that this should not be ingested.

Magical Herbal Tea Blend Recipes

Not all kitchen magic has to include baking and cooking—sometimes, it's just about establishing a mindful connection to the goals you wish to manifest, and one of my favorite ways to do this is through herbal teas.

In addition to the magical aspect of tea, it's delicious! You can buy or blend teas in a wide range of flavors and aromas, each with unique properties and benefits. They're typically made by steeping dried herbs or flowers in hot water, which allows the herbs to release their flavors, nutrients, and medicinal properties into the water. The steeping time varies depending on the herbs used and desired strength, generally ranging from 5 to 15 minutes. Brewing your own teas is pretty easy, but it can be helpful to have a few basic items in your kitchen before you get started.

- To contain the herbs while brewing, you'll need a tea infuser or a strainer. You can also use paper or cloth tea sacks. This allows the herbs to steep in hot water while keeping them separate from the liquid when you pour.

- Use a kettle or a pot to heat water. If you have hard water, use filtered or spring water for the best flavor. The water temperature may vary based on the herbs you're using; some herbs prefer boiling water, while others require lower temperatures. I have an electric kettle that allows me to check the water temperature as it heats up, so I can pull it off the heating coil before the water gets too hot. However, you can use a regular kettle or pot. Simply heat the water to boiling, and then allow it to cool for a few moments before you pour it over your herbs.

- Use a mug or teapot to brew your herbal tea. Make sure it's heat resistant and suitable for holding hot liquids. If you're making larger batches, a teapot with a built-in infuser is super convenient.

- Having a timer handy ensures you steep the herbs for the appropriate duration. Steeping times vary depending on the herbs used and desired strength.

- Honey, lemon, or other sweeteners and flavor enhancers can be added to your herbal tea blends based on personal taste preferences.

And of course, in addition to all of these items, you'll need some tea blends! You can certainly buy commercially prepared teas, especially if you have a local witchy shop that sells them. If you'd like to blend your own, try a few of these.

Prosperity Blend

Visualize success and financial stability while sipping this tea.

- 2 parts cinnamon for prosperity
- 1 part clove to attract abundance
- 1 part ginger to bring success
- 1 part chamomile for financial gain

Love and Harmony Blend

Brew this blend to promote love, harmony, and passion in relationships. Drink it during moments of connection or shared relaxation.

- 2 parts rose petals for love
- 1 part lavender to inspire harmony
- 1 part hibiscus to ignite passion
- 1 part cinnamon for warmth

Protection and Clarity Blend

Drink this when you need to cleanse your space or your spirit of negative energies.

- 2 parts rosemary for protection
- 1 part sage for cleansing
- 1 part lemon balm for clarity
- 1 part thyme to ward off negativity

Healing and Vitality Blend

Sip this brew when you're feeling under the weather or just feel like you need a bit of rejuvenation.

- 2 parts peppermint for healing
- 1 part echinacea to inspire immune support
- 1 part elderflower for health
- 1 part ginger for vitality

Tranquility and Serenity Blend

Brew this blend for relaxation and inner peace. Enjoy it before meditation or during quiet moments to promote tranquility and calm.

- 2 parts chamomile for peace
- 1 part lemon verbena to inspire calmness
- 1 part valerian to promote relaxation
- 1 part passionflower for stress relief

These blends can be adjusted in ratios or by including additional ingredients to suit your personal preferences and tastes. When brewing teas, focus on your magical intentions and visualize them manifesting as you sip the tea.

Be sure to store your dried tea blends in airtight containers away from light and moisture to maintain their freshness and potency. Keep track of your recipes by labeling them and taking notes on the combinations you enjoy. This helps in replicating successful blends and adjusting the flavors as needed in your future creations. Experiment with different combinations, proportions, and brewing times to discover your favorite flavors and the potential magical benefits of each blend.

Before consuming any herbal tea blend, do your homework to make sure the herbs are not contraindicated by any medical condition you may have.

MAGICAL BERRY INK

If you've got access to berries—either on your own property, from a local farmer's market, or purchased from the grocery store—you can make magical ink to use in your spellwork. I like to use pokeberries myself—they grow wild in my yard and also happen to be super toxic—but you can make this ink with any other berry that secretes a dark-colored juice. Before you decide which type to use, consider some of their magical properties.

Pokeberries are associated with the banishing of unwanted influences, while blueberries are known to help keep trouble at a distance, and juniper berries are tied to psychic protection. If you want to do a working for longevity and hardiness, consider using mulberries. Try blackberries for spellwork related to healing and charms against illness or black currant berries if you need to bolster your courage. For magic related to overcoming stagnation and obstacles or just overall good fortune, try to get your hands on some bilberries.

If you're working with a berry that has toxic properties, such as the pokeberry, be sure to take proper precautions when you're handling them—gloves are your friend here. You'll need:

- 1 cup fresh berries
- ½ to 1 teaspoon white vinegar
- ½ to 1 teaspoon salt
- A mortar and pestle set
- A fine mesh strainer or cheesecloth
- A glass or plastic container with a lid for storage

Carefully remove the stems and leaves from your berries and discard them; you'll only use the ripe berries themselves. Place the berries in the mortar and crush them with the pestle to release the juice. Strain the mixture through a fine mesh strainer or cheesecloth into a glass or plastic container to separate the liquid (your ink) from any solids or seeds. Discard anything that remains in the strainer. Add the salt and vinegar to the crushed berries. This will help thin the juice out enough that you can use it for writing.

To use your ink in magical workings, use a calligraphy pen or a quill feather to inscribe your intention onto a piece of parchment or fancy paper, and then proceed with the rest of your spell.

KITCHEN DRAWER DIVINATION

Most of us have a weird space in our kitchen that we refer to as the junk drawer. It's full of all kinds of stuff that doesn't seem to have a home anywhere else. Mine is stuffed with pens, paperclips, batteries, rubber bands, wine bottle corks, a few keys (I have no idea what they unlock, but I'm scared to throw them away just in case I need them in the future), loose screws and thumbtacks, a couple of magnets ... the list goes on forever. The junk drawer is a magical, mystical place where things go in and rarely come out ... but if I ever need a paperclip, battery, or cork, I know exactly where in my home they live.

Because the contents of my junk drawer are so varied, I realized a while back that it might actually make a good method of divination. This was inspired—sort of—after I read about the use of divination bags during a class on pantheism and shamanism in ancient cultures around the world. Although it's commonly associated with African nations, the use of a collection of knickknacks for divination has been discovered in the Americas, Greece, Romania, and parts of Western Europe, among other places. Although these areas and their cultures differ widely, there are some common threads found in divinatory practices—one would keep a bag of bones, stones, shells, rocks, coins, and trinkets, each assigned with a different meaning. When divination and guidance were needed, the practitioner simply pulled items out of the bag to see what symbolism was revealed.

You can do the same thing with your kitchen junk drawer—and again, this goes back to the idea that at some point, someone came up with correspondences, or attributes, for everything. The difference here is that you, yourself, get to assign meanings to the objects in your junk drawer—and that's going to be unique to *you*. While a small pad of sticky notes in my junk drawer might hold a specific meaning for me, the small pad of sticky notes in *your* drawer may mean something completely different to you. So, the first thing you'll need to do is, of course, inventory your junk drawer. What, exactly, is hiding in there? Take some time to write down each item in a list, and then assign it meaningful properties that make sense to you personally.

Just to get you started, I'll share some of the objects in my junk drawer and the qualities I've felt were most appropriate for them—feel free to use this as a template as you begin, or you can give them completely different meanings if it seems more logical to you.

- **Spare keys:** Access and opportunity, security, safety, problem solving
- **Rubber bands:** Flexibility or constraint, recovery, bouncing back, temporary solutions
- **Paper clips:** Unity and connection, order and organization, assistance with mental blockages (if you're old enough to remember Clippy, you'll understand this one)
- **Pens and pencils:** Communication and creativity, recordkeeping, expression, knowledge
- **Scissors:** Separation, boundaries, precision, craftsmanship
- **Pad of sticky notes:** Reminders, organization, attention to detail, temporary situations, collaboration
- **Batteries:** Energy, recharging, rejuvenation, balance between positive and negative, innovation
- **Roll of electrical tape:** Repair and restoration, quick but temporary fixes, concealment, resourcefulness, binding and unity
- **Lip balm:** Protection, nurturing, self-care, softness, renewal, sensuality

- **Pushpins:** Attachment and commitment, creativity, visibility, organization
- **Safety pins:** Solidarity, resistance, improvisation, inclusivity, remembrance
- **Buttons:** Closure, completion, tradition and heritage, control, simplicity
- **Random screws and nails:** Permanence, strength and stability, the home, determination, endurance
- **Charger cables:** Connection, energy and vitality, efficiency, adaptability, support
- **Take-out menus:** Choice, convenience, indulgence, social connections, celebration
- **Magnets:** Attraction, harmony, polarity, influence, navigation
- **Postage stamps:** Communication, travel and visiting, civic pride, tradition, exploration
- **A wrench:** Versatility, adjustment, problem-solving, empowerment, skill development, crisis management
- **First aid kit:** Healing, preparedness for emergency, resilience, prevention, responsibility
- **Box of matches:** Light in the darkness, transformation, new beginnings, resourcefulness, passion, courage

Once you've made your list of divinatory meanings, when you find yourself in need of guidance, close your eyes and place your hand in the junk drawer. Pull out the first thing you touch—or even two or three things!—and see what sort of insight they offer you toward answering your questions.

Chapter 10
OTHER MAGICAL ROOMS IN YOUR HOME

We've made our way through several rooms in the home already—and many of them are places people traditionally think of being prime sanctuaries for magic, such as the kitchen and the bedroom. But if you're fortunate enough to have other spaces in your home, don't stop now! You can make magic all over the place if you think about the items in each room creatively. Your garage, attic, basement, and even your home office have plenty of magical potential.

The Garage

No one really thinks about the garage as a magical space. For many people, it's where they park the car, store the lawn mower, and have a collection of stuff they only need a couple of times a year. However, that doesn't mean you can't make it magical! Not only that, there is magic you can do *in* the garage. Start by decluttering and cleaning the garage thoroughly. This physical cleaning should be followed by a spiritual cleansing using smoke cleansing or incense to purify the space from any negative or stagnant energies. Add protective charms or sigils around the space to keep the contents safe from theft or damage. If your garage connects directly to your house, make sure you add some magical protection on the door between them, such as a sigil, protective crystals, or other items designed to repel danger. Finally, you may want to designate a specific shelf or cabinet in your garage as a place where you can work magic with … well … garage stuff!

Repurposing old or unused items found in the garage can serve as a form of magical recycling. Transforming these items into talismans, amulets, or other magical objects imbues them with new purpose and energy. Tools you keep in the garage, such as hammers, nails, or wrenches, can symbolize strength, unity, or the power to build and transform. Use them in rituals for protection, grounding, or manifestation of intentions. Even repurposed containers, like empty cans, jars, or bottles, can become vessels for storing magical ingredients, crafting charms, or creating altars. Give them a thorough cleaning, and let them hold herbs, crystals, or other magical items. Metal scraps, wires, or old keys found in a garage can represent security, protection, or unlocking new paths. Incorporate these into spells or rituals focusing on transformation, protection, or unlocking hidden potential.

Duct Tape Magic

There's an old joke about how duct tape is a lot like the Force in *Star Wars*—it has a light side and a dark one, and it binds things together. These properties can help with all kinds of magical workings—and better still, it's available in a multitude of colors and patterns, which can be valuable in spells that include color magic. These are a few of my favorite ways to use that roll of duct tape that's sitting on a shelf in my garage.

+ Think of duct tape's strength and resilience, and use it in binding spells. Write down the name of the person you wish to prevent from harming themselves or others on a piece of paper, wrap it with duct tape, and visualize the person—or situation—being restrained or protected.

+ Create symbolic representations or sigils on duct tape. Cut out specific shapes or symbols representing your magical intentions or goals, charge them with energy, and affix them to objects or surfaces to imbue them with your intent.

+ Use duct tape to seal containers or envelopes holding herbs, written intentions, or magical items. As you seal them, visualize the energy being contained and preserved until the intended outcome is achieved.

+ Craft small protective charms or talismans using duct tape. Mold it into shapes or symbols representing protection or warding, charging them with your intent, and carry or place them in areas needing protection.

+ In group rituals or ceremonies, duct tape can symbolize unity. Participants can tear strips of duct tape and join them together, representing the unity of intentions or energies.

+ In a symbolic sense, using duct tape to mend or fix broken objects can represent restoration and healing. Perform rituals while repairing items, infusing them with energies of renewal and wholeness.

• Use duct tape to mark sacred spaces or create temporary symbols on floors or walls for rituals. Its adhesive nature makes it suitable for creating easily removable and nonpermanent markings.

Remember that while duct tape might seem mundane, its versatile nature and symbolism can be creatively utilized in spells and rituals to manifest your desired outcomes.

Toolbox Treasures: Hammers, Saws, and More

The tools that live in your garage (or storage shed, or basement) can be incorporated into magical workings as well. The great thing about tools is that they can be used to both destroy and create—they can damage and repair, which means they have a lot of potential when it comes to spellwork.

Use a saw to represent the act of cutting or transformation. It can be included in rituals or spells aimed at cutting ties, releasing negative energies, or initiating change. Visualize using the saw to sever connections to things no longer serving your purpose. When it comes to hammers, think about strength and power. Use it to "hammer out" intentions, goals, or manifestations into reality or build a foundation for your desires.

A wrench can be a symbol of adjustment and adaptability— the ability to adjust situations, energies, or circumstances. Use it in workings focused on adapting to change or fixing problematic situations. Need precision and control? Grab a screwdriver, and tighten up or secure your intentions, beliefs, or desires.

Nails and screws provide stability, anchoring, and binding. Use them to secure intentions, create talismans, or bind energies. Visualize driving nails as anchoring and securing your desires or goals so you can manifest long-lasting results.

Laundry Room

Not too many people love doing laundry, but it's a chore that's one of life's necessary evils. If you enjoy the process and find it meditative and relaxing, good on you. Personally, I only do it because I happen to appreciate having clean socks, underwear, and sheets. Whether you have a washer and dryer of your own, are using a shared set in your building, or make a weekly trip to the local laundromat, there are plenty of magical ways you can impact your laundry space. Look at this part of your world as an environment where all four of the elements come together—earth on your clothes, air and fire (heat) in your dryer, and water in the washing machine! It's the perfect place to eliminate things that are soiling your life or enchant your clothes and linens with magical intentions.

Remember that mundane actions always help the magical—keep your appliances in good working order by cleaning them regularly. Keep your washer level so the drum doesn't vibrate excessively, clean out the dispenser drawer, and maintain the water-fill hoses—if they look cracked or brittle, replace them before they flood your laundry room. Be sure to empty your dryer's lint trap after each use, and periodically clean out the duct. Finally, give them each a good wipe down when they start to look dusty or dirty. Try some of these magical tips to enchant the washer, dryer, and everything that goes in or comes out of them.

+ Charm the washing machine and dryer. In addition to using the appropriate settings and detergents (and fabric softeners if that's how you roll), you can offer a little incantation to your appliances, encouraging them to do a good job. For extra-clean clothes, try *In the washer's watery whirl, I cast my clothing with a swirl. With the dryer's warmth and fire, may I be given fresh attire.* If you've got a problem with socks going missing—and really, who hasn't had that happen?—do a simple sock reunion chant: *Socks that vanish in the washer's drum, back to your partner you now shall come. Socks that vanish in the dryer's heat, return to your mate, your journey complete!*

+ Put a few drops of essential oil into your detergent before doing your wash and "cleanse" while you clean. Four to five drops of your favorite essential oil—lavender, patchouli, or eucalyptus, for instance—can be added to your detergent to give an invigorating magical scent to your clothing. Be sure not to add too much, though, as it can cause staining and discoloration of your clothing's fabrics. If you're not a fan of essential oils, try choosing detergent fragrances based on magical herbal correspondences. You can also include a sachet of magical herbs in the load when you start the dryer.

+ Laundry rooms make a great place to cast a banishing spell—after all, if you've got something dirty, all that yuck will be gone after it cycles through the washer and dryer. Create a fabric doll, or poppet, to represent the person you want to banish. As you make the poppet, visualize all the negative energy this person brings into your life and see that energy being stored within the doll. When you're ready, place the doll in the washing machine and add detergent. Run it through a normal wash cycle, and as it spins around in the water, envision the negativity of this individual being washed away. Move it to the dryer, and see that negative energy being dissipated with the tumbling motion and heat. Once the poppet is completely dry, dispose of it somewhere far from your home, and either bury it, burn it, or cast it into moving water to take it away—make sure you're using biodegradable materials.

+ Use detergent to create patterns. In many traditions of modern witchcraft, patterns and directions have magical significance. For instance, moving in a clockwise direction, or *deosil*, is associated with attraction magic. Its opposite, *widdershins*, or counterclockwise, represents magic that repels or sends things away. When you're adding detergent to your washer, consider sprinkling it in the direction that best corresponds to your magical purpose. Alternatively, you might want to sprinkle it in the shape of a spiral, a pentacle, or any other symbols that are meaningful to you.

+ Hang your laundry in the sun to dry. While this isn't possible for everyone—and it certainly requires a bit more work than just tossing your clothes in Ye Olde Magical Drying Box—it's a nice option if you've got an outdoor space, whether it's a full yard or a small balcony. Not only that, it's energy efficient and earth friendly! As you hang your clothes on the line, visualize them absorbing the powerful energy of the sun. See your personal power growing as your wet washing warms up; this can be used as an excellent confidence-booster spell. You might even want to add a chant as you clip each clothespin: *Beneath the sun's warm embrace, I hang my clothing with effortless grace. As it dries, in the breeze it will spin, giving me the power to take charge and win.*

MAGICAL CLOTHING SPRAY

You can make your own magical clothing spray to spritz on your freshly washed laundry. This is a great way to customize your intentions based on what you're wearing on any given day, and you can tailor it to the needs of your own spellwork. It only takes a few moments to make and uses just a couple of ingredients. You'll need:

+ A spray bottle
+ 2 ounces witch hazel
+ 2 ounces distilled water
+ Essential oils of your choice

Place the witch hazel and water in the bottle, and add the essential oils. Add just a few drops at a time until you like the way it smells—you don't want the scent to be overpowering (I typically end up using a total of 30 to 50 drops, distributed between two essential oils). Shake well to blend, and spritz your clothes lightly the night before you plan to wear them. Remember that a little spray goes a long way. For different magical combinations, try one of these:

+ Lemongrass and lavender to uplift the spirits
+ Rose and citrus to invite romance into your life
+ Frankincense, clove, and mugwort to boost your intuition

+ Patchouli, peppermint, and juniper for cleansing and purification
+ Clary sage and eucalyptus for healing energy

No-Sew Herbal Dryer Sachets

A dryer sachet is a great alternative to commercially produced scented dryer sheets. As with the clothing spray, you can customize these to suit your own magical purposes. For each one, you'll need:

+ A 4 × 6–inch muslin bag with a drawstring
+ 1 ounce dried herbs

Stuff the bag with the herbs, and pull the drawstring tight, tying it in a knot to secure the herbs in place. To use your sachets, simply toss them into the dryer with your wet laundry—a single sachet should last through about two dozen loads, but if you find the scent is beginning to fade, you can give it a boost with a few drops of essential oil. Try one of these combinations to bring magic into your everyday life:

+ Rosemary and lavender to open up the possibility of rekindling an old love
+ Chamomile, feverfew, and cedarwood for healing magic
+ Hyssop, ivy, and mint for protection
+ Orange peel, catnip, and lilac to draw good luck
+ Comfrey, pine, and jasmine to ensure prosperity

Your Home Office Space

For my full-time job in the corporate world, I've had the luxury of working from home since 2013. Long before COVID forced the world into lockdown, I've started each weekday with a morning commute that consists of trying not to trip over the dog on my way to the coffee pot. I love my job, but the result of it is that I do put in a *lot* of time in my home office. It's where I write books and blog posts, and when I went back to school to complete my bachelor's degree in 2014, most of my evenings and weekends were spent at my desk.

Because I'm in it so much—sometimes as much as twelve hours a day—it *has* to be a magical space. I would go absolutely bonkers if it wasn't. Even if your work doesn't require you to be in your home office space all day, every day, it's still a great idea to give the space a magical vibe. Your home office might not even be a separate room but a simple corner in another space in your home—regardless, if it's a place where you do work, pay bills, or indulge in creative endeavors, it should be magical.

Creating a Place of Focus

Look around your office—can you dedicate a corner or a shelf as an altar or sacred space in your work area? Place items like crystals, candles, incense, or symbols representing your practice or your deities. Choose crystals for focus, clarity, protection, or creativity. Plants like sage, lavender, or aloe vera can bring calming energies. This area serves as a focal point for work-based meditation, rituals, or setting intentions. I work at my late grandfather's giant wooden desk—and along the top shelf, there is a collection of crystals, a goddess candle, and an incense burner. Hang artwork, tapestries, or posters featuring mystical or spiritual symbols, plants, or landscapes that evoke positive energies. One of my favorite pieces of office décor is a lovely triple moon painted on a purple background, a gift from my best friend in the whole world, and it hangs right above the doorway so I can see it from every angle.

Use essential oils, diffusers, or incense to fill the space with scents that promote focus, relaxation, or creativity. Certain fragrances, such as lavender, frankincense, or sandalwood, can enhance your mindset significantly as you work. Create or display sigils or symbols representing your magical goals. Place them discreetly around the office (or not so discreetly)—underneath the keyboard, on the back of a chair—to subtly infuse the space with your desired energies. I keep a prosperity symbol chalked on the underside of my center desk drawer.

MAIL AWAY YOUR PROBLEMS SPELL

If you've got someone causing you problems, a simple banishing spell is a good way to get them to back off, and you can do this one with items you've probably got in your office space already! You'll need:

- ✦ A piece of paper and a black marker
- ✦ An envelope
- ✦ A stamp
- ✦ Matches or a lighter
- ✦ A cauldron or firesafe dish

Write the name of your problem person on the paper three times, and then draw big black X's through the names. As you do, say, *Go away, be gone, leave me, trouble me no more!* Fold the paper three times, stuff it in the envelope, and seal the flap. Add the stamp. On the outside of the envelope, where you'd normally write a mailing address, write *Go Away!* in big letters. Light the corner of the envelope with your matches or lighter, and drop it into the cauldron to burn. As it does, envision the person's mischief and drama burning out of your life. Once the envelope and paper have burned to ashes, take them somewhere outdoors and scatter them into the wind.

Abundance and Prosperity Magic

Because it's the space in our home where we often take care of financial matters, the office area is a great place for prosperity and abundance magic. By focusing on manifesting wealth, success, and a plentiful life, you can attract financial stability, material and nonmaterial gains, and overall opportunities for improvement. Throughout history, various cultures and civilizations have practiced rituals and beliefs intertwining spirituality with material wealth.

In ancient Egypt, offerings and rituals to gods associated with prosperity, such as Hapi, Anuket, and Hathor, were common. The Egyptians believed in an afterlife where wealth and possessions were essential, leading to burial practices that included placing riches and treasures in tombs. In Chinese feng shui, practices such as the strategic location of objects, the use of specific colors, and the symbolism of elements aim to invite wealth and success into homes and businesses. Many indigenous groups worldwide have rituals and ceremonies dedicated to abundance and prosperity. These rituals often involve offerings, dances, chants, and prayers to nature spirits, ancestors, or deities for bountiful harvests, successful hunts, or thriving communities.

Money Manager Spell

In this day and age, it can be a challenge to stay financially afloat. For many people, learning to be a savvy money manager is a game changer. The first step to that is to know precisely where your money is coming from and where it's going to. Once you've determined the exact amount of your income and monthly expenses, you can start taking better control of your finances. For this working, you'll need:

+ A paper and pen
+ A calculator
+ Scissors
+ A green candle
+ Matches or a lighter
+ A cauldron or firesafe bowl

Begin by drawing a line down the center of the paper. On the left side, list your household's monthly income from each source—if your paycheck sometimes varies, you can guesstimate the numbers, but try to be as accurate as possible. On the right side, enumerate all of your expenses—this could be rent, utilities, credit card payments, groceries, daycare expenses, or anything else you know you and your household need to pay for. Use the calculator to tally them up. Is one number higher or lower than you'd like? For most people, there's an imbalance, so take a good long look at where you need to make changes.

Using the scissors, cut the paper in half along the line as you say, *I separate myself from unnecessary debt*. Place the candle on top of the income half of your paper in a firesafe dish and light it as you visualize abundance coming into your household. Say, *Abundance, I draw you. Prosperity, I call you. Bounty, I invite you into my home.*

Take the side of paper that contains your expenses and debt, and hold the corner to the candle's flame. Let it burn in your hand for a moment, as you say, *Debt, I banish you. Needless expenditures, I reject you. Financial struggles, I no longer allow you in my home.* Drop the burning paper into the firesafe dish. Dribble a little of the candle wax into the ashes, and once it has cooled, take the clump of wax and remnants of the burned paper someplace far away to dispose of it. Keep the list of income where you can see it, as a reminder to make smart financial choices. Finally, follow your household budget strictly, so you can rid yourself of any debt.

Simple Abundance Practices for the Home

With spellwork, rituals, and simple daily practices, you can draw abundance into your life. It's important to keep in mind that while prosperity magic can work in many ways, it's unlikely to result in you winning the lottery or finding a million dollars in an unmarked sack in your front yard. But what it *does* do really well is bring new *opportunities* for abundance—and often in amounts that cover what you're hoping for. I've generally found I get the best outcome from prosperity magic if I do my working focusing on need rather than greed.

+ Create a small pouch or sachet using green or gold fabric and fill it with basil, cinnamon, cloves, or bay leaves—herbs known for their association with wealth. Keep the pouch at your desk or wherever you sit to pay your bills to reduce debt and attract financial prosperity.

+ Place a small dish of salt and a few coins near the entrance of your home or the door to your office to draw abundance.

+ Use a green, silver, or gold candle to represent wealth and prosperity. Carve dollar signs into the candle, anoint it with cinnamon or bergamot essential oil, associated with wealth, and light the candle while visualizing your financial goals manifesting.

+ Implement feng shui principles in your workspace to attract success. This might involve arranging furniture to promote the flow of energy, or Chi, placing symbols of abundance like a bowl of oranges or a money plant in the room, or keeping mirrors to reflect and multiply bounty.

+ Bury a coin in the soil of a potted plant in your office to symbolically "grow" wealth. As the plant thrives, so too does your financial well-being.

Basements, Cellars, and Attics

Basements, cellars, and attics often carry a sense of mystery, seclusion, and sometimes even a connection to the spiritual realm. So why not take advantage of the energy of the space? Even if the area is unfinished, you can still turn it into a magical spot in your home.

Got concrete or plain wooden walls? Hang some tapestries or even colorful sheets! Is the floor just a slab? Pick up a small area rug.

Convert these areas into dedicated sacred spaces for rituals, meditation, or spellcasting. Set up altars, arrange magical tools, and fill the space with lighting, plants, and your favorite scents, and you'll be able to get to work. Use these spaces for divination practices like tarot readings, scrying, or meditation. The secluded nature of a basement or attic can enhance focus and concentration during these activities, especially if you live with other people and need some privacy. Attics with windows or skylights can be ideal for moon or sun rituals. Use these spaces during specific lunar or solar phases for rituals, meditation, or charging magical items under the natural celestial energies.

You can also work with the natural elements present in these spaces. Connect with earth energies in the cellar, air energies in the attic, or use the enclosed nature of the basement for water-related spells or rituals.

Because my house is old and sits at the bottom of a very steep hill—I mean, it's so steep, I'd probably need rappelling gear to climb it safely—I get a lot of water runoff during certain times of the year. My house, like many in my area, is designed with a trench that actually runs through my cellar, carrying water from the hillside into my sump pump, where it is then pumped out into the main storm drain. From mid-March, when the snow starts melting, until around the middle of June, when the rainy season ends, that sump pump is chugging away nonstop. Additionally, my cellar is only partially excavated—the front half is finished with concrete blocks and a slab floor, while the rear section is simply soil and really big rocks. This means that I have a *lot* of natural representation of both earth and water at the ready.

Sump Pumps and Cisterns

If your home has a sump pump like mine does, you've got a perfect delivery method for spells that call for banishing or elimination. Now, I'm going to warn you—don't ever drop solid things in your sump pump's pit. That includes crystals, candles, and even biodegradable stuff like paper—at best it will clog the outflow pipes, and at worst it can destroy the pump itself, which is an expensive thing to replace. However, what you *can* add is a small amount of… more water. After all, that's how you test the pump to make sure it is working. Do *not* pour dirty water into the pit.

To banish something—or someone—that's been causing you a problem, write the person's name on a small glass jar. Fill the jar with water, and light a black candle—remember that black is associated with banishing. Place the candle beside the jar and allow it to burn down on its own. Once the candle has self-extinguished, pour the water from the jar into the sump pit. The next time the pump runs, it will forcefully expel the water out of the pit and into the drain system, carrying it away from you. Place any remnants of the candle into the jar, and dispose of it somewhere far from your home.

If your home has a cistern, again, you've got a perfect avenue for water-based magic. My home's water cistern—which sits on the side of that ridiculously steep hillside—has been out of use since my village got municipal water in the early 1980s, but many of the homes in my area do still use them to collect water for gardening and other uses. If you have access to one, use it as a focal point for water-related rituals, meditations, or spells, harnessing the energy of the element for emotional healing, purification, or enhancing intuition. You can also consider it as a vessel for abundance and prosperity magic. Collect rainwater in the cistern during auspicious times, charging it with intentions for abundance, financial prosperity, or fertility.

Utilize the reflective surface of the water in the cistern for scrying or divination practices. Gazing into the water's surface during specific moon phases or under certain celestial alignments can be a valuable opportunity to receive insights or visions.

Magic in Your Rafters

Does your home include an attic space? If you can safely access it, create a sacred circle, spread out tarot cards, scry using reflective surfaces, or conduct pendulum work to tap into higher realms of consciousness while you sit in the highest point in your home. Try incorporating symbols or representations of air, as the attic often connects with this element. If the space has windows, open them up—or clean them so you can see the outdoors—to tap into the power of the sun as a representation of fire.

The attic can be a great spot to do workings focused on mental clarity, communication, inspiration, or harnessing the power of thoughts and intentions. Draw or carve symbols of your magical intentions on wood, cloth, or paper; hang your sigils in the rafters or place them around the attic to imbue the space with specific energies. You can also hang symbolic items like charms, ribbons, or herbs in the rafters. These high spaces can serve as symbolic gateways to higher energies or realms, helping you manifest your magical intentions.

Craft Room

Not everyone has a specific room for crafting, sewing, or creating artwork—I've lived in places where I had a single table in a corner as the only space available for me to make things. However, if you're a creative sort, you've probably figured out your favorite spot in your home to craft in whatever your preferred medium is, whether it's sewing, fiber arts, painting, or paper projects. A dedicated crafting space—whether it's an entire room, a large closet, or a small spot in the back of the kitchen—allows for better organization of materials, tools, and supplies. Organization makes it so much easier to find and access what you need for projects, which in turn saves time and reduces stress. A crafting space can inspire and stimulate creativity and serve as a sanctuary where you can freely explore ideas, experiment, and immerse yourself in creative processes without distractions. It's also a great place to make some magic! Personalize your crafting space with artwork, colors, symbols, or other décor that resonates with your practice. Encourage your own creativity by integrating crafts or artistic projects into your magical workings.

Button Magic

Do you have a stash of buttons? I've got a huge mason jar filled with them sitting on the shelf near my sewing machine. Some are left over from previous projects—for instance, I bought a dozen buttons but only needed six—and others are spares from clothing that has long been consigned to the dust rag pile. A few even came from a box found in my grandmother's sewing kit when she passed away many years ago. No matter what style of button you have on hand, there are plenty of ways you can use them in magic.

+ Use them in poppet magic to form eyes on magical dolls.
+ Incorporate them into spells related to keeping things connected; much as a button holds together a coat or

a shirt, it can represent holding together a family in rough times.

+ Multicolored buttons can be used in the same way multicolored cloths are used for aligning, activating, and balancing the chakras, or energy centers of the body. As each chakra has an associated color, the same color button could be used to represent that chakra.

+ Use in a charm to "keep your mouth buttoned," reminding you to think before speaking, or create a buttoned charm to put around your Book of Shadows to discourage potential prying eyes.

+ Include buttons in between the knots of cords used in knot magic or as part of a Magpie Tangle, as referenced in chapter 11.

Cutting Machine Magic

Do you own a cutting machine? There are several brands out there on the market but Cricut, Silhouette, and Brother make the best known models. They really have revolutionized the world of crafting by offering limitless creative possibilities to hobbyists and professionals alike. These ingenious gadgets allow you to precisely cut intricate designs, shapes, and lettering on various types and colors of vinyl, paper, or other materials. You can use cutting machines to customize everything from T-shirts and mugs to home décor items, which allows for some highly creative magical opportunities. There's user-friendly software to help you bring your artistic visions to life, and although there's a bit of a learning curve when you first get started, there are literally thousands of tutorial videos available online for beginners.

You may feel a cutting machine is outside your budget, but don't worry! More and more public places are making available what they call "maker spaces," in which patrons can come on-site, pay for supplies, and use items like cutting machines, sewing machines, and 3D printers for a nominal charge. In my area, many public libraries offer maker spaces, as do a few independently owned galleries and shops. In addition to being super helpful for those who are budget conscious, this is a great alternative for anyone who's thinking about buying a machine but isn't sure they want to take the plunge yet—you can take it for a test-drive before you spend the money. It's also a great resource if you'll only have a few small projects to make now and then and you don't think it's worth it to spend full price on a machine you'll only use once in a blue moon.

If a maker space isn't an option for you either, consider asking your friend circle if anyone has one! Most people who have cutting machines absolutely love them, and we *really* love showing other people how they work. Offer to pay for vinyl or paper, and find a friend who will teach you about the ins and outs of their own machine while you make magical projects together.

I had been toying with the idea of purchasing a cutting machine for a while, and then my best friend brought hers over for a playdate so I could see how it actually worked. I went out and bought one the next day—I was able to find a bundle on sale at 40 percent off the regular price—and was completely hooked. If you're creative and willing to think outside the box, the possibilities are pretty much limitless. One of the first magical uses I found for my machine was a Mailbox Protection

Spell, which you can read about in chapter 3. However, since then, I've discovered all kinds of ways to make magical mayhem with this handy-dandy gadget.

- **Enchanting sigils:** Use your machine to create sigils on various materials, such as paper, wood, or vinyl. These sigils, charged with intention, can be used in spells, rituals, or talismans to manifest specific desires, protection, or spiritual guidance.

- **Elemental altar décor:** Cut out elemental symbols or representations of earth, air, fire, and water—incorporate them into altar decorations to enhance your connection with the elements during rituals. For instance, earth symbols can be added onto stones or wood, while air symbols can adorn your incense holders.

- **Personalized spell candles:** Create personalized spell candles by cutting out intricate designs on candle labels or vinyl. Add the labels to a blank jar candle and *voila*! You can boost the power of your candle workings, focusing on healing, love, protection, or any other magical intention.

- **Witchy home décor:** Craft magical home décor items—pentacles or moon phases can be cut out and applied to mirrors for protection or scrying purposes. Make botanical motifs to use in spell jars or sachets, bringing the energy of specific herbs into your spells.

- **Divination tools:** You can even use a cutting machine to create unique divination tools, such as oracle or tarot cards, if your machine has a pen feature. Each card can feature carefully chosen symbols, colors, or patterns, charged with magical energy, enhancing your divinatory practices and connecting you with the spiritual realm.

CONTAINER SPELLS

The use of containers in magic is an old practice. A clay pot was found with an Egyptian papyrus dating from around the fifth century CE. The following was written on the papyrus:

Awaken, demons who lie here, and seek out Euphemia … may she not be able to find sleep the whole night long, but bring her until she comes before his feet, lusting after him with crazed lust, with love and with sexual congress. For I have bound her brain, her hands, her upper belly, her vulva, so that she loves me.[21]

This is a binding attraction spell, found sealed in a container, with two embracing dolls accompanying it.

In ancient Middle Eastern settlements, archaeologists have discovered clay bowls used for protection from demons.[22] The demon's face was carved into the inside of the bowl, which was then sealed and placed upside down, preventing the demon from escaping and causing harm. During the Middle English period, witch bottles were buried under the threshold or hidden up in a chimney to keep witches or evil-intentioned people away. These

21. Ogden, *Magic, Witchcraft, and Ghosts in the Greek and Roman Worlds*, 232.
22. Thrope, "Magic Bowls of Antiquity."

bottles, many of which are still being discovered today, contained sharp, jagged items like bent pins or nails.[23] Today, many practitioners include modern objects like shards of glass or broken razor blades in their witch bottles. In the magical traditions of the African diaspora, honey jars—sometimes called sweetening jars—are designed to turn a situation, or even a person, favorable toward the practitioner. On the opposite end of the spectrum, a vinegar jar, or souring jar, is used to cause discord.

Boxes, jars, bags, bowls—you name it. If you've got any sort of container on hand, put it to use with one of these simple spells.

+ **Protection jar:** Add sea salt, red brick dust, protective herbs like basil and rosemary, and three small crystals such as black tourmaline, hematite, or obsidian to a jar. Write your intention for protection on a piece of paper and place it in the jar. Visualize a shield of protective light surrounding you and your home as you seal the jar. Keep it in your home for continuous protection.

+ **Love bag:** Place rose petals, lavender, and a small rose quartz crystal in a pretty cloth bag. Use the fingers of your dominant hand to move them around in a clockwise direction, swirling gently while focusing on attracting to you the sort of loving relationship you need, want, and deserve. Tie the bag shut and keep it in your bedroom or a prominent place in your home.

+ **Abundance box:** Write your financial goals on bay leaves and place them, along with a citrine crystal and

....
23. Meier, "Is There a Witch Bottle in Your House?"

a silver coin, inside the box. Light a green candle and focus on the flame as you call prosperity and blessings toward you. Allow the candle to safely burn out on its own. Keep the box near the center of your home.

+ **Confidence jar:** Write positive affirmations about yourself on a piece of paper. Light a yellow candle and focus on its warm glow as you're reminded of just how awesome you truly are, even if you don't always feel that way. Fold the paper and place it, along with sunflower petals, into a jar. Seal it with a few drops of yellow candle wax, and keep it on your dresser as a reminder of your worth.

No access to bottles, boxes, or bags? No worries! Anything can be a container—think creatively, and consider using something else, such as an envelope or folded paper, a strip of aluminum foil, a food carryout container, or a paper sack. One of my favorite containers to use—and it's something just about everyone can get their hands on—is the cardboard tube from the inside of a roll of toilet paper. Fold the two open ends shut, and you have an instant container waiting for you to place ingredients within.

CHARM BAGS

In his amazing book *The Magical Art of Crafting Charm Bags*, author Elhoim Leafar explains these handy magical tools in the simplest of ways. He says a charm bag "contains a cohesive and vibrationally harmonious group of enchanted objects,"[24] and I'm certain that's one of the most accurate descriptions of a charm bag I've ever read.

Like many other magical items we use today, charm bags have a long history. Whether your tradition refers to them as mojo bags, gris-gris bags, or sachets, they're found in spiritual traditions around the world, although the specific practices and ingredients vary widely across cultures. These small pouches filled with herbs, stones, and other items can carry protective, lucky, or healing properties.

Easy Charm Bag Projects

- **Home protection:** Use fabric in black or deep purple. Add rosemary, bay leaves, and juniper berries. Place pieces of black tourmaline and hematite in the bag as well. Include something made of iron—ideally a nail or needle (and if the nail comes from your home, that's even better!). Finally, add some garlic cloves, red pepper flakes, and a pinch of black salt.

- **Healing:** Choose a fabric in light blue. Fill it with lavender for relaxation, rosemary for mental clarity, and calendula or chamomile for soothing energy. Include amethyst for spiritual healing and balance and clear quartz to give that healing energy a boost.

- **Prosperity:** Try a fabric in green or gold. Add herbs known for their prosperity-enhancing properties such as basil, cinnamon, and bay leaves, along with crystals like green aventurine, citrine, and pyrite. Use dried

....

24. Leafar, *The Magical Art of Crafting Charm Bags*, 31.

flowers such as marigold for financial gain and orange blossoms for prosperity and success. Last but not least, place a few shiny coins in the bag to represent wealth flowing into your life.

+ **Self-love:** Work with a fabric in pink, red, or rose. Include herbs like rose petals, lavender, and chamomile. Add rose quartz and amethyst as well as a small pocket-size mirror to symbolize self-reflection and self-acceptance. Finally, include a written affirmation stating, *I am worthy and deserving of love and happiness.*

CORD CUTTING SPELL TO END A RELATIONSHIP

We've all found ourselves, at some point, in a relationship that's unsatisfying. Whether it's a friendship that has run its course or a romantic connection that isn't fulfilling our needs anymore, sometimes, you just have to walk away—but that's not always easy! Do this spell to cut the cord and sever the ties to make it a little less challenging to put an end to things. You'll need:

+ A length of black cord or twine
+ Two pieces of paper and a pen
+ Scissors

Write your own name on one piece of paper, and the other person's on the second. Place the papers together with the blank sides facing each other and the names on the outside. Use the cord to wrap the papers together tightly.

With the scissors, slowly begin snipping away at the paper and the cord. As you do, say, *This relationship is broken and cannot be mended. I cut the cord, this relationship is ended.* Repeat this with each snip, cutting the paper and cord into the tiniest pieces you can. Once you're all done, dispose of the remnants, and take whatever mundane actions are necessary to put an end to the relationship.

Chapter 11
MAKING MAGIC ANYWHERE

I've encountered plenty of people over the years who have told me they'd love to spend more time focused on their spiritual growth, but they feel stifled by their living situation. Years ago, a friend decided that she, her wife, and their large goofy Labrador were going to hit the road and live the van life, traveling the festival circuit all over the country. There was quite a lively discussion about what to keep and what to eliminate as they moved out of their apartment, put their furniture in storage, and prepared for life on the road. At one point, I said, "Okay, but you have more magical stuff than anyone I know. What will you do without it?" And she grinned, booped me on the nose, and said, "Magic is wherever I am."

I've since lost touch with her, but that one sentence stuck with me, even now, decades later. The key to living magically—no matter what challenges there may be—is to find the magic wherever you are, whether you're living in a van, an apartment, or a house. Whether you're living on the road, in a suburban neighborhood, on a country farm, or in a bustling city, it's out there. You just have to look for it, and learn to recognize it when you see it.

Bricks, Glass, Steel, and More

In a cityscape, where modern materials dominate, you can still find magical correspondences in the surroundings that make up your urban environment. Bricks can symbolize security, endurance, and foundation. Use them in spells or rituals aimed at building or strengthening foundations in life, creating stability in uncertain situations, or laying the groundwork for new endeavors.

Glass holds qualities of reflection, clarity, and transformation. Incorporate it into scrying rituals or divination work, harnessing its transparency to gain insight or clarity into complex situations or to reveal hidden truths. Even asphalt—which certainly isn't limited to cities alone—can represent connectivity and transition. Work with it in spells focused on travel, movement, or transition phases in life. It can also symbolize the road to transformation or new beginnings.

While not traditionally associated with ancient magical correspondences, plastic can symbolize adaptability, innovation, and malleability. In your magical practice, you might see it associated with the ability to adjust to changing circumstances or the power of transformation. I've been known to use plastic in spells aimed at flexibility or reshaping aspects of my life.

Even metals can be used in magical workings—think about the durability of iron! It's well known for its use in protection magic and is useful for spells related to fortitude and stability. Copper symbolizes communication; use it to amplify energy, promote positive interactions with others, and enhance your intuitive gifts. If you need strength, resilience, and protection, consider using steel in rituals or charms aimed at fortifying personal boundaries, enhancing your inner strength, or creating protective shields against negative energies.

Each of these materials in an urban landscape can be seen through a magical lens, offering correspondences that can be used any way you like in spells, rituals, or meditations. The key is to ask yourself what your city's features mean *to you* and draw your own associations from them.

Working in Small Spaces

Living in a small space doesn't have to hinder your ability to practice magic. In fact, a more compact setting can often foster creativity and resourcefulness in magical practice. Small spaces encourage minimalistic approaches to spellcasting. By learning to focus on spells or rituals that require minimal tools, you can become a more efficient practitioner. Candle magic, for instance, is super adaptable to confined spaces.

In small spaces, everyday items become magical tools. Kitchen herbs, household crystals, or even common stationery can serve as potent ingredients or symbolic representations in spells. Digital platforms offer a wealth of resources for magical practice. I've lived in apartments that were far too small for more than two guests at once—but this experience allowed me to start exploring online communities. With the boom in social media platforms, you might join virtual covens or groups, access guided meditations or rituals, and even learn about new practices and spells just by tapping an icon on your phone.

Limited space encourages a focus on internal work and mindfulness. Meditation, visualization, and energy manipulation require no physical tools or large spaces. If you practice grounding, centering, and visualization exercises, you'll be able to enhance your magical abilities regardless of the space constraints.

Is living in a small space a challenge? Sure. Is it manageable? Absolutely. You'll learn to adapt and innovate in your magical practice.

Making Your Small Space Work for You

If you're functioning with limited space, you can still turn it into a magical sanctuary—you just have to be mindful of what you bring into it. When possible, choose multipurpose magical items—for example, a beautiful kettle for brewing herbal teas can be both practical and a tool for potion making. Kitchen herbs and spices can be used in your magical workings. Make the most of vertical space for storing magical tools and books—and if you don't mind using an e-reader, consider eliminating some of the paperback and hardcover books you own and moving to digital versions to save on valuable space. Use hanging organizers, shelves, or hooks to keep essential items accessible without cluttering limited surface areas. Maximize light using mirrors and reflective surfaces to make the space feel larger and more open. Mirrors also have the added bonus of their magical qualities—they can amplify energy and aid in spells and introspection.

Learn to make magic without tools—they simply serve as a focal point. If you can work a spell or ritual simply by visualizing your goal and projecting your will out into the universe, you're making magic. You can still track the phases of the moon and the changing seasons, and you can establish a daily practice of reciting magical affirmations, making offerings to your deities, or saying a blessing in your space—none of which require tools.

If you're living on the road, either in a camper or some other vehicle, why not include magic as part of your travels? Use a pendulum, numerology, or other divination methods to select where you'll go next! When you stop for the night, set up protective wards around your sleeping space. If you're crashing in a tent for the night, enchant the tent stakes with protective energy. Collect a small bit of soil or water from the different places you go, and use it in future spellwork; they both take on the energies of the location you found them. Allow yourself some flexibility when it comes to workings. If the instructions call for a ritual bath and you're out at a wooded campsite far from a bathtub, what can you do instead? Is there a stream nearby? Can you fill a bowl with clean water and bathe with a sponge? You're only limited by your own creativity and imagination.

Sharing Space with Non-Witchy Folk

Living with individuals who don't share your beliefs or practices can present unique issues. If you've got roommates or family members in your home who just don't get it—or even think it's weird—you can still find ways to coexist respectfully. The key here is communication. If you're angry and slamming doors because someone scolded you about leaving a burning candle out … well, you've both got to learn to use your words like grown-ups.

It's crucial to respect others' beliefs and boundaries. Just as you wish your practices to be respected, extend the same courtesy to others. Avoid imposing your beliefs or rituals on those living with you, and ensure that your practices don't disrupt their lives or spaces. If you prefer to keep your magical tools or practices private, ensure that your tools are stored discreetly and your rituals are conducted in a way that respects the shared living space. Consider using portable altars, which we'll discuss in the next section, or keeping your tools in a private area to maintain personal boundaries.

If you have an otherwise good relationship with the people who share your home and you feel comfortable, offer to educate them about your practices. Explain the significance of your rituals or tools without pressuring them to participate or believe. Mutual understanding can foster a harmonious living environment—but if they tell you they're not interested in hearing about "all that witchy stuff," respect that as well.

You might feel safer if you opt for neutral or discreet tools and decorations. Utilize items that can be interpreted in various ways to avoid unnecessary attention or discomfort. Crystals, candles, and decorative elements can be chosen in styles that blend with the overall décor.

Be mindful of timing your rituals or spellwork. Choose times when your housemates are less likely to be inconvenienced or disturbed by your practices. Consider noise levels, especially during meditation, chanting, or ceremonies. If you regularly do a smoke cleansing in your living space, ensure it doesn't interfere with others' sensitivities. You may need to go with methods that don't produce strong scents or smoke—or find a compromise that respects everyone's comfort and health needs.

When using shared spaces for rituals or activities, seek consent and find mutually agreeable times. Be considerate and ensure that your practices don't hinder others from utilizing the shared spaces comfortably.

By prioritizing respect, open communication, discretion, and consideration for others' boundaries and comfort, you can navigate living with non-practitioners while developing and growing your own spiritual practice.

Mini/Portable Altar Setup

The portable altar is one of my favorite life hacks for being on the go. Certainly it comes in handy when traveling— airplane trips, subway rides, etc.—but it's also a great way to have a usable, functional altar when you don't have a lot of space to work in. Once, when I was between apartments and couch surfing at a friend's for a few weeks, I put a lot of my belongings into storage totes—after all, I didn't want to take advantage of her generosity by cluttering up her living room with all my stuff. So, in the interest of maintaining a temporarily minimalist lifestyle, I tucked most of my magical tools away where they wouldn't be underfoot.

But at the same time, I really, *really* needed to work some magic—remember that I was crashing on a buddy's sofa and didn't want that to be a long-term thing—so I decided to create a small portable altar kit. I could tuck it away when it wasn't in use and easily pull it out when I needed it. I used a small plastic storage container—I think it once held lunch meat?—but yours can be anything you like. Use a small case with a secure top, a pretty drawstring bag, or, if space is really at a premium, a breath mint tin or film canister with a snap-on lid.

I'm partial to boxes myself—I really like vessels of any kind, because they're things you can put other things in—and there are plenty of options to choose from. Visit a thrift store and find a plain wooden box and then take it home and decorate it with painted magical symbols and other embellishments, find a plastic container and cover it with your favorite stickers, or stop by your favorite local metaphysical shop and see what's available premade. Many cigar shops, if you have one near you, sell empty cigar boxes inexpensively—and they often have really pretty decorations on them.

If you want to use a bag and you've got some sewing skills, you can transform a circular altar cloth. Simply stitch a hem around the edge of the circle, leaving a small spot open, and thread a cord through the hem. Tie a couple of knots at the end, and then stitch the opening closed. Pull the cord tight and you've got an instant drawstring bag; when it's time to make magic, loosen the cord, unpack your loot, and presto! It's back to being a round altar cloth.

Regardless of whether you go with a box or a bag, it needs to meet only two criteria. First, it has to have room for the tools you need. Second, it should be small enough that you can carry or move it easily. Any requirements beyond that are entirely up to you.

As far as what you want it to hold … well, we're going for a portable and minimalist approach here. You don't need to put every single magical tool you own—or even a representation of it—into your portable altar kit. To paraphrase *Jurassic Park*'s Dr. Ian Malcolm, you *could*, but that doesn't mean you *should*. This is about prioritization—what things do you need to feel as though your magic is effective? For some people, it might just be some divination tools, while others might want to have physical symbols of the elements or small statues of their deities. A few items to consider:

+ A small notebook and pen
+ A few of your most-used crystals; for me, it's hematite, amethyst, rose quartz, and tiger's eye.
+ A couple of small pouches of dried herbs; I keep dried lavender, mugwort, and sage on hand.
+ To represent earth, a small container of soil
+ To represent air, a feather
+ To represent fire, a tealight candle and a match
+ To represent water, a seashell

+ A square of fabric for use as an altar cloth

+ Divination items; I take a pendulum with me
  wherever I go, but you could also include a miniature
  tarot deck, oracle cards, runes, or anything else you've
  got space for in your container.

I keep all of these things, along with a couple of other handy magical items, in a single zippered pouch that says *Ye Olde Bag of Witchy Shit* on it. I travel a lot, and it accompanies me wherever I go.

Consecrate your portable altar kit in whatever manner your tradition calls for, and use it when you're short on space, traveling, or just need to work some magic in a pinch.

Hold a Journal Ritual

I would love it if every single one of us—myself included—had a ton of space to perform rituals. In my perfect magical world, I'd have access to a big field, somewhere out in the middle of nowhere, surrounded by tall trees with soft green grass underfoot and perhaps a few standing stones for good measure. I wouldn't have curious neighbors peeking into the backyard; my altar would be a perfectly flat rock where I could set up my candles and magical tools while the moon glowed gently above me in the clear night sky as I frolicked barefoot…

Reality check: That is not the situation for most of us. In fact, for some people—especially if you live in an urban environment where space is at a premium and you're surrounded by other humans—it's hard to find any form of privacy whatsoever. In that case, you're pretty much stuck. You can either do your spellwork or ritual in a space that's less than ideal, or you can skip it altogether. Years ago, when I was living in a city with two roommates in a teeny tiny apartment, I began performing what I call a "journal ritual."

Most people have no qualms at all about interrupting people who are lighting candles, meditating, praying, or even reading—my roommates at the time certainly had no boundaries whatsoever, and holy cow, they were *loud*. But I learned quickly that they'd leave me alone if I was in the act of writing. This meant that if I had access to a blank notebook or journal—which I always did because, like a dragon, I hoarded pretty journals—I had an escape route from the roomies. I could write all evening long and *no one bothered me*.

To hold a journal ritual, get your journal out and find yourself a comfortable spot—ideally a place where you can work undisturbed. If you're fortunate enough to have a balcony or patio or a nearby park, take advantage of that and go outside. Want to set the mood just right? Light your favorite incense or a candle, put on some quiet background music—I like nature sounds myself—and meditate for a moment to get yourself focused.

Now, think about what the purpose is for your journal ritual. Maybe it's time to celebrate one of the eight Pagan sabbats or some other date that's important to your magical tradition. Perhaps you'd like to perform a specific ritual for prosperity or healing or protection. Maybe you'd like to offer a prayer of gratitude to the gods and goddesses of your pantheon. Once you've determined your intention, get your thoughts in order.

Allow yourself to write whatever thoughts go through your head—you can be structured and orderly or let things go free form. Visualize yourself performing the ritual actively, and narrate exactly what you would do. For instance, a ritual that begins with casting a circle and then asking your deities for protection might look something like this:

Tonight, I call upon my gods and goddesses, and I ask for their blessing as I direct my will toward healing. Before I begin, I will call the quarters. I place a bowl of fresh, clean soil to the north to represent the element of earth, invoking its secure and stable power. I place a soft feather to the east, representing the element of air, invoking the winds of change. I place a candle to the south, the element of fire, with its burning passion and energy. To the west, I place a chalice of consecrated water, welcoming its cleansing, purifying energy. The circle is now cast. Gods and goddesses, I honor you! I bid you welcome and ask your aid in healing ... and so forth.

Continue writing as long as you like, with the full ritual unfolding first in your mind and then upon the pages. If you're not interested in casting a circle or calling the gods, don't worry about it! Your path is as unique as you are, and you can tailor a journal ritual to fit the needs or structure of your individual belief system. If it helps you to visualize it, sketch a picture of what your ideal altar might look like if you were actively performing your ritual rather than just writing it down. There have been times when I've done this and found myself in almost a trancelike state, just freewriting all the things that pop into my head. If that happens to you, don't panic—it's perfectly normal. Once you've reached the natural conclusion of your written ritual and you finish jotting things down, close your journal and put it away.

I'd recommend putting a date on each journal ritual you write—this will be helpful in the future if you need ideas for performing an active ritual. Additionally, as time goes by and you fill your journal with a collection of written rituals, you can look back at your own spiritual development and see how you've changed, grown, and evolved.

Magpie Tangle Magic Using Found Items

I've lived in cities and I've lived in small towns, and no matter where I claim my home to be, I've found I'm a bit like the stereotype of a magpie—I like to stop and pick up interesting bits and bobs here and there. Over the years, I've collected all kinds of random items and stuffed them in my pockets just because I found them appealing. After a while, I realized that this habit of mine could have some significant magical potential. Thus, the Magpie Tangle Magic spell delivery method was born. It's especially useful for times when I'm exploring an urban environment because, unlike many other magical spells and rituals, it doesn't require natural items unless you want it to. With the exception of some string, which you'll use as the foundation, you can use anything you find lying about.

As a slight side tangent, after I'd been doing this—and calling it Magpie Tangle Magic—for several years, I read Terry

Pratchett's *The Wee Free Men*, in which he describes witches doing something called a *shamble* spell. I quickly realized there were a lot of similarities between my Magpie workings and what Pratchett was describing. Since I know for a fact this method works, I can only conclude that Terry Pratchett was probably a witch too. But that's neither here nor there.

Anyway, the Magpie Tangle Magic delivery method works essentially the same way as a witches' ladder or any other form of knot magic. It's a handmade device that, once constructed, serves to *activate* the spell. The Tangle is designed to hold the things you collect as you tie them together, focusing on your intent. When it's done, it's done, and you walk away from it.

To make a Magpie Tangle, you'll simply need a piece of biodegradable string, ribbon, or yarn—it can be as long or as short as you want, but I like to keep mine to about a yard. That's a length that's easy to stuff in my pocket, and it's long enough that I can attach things to it without running out of room at the end. Armed with your string, it's time to go for a walk.

As you walk—wherever it may be—focus on your intention for the spell as well as its *purpose*. We talk a lot about intention, but we often forget to think of purpose. Look at it this way—while your *intention* may be for prosperity, your *purpose* can be any number of things. Maybe prosperity means bringing in extra money to pay your kid's tuition or the electric bill or going on a fun vacation. Perhaps it means simply eliminating existing debt or coming up with additional revenue each month. Think about purpose as well as intent for this spell method.

Let's use prosperity magic as an example for how to create a Magpie Tangle—but remember that you can use it for any type of spell at all: protection, healing, banishing, romance, etc.

In this hypothetical example, our intention is prosperity, and we'll say our purpose is to manifest additional money to pay for a luxury item we wouldn't normally splurge on. You know, the kind of thing you wouldn't typically buy yourself because it seems extravagant—a piece of jewelry, a trip to someplace new, an expensive piece of electronic equipment, etc.—but it's an item that, if money wasn't an object, you'd feel was worth the investment.

You've got your string in your pocket, and you're ready to go. As you begin to walk, with each step, take the time to focus on your intention and your purpose. You may be visualizing that end purpose—that new tablet you've been wanting—and the source of extra funding, such as a raise at work. Whatever your goal may be, clear your mind of everything but this. Don't think about how your parents are doing this week, whether you cleaned the cat box, or that jerk down in the accounting department who stole your lunch from the work fridge. Dump everything out of your head but your magical intent and purpose.

While you're focusing on these things and walking, allow yourself to be aware of the world around you. Sense the pavement or soil beneath your feet. Feel the touch of the wind breezing over your skin. Take calming breaths and inhale the scent of the grass, the sky, the asphalt, whatever. Finally, *look*. As in, look around for things you can pick up.

What should you collect? Well, what strikes your fancy? Is there an interesting stone peeking out at you from a hidden corner? Maybe there's a small bit of metal from a discarded item lying on the ground, an old key, or a bit of brightly colored plastic. If something doesn't appeal to you, leave it be... but if you think, *Oh, that's neat*, go ahead and collect it.

As you pick each item up, stop and securely tie it to your string. You can spread your goodies out evenly or just tie them wherever along the string seems right to you—there are no rules here! While you're tying your object—key, stone, bead, etc.—onto the string, again, focus on the intent and purpose of your spell. Continue doing this as you walk, picking up items here and there and tying them to your string, until either the string is completely full or you just feel like it's done. I've done Tangle spells with just a few items on my string and others where it looks like a jumbled nest of pure chaos.

Once you've completed your Tangle, it's time to launch your spell out into the universe. Now, you can do this literally or figuratively. If everything you've collected is a natural item—rocks, twigs, seedpods, and so on—there's nothing at all wrong with leaving your Tangle out in nature. You can take it to a moving body of water and drop it in, toss it out into the woods, or just leave it somewhere unobtrusive—again, this is why we're using a biodegradable string or ribbon. On the other hand, a Tangle full of human-made items—essentially, litter you've collected—should probably go home with you and be hung up or tucked away. You don't want to just move other people's discarded trash from one outdoor spot to another. I've been known to launch a banishing Tangle into a dumpster or landfill simply because it seemed appropriate. Use your best judgment about how eco-friendly your launch is going to be.

Either way, the launch is where you envision your intent and purpose coming together, and then, with a great big mental *push*, you send it out and away from you. I like to verbalize my launch and will typically say something along the lines of *I send my will out to the universe, and so it shall be done. Aaaaaaaand release*. Once you've completed the launch, walk away. The spell is complete, and now your only remaining task is to wait for the results to begin manifesting.

For an alternative to walking around and picking up spell components outside, you can create your Magpie Tangle the same way using a collection of random items that are lying around your house. If you've got a junk drawer, a jar of mismatched buttons, or a collection of weird twigs, the potential is the same. The key is to focus your intention and purpose, then release the spell into the universe once the Tangle is complete—set it, and forget it!

City Magic Correspondences

We've all seen correspondence tables, and they're typically designed with the focus on items found in nature. However, not all of us have access to all the herbs, crystals, and what-have-yous, so this one is a little different—because it's based on objects not traditionally associated with magical workings. If you live in a city, try looking at some of the items on this list, and think about ways you can use them to make your own unique urban magic.

Symbolism or Correspondence	Items in Your Urban Environment
Earth	Asphalt/bricks, concrete, clay, iron
Air	Airplanes, air conditioners, balloons, clotheslines/dryers, fans, feathers, smoke
Fire	Barbecue/grills, lighters, streetlights, flashlights

Water	Fountains, plumbing, dams/lakes/rivers, washing machines/dishwashers, drains
Spirit	Birds, circles, wheels
Communication	Cell phones, comm towers, copper, mercury, electrical cords or outlets
Healing	Doctors' offices, copper, ambulances, test tubes or other medical supplies, pharmacies or pharmaceutical symbols
Protection	Alarm systems, police or fire symbols, silver or iron, condoms, fences, blue painter's tape to mark boundaries
Love	Candy hearts, chocolate, doves, tin (sexuality)
Money and prosperity	Stock market, banks, cakes, calculators, grain, lottery tickets
Transformation/change	Caterpillars/butterflies/moths, highways and roads, keys, bridges, food processors, sports car or wheels/tires
Banishing	Toilets/port-o-johns, balls, baseballs/tennis balls/footballs, scissors to cut away things that are negative

Chapter 12
AFFORDABLE MAGIC
AROUND THE HOUSE

O kay, I feel like I have to put out a disclaimer here, because whenever I talk at workshops about finding magical supplies around your home or in inexpensive or non-magical places, I inevitably get someone who's miffed because they think I'm trying to undermine the business of Pagan shops. I'm not, honestly. I'm a huge believer in the idea that we, as a magical community, *absolutely* need to support local witchy and metaphysical businesses when we can. After all, they don't just offer supplies like candles and herbs and crystals and books—they also present our community with a sense of place, a gathering spot where we can network with like-minded individuals.

However, I also recognize that there are a variety of reasons someone may not have the ability to shop at Ye Olde Wytchy Emporium around the corner. You might be living on a supertight budget. Maybe your local witchy shop operates on limited hours, and your work schedule doesn't mesh with their availability. Perhaps you don't have reliable transportation and the nearest metaphysical joint is a two-hour drive from you in a big city. Whatever your reason, it's perfectly okay to obtain magical supplies from places that aren't magical supply retailers. Should you support those shops when you can? Undeniably yes, and I wholeheartedly encourage you to do so. But if you can't, I'm the last person who's going to make you feel bad about it. What we're talking about here is *affordability* and *accessibility*.

One little nugget to keep in mind—while I always recommend cleansing for new magical supplies, it's *extra* important to do this when you don't know whose paws have been on an item before it got to you. Don't skimp on the cleaning and cleansing, *especially* with pre-owned objects. See later in this chapter for tips on how to do this.

Non-Magical Items Around Your House

Believe it or not, you've already got a treasure trove of magical ingredients around your home—they're just disguising themselves as mundane items. The trick is to start thinking magically about non-magical items. After all, every magical correspondence we use today exists because someone, at some point, said, *To me, this item represents that concept.* It's why we associate iron with protection magic, lavender with calming energy, copper with communication, and so on. It's also why many of the spells, rituals, and other practices in this book feature things other than traditional candles, herbs, and crystals—although you'll see some of those as well.

Consider for a moment all the stuff in your kitchen junk drawer, that weird box in the back of the basement, or that compact mirror sitting unused in your nightstand. What do those things represent to you? Could the batteries in your junk drawer symbolize power and energy? How about the coins in your basement box—do they make you think of wealth and prosperity? Could you do some divination with the mirror you'd forgotten about?

There's a full list of my fifty favorite household correspondences in the appendix, but to get you started, here are a few mundane household items that can be magical if you look at them the right way:

+ **String or yarn:** Different colored strings can be braided or knotted to create magical bracelets or charms. Each color represents different intentions—see the section on color magic at the end of this chapter. For instance, red can symbolize love and passion, while blue can represent peace and tranquility.

+ **Coins:** Old or new coins, especially those made of copper or silver, are associated with wealth and prosperity. You can bury them in your garden or place them in a jar along with herbs and oils to create a money-drawing charm.

+ **Keys:** Keys can symbolize unlocking potential or opening new opportunities. Use an old key as a charm for protection or wear it to symbolize moving forward in life. Visualize your goals as you hold the key, imbuing it with your intention.

+ **Salt:** Purifying and protective salt can be sprinkled around your home to create a defensive barrier or added to your bathwater to cleanse yourself energetically. Salt can also be used in rituals to represent the element of earth.

+ **Coffee mugs:** Use your favorite mug for tea magic. Choose specific teas or infusions based on their magical properties, such as chamomile for relaxation or peppermint for energy. While brewing, focus on your intention, and as you drink, visualize your desired outcome—see chapter 9 for some specific magical tea blend recipes.

+ **Bubble pack or craft foam:** Got something that needs protection? Wrap something symbolizing that item (or person) up in foam or bubble pack to keep it safe and secure.

+ **Kids' toys:** Use dolls, plastic bricks, or toy cars to kickstart a spell—a doll can represent a person, you can build anything you like with bricks, and toy cars are handy for protection spells when it comes to travelers and young drivers.

+ **Pillows:** Your pillow can be used in dream magic and manifestation. Place herbs such as lavender or chamomile inside a small sachet and tuck it inside your pillowcase to enhance relaxation and psychic receptivity, potentially leading to insightful dreams or visions.

+ **Matches and lighters:** Use a match or lighter not just to ignite candles but also to represent fire or to do some scrying. Lighting a flame can symbolize the ignition of energy and intention.

+ **Coffee:** Try using coffee grounds for divination and scrying, much like reading tea leaves. Gaze into a cup of grounds after drinking the coffee, seeking insights or answers to specific questions. The shapes and patterns formed can provide guidance. Coffee beans can also act as a neutralizer in spellwork.

+ **Shoes:** Use your shoes in protection spells. Placing a pair near your front door is believed to keep negative energies and unwanted visitors out of your home. You can also fill one with protective herbs and place it under your bed for protection while sleeping.

+ **Photographs:** Use photographs in sympathetic magic— write your intention on the back of a photo and place it on your altar, visualizing your desired outcome. This can be especially effective for spells related to relationships or healing.

+ **Citrus fruits:** Lemons, oranges, and limes are associated with purification and cleansing. Incorporate them into natural cleansers for ritual tools or your living space. Citrus peels can also be dried and used in various spells for their vibrant energy.

Craft Stores

Craft stores are full of endless possibilities for the resourceful witch! Be sure to think outside the box, because there's magical potential in just about everything. Just because an item is designed for one use doesn't mean it can't be used for some other purpose.

+ **Fabric:** Create your own magical dolls, altar cloths, bags and sachets to stuff with herbs, or wrappers for your magical tools. Consider stitching up some color magic items to decorate your home, like pillows, tablecloths, or curtains. You can also find some great prints with mystical symbols.

+ **Yarn, ribbon, and string:** Use these to craft a witch's ladder, make charms, or for other spellwork.

+ **Paint, canvas, and brushes:** Want to get really personal with your home's magical décor? Grab some inexpensive canvas and acrylic paints, and let your intuition guide you as you paint your own spiritually inspired wall art.

+ **Jewelry findings, beads, and charms:** It's easy to make your own magical jewelry with a bit of patience. Make a set of prayer beads, a necklace full of sacred symbols, or bracelets and earrings that have magical purpose.

+ **Precut wood shapes:** If possible, raid your craft store during the holidays, especially around Samhain and Yule! It's a perfect time to stock up on unpainted wooden shapes: circles, crescent moons, stars, trees, and more. Paint them as needed for magical ornaments to hang around your home, or craft some altar tools such as a pentacle, deity symbols, or other sigils.

+ **Paper, pens, stickers, and markers:** You can work just about any kind of magic with a good old-fashioned piece of paper and a pen. Write out your spells to use in fire magic, which sends your intentions out into the universe, or draw sigils and symbols to include in your rituals and other practices.

Hardware Stores

While I realize it might be a bit unconventional, some of my most commonly used magical items come straight from the local home improvement/hardware store. If you think creatively, there are a number of magical goodies to be found in the various aisles of Lowes, Home Depot, and other similar stores.

+ **Iron nails and rebar:** If you have a yard, bury pieces of iron in the soil around the perimeter for protection. If you don't have a lawn, don't worry—you can tuck them into the corners in the interior of your home. Just make sure you place them somewhere out of reach from kids, pets, and your vacuum cleaner.

+ **Garden supplies:** Pick up some inexpensive pots and paint them with magical symbols. Fill them with fresh, clean soil, and add some seeds to grow your own magical herbs and flowers.

+ **Rope, tape, or lengths of chain:** Create a poppet and wrap it in rope or tape as a way of binding the person from doing harm to themselves or others.

+ **Paint, brushes, and rollers:** Paint sigils of prosperity, happiness, protection, or any other magical intention on your walls, or use color magic to make an entire room a magical space.

+ **Birdseed:** Birdseed makes an excellent way to mark a ritual circle if you're practicing outdoors—scatter the seed around your circle, and once you're finished, the birds can feast on the leavings.

+ **Wood:** Make your own spirit board with a flat piece of wood, some paint or markers, and a stencil.

Yard Sales and Thrift Stores

+ **Picture frames:** A good frame can be cleaned up and repurposed to display magical artwork or altar items. Additionally, you can remove the glass and use it to make a scrying mirror by painting one side with a matte black spray paint; use the unpainted side as a reflective surface to gaze into and look for images and messages during divination sessions.

+ **Chalices, bowls, and jars:** Your local thrift store probably has a ton of these in their kitchenware area! You can use a chalice on your altar to hold consecrated water or offerings to your deities, and jars can be filled with crystals, herbs, or other magical items.

+ **Candleholders and candles:** Polish up some grubby candleholders until they shine and use them in ritual. You may be fortunate enough to find unused candles in a variety of colors, shapes, and sizes that you can incorporate into spellwork.

+ **Board games:** Take advantage of board game pieces to use in spellwork—for instance, try using a Monopoly house to land a new home or paper money for prosperity. Enchant a pair of dice for good luck at a casino, inscribe a sigil on a Scrabble tile and carry it with you as a talisman, or use one of the cars from the game Life to help yourself get a new set of wheels.

Dollar Store Magic

Does your neighborhood have a store where everything sells for the same price? Just a buck or two—five at the most? You'd be amazed at some of the cool things you can score at a dollar store that are easily adaptable for magical shenanigans, and you can source them in a way that's reasonably affordable. Consider some of these items when you're out scouring the local discount shops for goodies:

+ **Jars and boxes with lids:** Use them for herb or crystal storage or for spell jars.

+ **Candles in a variety of colors, shapes, and sizes:** Include these in any type of magic you like! Many discount stores also sell the tall jar candles referred to as saint candles, and these can be decorated any way you like with a bit of paint or a sheet of paper wrapped around the glass.

+ **Holiday and seasonal décor:** Look for wreaths, ornaments, flowers, and ribbons that can be displayed around your home or placed on your altar.

+ **Blank notebooks:** Use for journaling or written spellwork, or use one as your Book of Shadows.

+ **Incense and burners, scented oils, and fragrant wax warmers:** These can often be found in discount stores, and a bit of aromatherapy helps set the mood for just about any ritual, meditation, or divination session.

+ **Suncatchers:** You can often find these unpainted, and you can decorate them however you like—look for suns, moons, stars, and animals to hang around your home.

+ **Spritzer bottles for sprays:** Blend your own laundry freshening spray—mentioned in chapter 10—or create a magical cleansing wash with a bit of consecrated water and your favorite essential oils. Spritz them around your house as part of purification and cleansing rituals.

+ **Herbs and spices:** Although they're marketed for culinary use, grocery goods like cinnamon, sage, rosemary, and sea salt have significant magical properties, and they can be found in most discount stores.

+ **Fantasy decorations:** Does your vibe include fairies, mermaids, dragons, and more? You'd be amazed how many of these things you can find at a low price!

+ **Battery-operated fairy lights:** String them around your altar, above your bed, or in your bathroom for a magical feel.

+ **Herbal teas:** Your tea doesn't have to come from a fancy store to be effective—find a blend that matches your magical intention, and brew it up for a delicious warm beverage while you focus on your spell or ritual. There's a selection of my favorite combinations in chapter 9.

+ **Craft supplies:** Pick up yarn, paintable wood, paper and vinyl for cutting machines, art canvases, straw and cinnamon brooms, and ribbons on the cheap for some crafty witchery.

Foraging

I love finding random stuff just lying around. Not that I'm going around rooting through other people's garbage cans every Wednesday morning when it's trash day, but if I'm out driving or walking around and I see something that looks interesting, moderately clean, and usable? Yeah. I might just pull over and bring it home with me. After all, I figure our ancestors used whatever they stumbled across, so I reckon I'm carrying on an old tradition.

Keep in mind that if you're foraging natural items like plants, you should only collect items that have either already fallen to the ground or those that you can take without causing damage to the remaining items nearby. I try to never harvest more than 10 percent of the growth of a plant I've found in the wild—that leaves plenty for the birds and other animals in the area to eat, and it also ensures the patch will continue to thrive year over year. Additionally, if you're going to handle, eat, or otherwise ingest something you've foraged, be sure to use a reliable plant identification guide. Nothing ruins a ritual faster than suddenly realizing you've poisoned yourself by using something dangerous in your herbal tea.

Some of the things I've collected over the years:

+ **Flowerpots:** Perfect for painting with magical symbols and growing herbs and flowers.

+ **Baby food jars:** I found an entire case of them, washed and rinsed, sitting at the end of someone's driveway with a "free stuff" sign. They're awesome for storing magical goodies in.

+ **Beach items, like seashells, driftwood, and dried seaweed:** Use them items in rituals related to water magic, for healing workings, or to honor deities related to the sea. You can even write the name of something or someone you'd like to banish on a shell or piece of wood and return it to the ocean.

+ **Two full sets of tires:** Someone had discarded them on one of the hiking trail access roads in the forest by my house, so I picked them up, brought them home (it took me two trips), and cleaned and painted them. They're now stacked in my yard, filled with soil, and I use my tire towers as three separate raised garden beds for magical herbs.

+ **Rocks, interesting leaves, acorns, twigs, plants, and pine cones:** These natural items can be used in just about anything. Dry out plant material you've found in your neighborhood and blend your own home-based magical incense. I live in the northern foothills of Appalachia, and there is a lot of biodiversity here. I've harvested mullein, chicory, wild oregano, hawthorn spikes, purple coneflower, yarrow, angelica, and more.

+ **Animal items such as bones, antler sheds, and the occasional snakeskin:** We have plenty of snakes here, so finding a discarded skin is a regular thing for me. One time, my partner was coming off a hiking trail and found an entire tanned and treated fox pelt—we have *no* idea how it came to be there, but as you can probably imagine, it soon made its way to my house.

Learning to Barter, Make, and Improvise

I've been a practicing witch since about 1987, and if you do the math, it's pretty clear I've been at it for a long time. Over the years, I've acquired plenty of magical tools and supplies, from books to herbs to candles to décor, that I loved when I got them. But over time, I realized I wasn't actually *using* all of them. This was when I started giving things away.

And if I've learned one thing about the magical community, it's that when you give someone something, often they give you something in return. It's not out of any expectation or obligation—that makes a gift something other than a gift—but more because many of us feel an exchange of energy is a good thing. So, I might give someone that extra jar of dried mugwort that I didn't need, and a few weeks later I'd bump into them at an event and they'd say, *Oh, I'm so glad you're here. I have a crystal I want to give you!* Or a person would present me with a lovely thing they'd carved from wood, and I'd be appropriately grateful… and the next time I crocheted a scarf I'd tie off the final stitch and realize it was perfect for that same individual. Sometimes, exchanges happen organically, as in the two cases I just mentioned. Other times, they can be organized.

Have you ever thought about putting together a magical swap meet? You can keep it limited to specific items—books or herbs, for instance—or you can open it up to just about any kind of witchy thing, from crystals to statuary to candles and so on. If you've got a solid magical community near you—or even if it's just you and four or five friends—why not plan a get together in which everyone brings the things that no longer serve them magically? Everyone can swap stuff, and each person will get to take home something new while eliminating the things they don't use or want anymore.

You can also make your own magical items when you don't have the exact thing you need on hand. Now, obviously, there are going to be some things you might not have the skill or time or resources to make—most of us don't have the wherewithal to create a cast-iron cauldron of our own, or you may not have a sewing machine to craft your own ritual robe. But there are plenty of other ways you can make your own items. However, just to give you a few things to think about, some items that are fairly simple to make include altar cloths, poppets or magical dolls, candleholders (and candles themselves if you've got access to wax), and spell jars.

Finally, one of the hallmarks of a truly competent practitioner is the ability to adapt and improvise. Don't have any lavender on hand for that healing spell you want to do? Fine. What other healing herbs do you have available? Do you have angelica or dandelion or fennel? Could you use a crystal instead, such as citrine, amethyst, or clear quartz? Perhaps you've read about a spell that requires a photo of the person it's aimed at and … you don't have a photo. Is there something else you could use as a magical link, such as a business card, a piece of clothing, or a screenshot of their social media profile? Learning to think in new ways, with natural curiosity, is one of the most valuable abilities you can develop as a practitioner of magic.

Magical Tools for Home-Based Magic

When you first begin studying Paganism, witchcraft, or just about any other form of metaphysical spirituality, you're going to run into a lot of lists of tools. Many times these are painted as must-haves, and you might find yourself thinking, "Well, I don't have all nine of these tools that this book said I need, so I guess I just can't do magic yet." I can't begin to tell you how many times people have come up to me and said they'd like to practice but they *didn't have the tools.* Plot twist: You don't actually need tools to practice witchcraft or to celebrate your deities. Tools are just that—tools. They certainly can make things easier by helping us focus our minds on the tasks at hand, but they're not a hard-and-fast requirement.

However, I'd be remiss if we didn't at least talk about some of the most popular tools found in modern magical practice—but let's also look at things you can use if you don't have access to the traditional versions. Do you need every single one of these? Absolutely not. Will they make it easier to follow some spell instructions? Sometimes, yes. Other times, maybe not. You're the only one who can decide what you need for your practice, because it's as unique as you are. Before you use an item—whether it's the traditional version or a substitution— cleanse or consecrate it for magical use.

Altar Cloth

In witchcraft, an altar cloth serves as a significant and versatile tool. The purpose of an altar cloth extends beyond its aesthetic appeal, because it's both practical and symbolic. You can use your altar cloth to designate a sacred and consecrated space—one minute your coffee table is just a coffee table, but once you've cleansed the space and added an altar cloth, it's an altar. For many practitioners, the choice of fabric, color, and design can carry specific magical meanings, aligning with magical intentions and the nature of the working. The altar cloth can also serve as something of a barrier, separating the mundane from the magical, helping you focus your energy and intention during spellwork or ceremonies. Additionally, on a practical level, it serves as a protective layer for the flat surface of the altar, protecting it from things like drippy wax, leaky oils, and more.

Substitutions: Lengths of pretty fabric, large scarves or pashminas, fiber materials that hold special meaning to you or your family

Athame

Traditionally, the athame is a double-edged daggerlike blade with a black handle, though variations exist. Its primary purpose lies in directing and manipulating energy during magical workings. You can use an athame to cast circles, invoke the elements, or channel intention and focus. Historically, the athame represents the element of fire and the power of transformation and the will. It's typically not used for physical cutting but rather as a metaphysical instrument, cutting through energetic barriers and boundaries. Through its use, the athame becomes an extension of our personal energy, enhancing our ability to harness and direct magical forces.

Substitutions: The pointer finger on your dominant hand, a kitchen knife, or some other sharp-bladed instrument

Besom/Broom

Symbolizing purification, the besom, or broom, is often employed in ritualistic sweeping to cleanse and prepare a sacred space before magical workings or ceremonies. Witches use the besom to symbolically "sweep away" negative energies, creating a clean and consecrated area for spellcraft. The besom is also associated with the element of air, representing communication and the power of the mind. You can even move your broom in sweeping motions to raise and direct energy, making it a versatile tool for spellcasting.

Substitutions: A brush, a cluster of lightweight twigs wrapped together, a feather, or make your own as outlined in chapter 2

Candles/Incense

Candles and incense are super-useful elements in witchcraft, serving diverse purposes. Candles are often chosen for their color and corresponding elemental associations, and they can help us focus intent and harness energy. They symbolize the illumination of knowledge, spiritual insight, and the presence of the Divine. The act of lighting candles can also mark the beginning of a magical working, creating a sacred space and enhancing concentration. Incense, with its aromatic smoke, holds similar importance. It not only pleases the senses but also serves as a vehicle to carry prayers, intentions, and magical workings into the ethereal realm. However, candles and incense are items that many people are unable to use for a variety of reasons—perhaps you or someone in your home has allergies or fragrance sensitivities, or maybe you live in a place where you're unable to have an open flame.

Substitutions: Battery-operated tealights, wax melts, diffusers, aromatic oils

Cauldron

Serving as a vessel for transformation, the cauldron is deeply associated with the element of water; its rounded shape symbolizes the cyclical nature of life, death, and rebirth. You can use cauldrons in a variety of rituals and spellwork, such as brewing potions, scrying, and creating sacred brews. Two of my favorite uses for a cauldron are holding lit candles or burning petition papers in, as an iron cauldron is a firesafe vessel. The cauldron is a symbol of the transformative and nurturing powers inherent in the craft, and it can be a focal point for combining and melding elements. The act of stirring within the cauldron in one direction or another can help us manifest change.

Substitutions: A cast-iron pan, any type of fireproof dish

Chalice

Often crafted from materials such as silver, pewter, or glass, the chalice is employed as a ritual vessel for holding and consecrating liquids, most commonly water or wine, during ceremonies and magical workings. It symbolizes abundance and spiritual nourishment. The act of consecrating and drinking from the chalice can help build a connection with the energies invoked by way of ritual or spellwork. Through the use of a chalice, you can attune yourself to the endless flow of life, love, and spiritual insight, deepening your connection to the Divine.

Substitutions: A cup, glass, or other drinking vessel

Offering Plate/Dish

If you want to make an offering to your deities, ancestors, or household spirits, it's a good idea to have a designated dish for this, particularly if you're presenting food. The offering plate serves as a ceremonial vessel for presenting gifts and can symbolize the reciprocal nature of your relationship. Offerings placed on the plate can vary widely, from herbs and food to crystals or representations of personal intentions. Using a dedicated dish or plate helps to create a tangible link between us and the spiritual world.

Substitutions: Any clean dish, ideally made of ceramic, glass, or wood

Staff

The staff is used to direct and channel energy during rituals, ceremonies, and spellwork, acting as an extension of the practitioner's will and helping to focus intention. It can be plain, or it can be adorned with symbols, crystals, or other correspondences to enhance its potency and align with specific magical purposes. Beyond its functional aspects, the staff represents spiritual authority, personal power, and the connection between the earthly and the Divine. Whether used for casting circles, invoking energies, or directing spells, the staff becomes a conduit for our energy and intentions.

Substitutions: A large stick, broom handle, or your dominant hand with your arm extended

Statues of Deity

If you work with a specific deity—or deities—you may want to have them represented on your altar space during ritual. One of the best ways to do this can be with statuary—but that can get expensive! Statues serve as physical embodiments of the Divine, acting as conduits through which we can invoke, honor, and commune with the deities they represent via rituals, offerings, or simply the act of gazing upon the statue. For many of us, these sacred images become focal points for meditation, prayer, and spellwork.

Substitutions: Your own drawings, figures created from clay or wood, or images printed on paper

Wand

Symbolizing the element of air and the power of intention, the wand is used to direct, focus, and amplify energy during rituals and spellcasting. Wands can be crafted from various materials, each with its own magical associations, and often become personalized extensions of the practitioner's energy and will. You might wish to inscribe or adorn your wand with symbols, crystals, or other correspondences. The sweeping, swishing motions of the wand through the air help shape and direct energy. This tool allows us to connect the earthly realm with the spiritual, navigate the realms of the unseen, and forge a link between ourselves and the sacred.

Substitutions: A stick, the pointer finger on your nondominant hand, a wooden kitchen spoon

Cleansing Your New Stuff

Your magical tools don't wield incredible power—that comes from *you*—but they may arrive in your possession tinged with energies from their previous adventures. Cleansing your tools is an essential practice in the craft, much like washing a new mug before pouring that first cup of coffee into it.

Here's why: Every magical tool carries remnants of the energies it encountered, be they from the hands that crafted it or the places it journeyed. Clearing these residual vibrations will help attune the tool to your energy and intentions, but more importantly, it can liberate the instrument from any lingering negative influences. Cleansing your tools isn't a complicated process, but for many of us, it's a necessary one.

Elemental Cleansing Ritual

When you bring new magical items into your home, you can do a simple elemental ritual for cleansing. This is one I've used for ages, and I've found it highly effective. You'll need:

- Your magical tools to be cleansed
- A small dish of salt or soil
- Incense or feathers
- A white candle
- Matches or a lighter
- A bowl of water

Begin by designating a space where you can perform the ritual undisturbed. Light the candle and set it at the center of your workspace. Place your tools in front of you, arranging them in a way that feels natural and respectful. Hold your hands above them, closing your eyes and feeling their natural vibrations. Say, *I send away all negativity, I cast out any energy of sadness, anger, hate, or discontent from these tools.*

Open your eyes. Take the dish of salt or soil and sprinkle a small amount over the tools, saying, *With the power of earth, I cleanse and ground these tools, purifying them for my magical work.* Wave the incense or feathers around the tools, allowing the smoke to envelop them if you're using incense, and say, *By the breath of air, I bless and infuse these tools with clarity and intuition, aligning them with my sacred purpose.*

Carefully pass each tool over the flame of the candle, or if safe, gently run the flame over the surface of the tools. Say, *Through the flame of fire, I ignite and empower these tools, awakening their magical potential.* Finally, dip your fingers into the bowl of water and sprinkle droplets over the tools as you say, *In the waters of life, I consecrate and purify these tools, charging them with the flow of magic.*

Once each element has been invoked, hold your hands over the tools once more. Say, *I claim these tools as my own, with positive energy and a grateful heart, and will use them for my highest purpose.* Meditate for a few more moments, and allow yourself to feel a sense of completion and connection to your consecrated magical tools. When you're done, store your tools in a place of honor at or near your altar if possible.

Remember that witchcraft is uniquely personal, so feel free to adapt this ritual to resonate with your own beliefs and spiritual practices.

SIMPLE CLEANSING PRACTICES

If you don't have time to do a full ritual, don't panic! There are a number of simple cleansing practices you can use for various tools. Try one of these if you need to cleanse a tool with minimal effort.

- Pass your tools through the smoke of cleansing herbs like sage or mugwort to clear away residual energies. Alternately, place them in a dish of dried purification herbs, cover them, and allow them to sit overnight.

- Give your tools a moonlight bath—leave them out under the light of a full moon to absorb its purifying energy.

- Allow your tools to bask in the sun's rays to recharge and revitalize their energies.

- Bury your tools in a bowl of salt or sprinkle salt over them to absorb negative energies. Be sure to clean the tools afterward to remove the salt. Only use this method if you know the item won't be damaged by exposure to salt.

- Use singing bowls, bells, chimes, or even your voice to create sound vibrations to clear and refresh the tools' energies.

- Place your tools on a bed of cleansing crystals like clear quartz or selenite to absorb negative energies and restore their vibrancy.

+ Use consecrated oils to anoint your tools, taking advantage of the oils' cleansing properties. Again, only use this method if you know the item won't be damaged by contact with oil.

Color Magic in Your Home

One of my favorite cost-effective ways to make magic in my home is with color—and you can use it in so many different ways, from mindfully choosing wall paint to adding a quirky tablecloth or a plant with flowers in a very specific shade. So, before you go out and stock up on blankets, pillows, and wall art to decorate with, let's talk about color magic. Each color has its own unique set of magical correspondences, so keep that in mind when you're decorating your home. If you want a calming, soothing space, choose colors that are tranquil and relaxing, not high energy. Likewise, if you'd like your space to inspire joy, select colors that reflect that. Also, don't be afraid to experiment by combining multiple colors in the same space. If watermelon pink combined with neon green makes your heart happy, go for it, and don't let anyone tell you it's wrong!

+ **Red:** Shades of red—and that includes deep tones like plum and burgundy—can invigorate energy, power, and passion. Use red to inspire confidence and assertiveness. This color family is sensual and sexy, which is why we often see it in bedrooms. If it seems a bit too much, balance the red with something neutral and light, like cream.

- **Pink:** Available in everything from a pale pastel to an effervescent Malibu Barbie's Dream House shade, pink is associated with romance, sweetness, and friendship. It can be valuable in promoting a feeling of domestic harmony, nurturing love of family, and positive bonds.

- **Orange:** If you're a creative spirit—an artist, musician, writer, or maker of any sort—orange might be the color for you. Try different shades of orange to bring about a connection to your muse, spark the creative fires, and stimulate exuberant energy.

- **Yellow:** It's nearly impossible to look at yellow and not feel happy! Whether you like a pale, soft shade or a bold, sunny tone, yellow can bring out joy in any room. It's tied to mental stimulation as well, so if you want to feel energetic all over—mind, body, and spirit—give yellows a whirl.

- **Green:** In magic, green often represents abundance, but it can also inspire a sense of stability. If you want to connect with the rooms in your home on a deeper level and feel calm and relaxed at the same time, varying shades of green might be the colors for you.

- **Blue:** Traditionally, blue is a color of healing, and in its many forms can add a sense of serenity. While light blue is calming, darker blues can represent responsibility and wisdom. In some magical folkloric traditions, blue is used to keep evil spirits and negativity away, such as with the evil eye protection symbol and the use of "haint blue" in the Lowcountry of the southern United States on porch ceilings.

+ **Purple:** Purple is a popular color in the witchy community, and there may well be a reason for it. It's not just pretty—it's the color of intention and manifestation as well as spiritual growth and development. If you've got a dedicated space in your home for spellcrafting and ritual work, purple could be the perfect addition to that zone.

+ **White:** A plain white color doesn't have to be boring—it's associated with cleanliness and purification as well as our higher truth. If your style is more of a minimalist vibe, white might be just the right color to incorporate into your space. Even a little bit of white, strategically placed, can complement other colors.

+ **Black:** Typically associated with magical purposes like banishing and protection, black can be a power color as well—it expresses a feeling of prestige, discipline, and sophistication. If you're not quite ready to go for a fully black space, blend it in combination with other colors for offset.

+ **Brown and tan:** Earth tones like brown and tan are perfect for giving your space the feel-good vibe of a natural sanctuary. Brown is the color of hearth and home—and of nature itself. It's grounding and mature, and it can provide an environment that feels rich and meaningful but, at the same time, unpretentious.

+ **Gold and silver:** Think about accessories and accents in gold and silver—they're a great way to bring a connection to the Divine into your life. Silver is the color of the moon and often represents the sacred feminine, while gold symbolizes the sun and masculine energy. If you're looking for a harmonious balance between the two, add a bit of both!

When I bought my cottage, it was just…meh. Sometime in what was probably the late 1980s, a previous owner decided the entire first floor would benefit from being covered in fake wood paneling. All the rooms had a dark, gloomy feel—but I saw the potential and possibilities that could be had. Before I even moved a single piece of furniture in, I knew I had to bring the whole place to life with bright, vibrant color, comforting textures, a variety of fabrics, and a cozy, magical aesthetic. I painted my living room and hallway a lovely butternut squash color, the bedroom a bright, sunny yellow, and my office a calming sage green. Within just a few days, the whole house was transformed from boring and blah to uplifting, welcoming, and warm.

You might not be able to paint your walls—perhaps you're renting or living in a dorm, or you know you'll be selling your home and you've followed your realtor's advice to keep everything neutral. If that's the case, don't worry—you can still bring the magic of color correspondences into your home in other ways.

- **Textiles:** Do you like blankets? I love them! I've got them all over the place and in a variety of fabrics— there are some vintage quilts, a few handmade crocheted pieces, and soft, fuzzy fleeces. They're in a number of different colors, nuzzled up against the backs of chairs, draped across the couch, and displayed on an old wooden ladder I found at an antique mall. I also use scarves as décor, covering plain tabletops with a splash of color and whimsy. Pillows serve a similar purpose—I probably have more throw pillows than I need, but I love the way they stand out and add an extra dimension to my space.

+ **Vessels:** I adore anything I can put other things in, so I have a collection of colorful thrifted bottles, jars, bowls, and boxes that double as storage for smaller items. If you like baskets, get a few of those and either fill them with treasures or hang them on your walls for a unique and fun display.

+ **Candles:** Colored candles are obviously useful in spellwork and ritual, but that doesn't mean you need to hide them away from prying eyes. Place a few in your favorite magical colors around the house in decorative holders; a few arranged on a tabletop or shelf can help draw the eye upward and add a pop of brightness.

+ **Wall art:** My hallway is decorated with what I call my Thrifted & Gifted collection of plant art. It's a long wall adorned with paintings and drawings of flowers and herbs that have either been presented to me as gifts or found in a thrift store or yard sale (I set a rule for myself that I'd only hang things on this wall if they cost me under fifteen dollars). They're in a variety of sizes, arranged closely together, and turn an otherwise uninteresting hallway into a small nature-focused art gallery. If you're crafty, consider making some of your own magical wall art to display, or ask the people you love the most to create something just for you.

+ **Plants:** If you love plants, fill your space with them! Plants are more than just blobs of greenery scattered around your home; flowering plants in plenty of different colors are available in many places. Additionally, you can decorate the pots as you see fit. If you have pets or tiny humans in your home, make sure you check to see if the plants are safe, or put them someplace where they're out of reach to anyone who might want to nibble them.

Conclusion
PUTTING IT ALL TOGETHER

House, apartment, dormitory, camper, ranch, sailboat—whatever it may be, it's your home. Whether it's shared with others or you bask in solitude, it's your sanctuary. Your home is where you eat, sleep, laugh, and love. It's where you create and maintain relationships with the people who matter the most to you, and it's where you take extra time to care for yourself. Your home is an expression of your tastes and emotions, and it reflects every bit of who you are as a person. Why *wouldn't* you want to keep it sacred and magical?

As you're making magic around your home, don't be afraid to try new things. We've all made plenty of magical mistakes—but that's how we learn and grow. As you've worked your way through this book, I hope you've kept an open mind—after all, in magic (as with many other aspects of life), what works for one person might not work for the next. While I've shared many of the things I've learned over the past several decades of practice, *you* know your practice far better than I ever will. It's why I encourage you to be creative and think in unconventional ways—if I've suggested something that you don't think will be effective in your situation, that's totally okay. You get to put on your witchy thinking cap and come up with an even better alternative that will offer you a solution.

Wherever you live, in whatever kind of home, I'm confident you have the ability to make it just the kind of sacred, magical space you want. Remember that you're a magical being, and you deserve to live in a place that is happy, harmonious, safe, and blessed. With a little reflection, some insight, and a sprinkle of pixie dust, your home is going to be the most magical place on earth.

Appendix
MAGICAL HOME CORRESPONDENCES

L ook around your home, at some of the mundane items, and think about what you see. What magical attributes can you assign to the non-magical things you have on hand? Here are several of my favorites to get started—many of these are a direct result of the Household Magic workshop I referenced way back in the beginning, and they are some great examples of clever ideas that workshop attendees came up with on their own.

Symbolism or Correspondence	Items in Your Home
Communication	Feather, journal, pen or pencil, bell, tea leaves, stationary, stamp, envelope, dictionary, map, writing desk, echoing sound
Healing/rejuvenation	First aid kit, adhesive bandages, prescription bottles, a set of scrubs, blanket, cozy socks, tea mug, mandala, yoga mat or block, humidifier, anatomical model, battery
Protection	Padlock, mirror facing outward, key, horseshoe, bell, security camera
Love and attraction	Heart symbols, magnet, dove, a book of poetry, knotwork, apples, jewelry, candle, romance novel, chocolate
Money and prosperity	Coin jar, cornucopia, globe, checkbook, financial planning book, family heirloom
Transformation/change	Butterfly décor, kaleidoscope, feathers, hourglass, puzzle game, compass
Banishing and binding	Black mirror, iron item, cord, tape, string, yarn, glue, salt water, doll

Finally, here are fifty items commonly found in a home, with potential magical correspondences.

1. **Artwork:** Creative expression, inspiration, and channels for magical energies

2. **Backpacks/bags:** Carrying intentions, desires, or magical tools

3. **Batteries:** Energy sources, power, and amplification of magical workings

4. **Bedsheets:** Rest, rejuvenation, and the realm of dreams and subconscious energies

5. **Books:** Knowledge, wisdom, and the gateway to different realms of understanding

6. **Candles:** Light, focus, and intention setting in magical workings

7. **Chargers:** Rejuvenation and energy replenishment for devices

8. **Clocks:** The cyclical nature of time, cycles, and phases in life

9. **Coasters:** Protection against unwanted energies, shields for surfaces

10. **Cooking utensils:** Tools for mixing and blending energies, symbolizing manifestation and creation

11. **Curtains:** Veils between worlds, privacy, and shielding from outside influences

12. **Cutlery:** The power to sever ties or connections when needed

13. **First aid kit:** Healing, restoration, and providing aid to oneself or others

14. **Flashlight:** Illumination, revealing hidden truths or energies in the dark

15. **Glasses:** Perception, clarity, and the ability to see beyond the mundane

16. **Glue:** Bonding, healing rifts, or joining energies

17. **Keys:** Unlocking mysteries, opportunities, and protection against unwanted entry

18. **Lamps:** Illumination, enlightenment, and invoking energies in the dark

19. **Locks:** Containment, protection, and safeguarding energies

20. **Matches/lighter:** Ignition, the beginning of rituals, and activation of energies

21. **Mirrors:** Reflection, divination, and revealing truths hidden from plain sight

22. **Notebooks/journals:** Capturing thoughts, setting intentions, and recording magical workings

23. **Pens and pencils:** Creation, manifestation, and casting intentions

24. **Photographs:** Memories and moments frozen in time, carrying personal energy

25. **Picture frames:** Capturing energies and memories, preserving moments

26. **Pillows:** Comfort, support, and receptivity to dream messages

27. **Planters/pots:** Containers for cultivating energies, nurturing growth

28. **Plants:** Nature's energy, growth, and connection to earth-based magic

29. **Plates:** Nourishment, abundance, and the ability to provide and share

30. **Pots and pans:** Transformation and alchemy in the kitchen, symbolizing change and adaptability

31. **Remote controls:** Control, commanding energies or devices

32. **Rugs:** Grounding, protection, and delineation of sacred spaces within the home

33. **Saltshaker:** Purification, protection, and warding off negative energies; salt is a potent tool for creating barriers and banishing unwanted influences.

34. **Scissors:** Cutting cords, severing connections, or boundaries

35. **Sewing kit:** Binding, stitching together energies or intentions

36. **Soap:** Cleansing and purification of oneself or objects

37. **Stationery:** Creative outlets, scripting intentions, and manifestation

38. **Storage boxes:** Containment of energies or intentions, safeguarding magical tools

39. **Sunglasses:** Concealment, hiding intentions or emotions

40. **Tape:** Binding or joining energies, sealing intentions

41. **Toilet paper:** Release, banishing, and removal of negative energies

42. **Toiletries:** Cleansing and purification, maintaining personal energy and hygiene

43. **Toothbrushes:** Protection, particularly against negative influences on speech

44. **Towels:** Cleansing, purification, and drying away residual energies

45. **Trash bags:** Containment, banishing, and disposal of unwanted energies

46. **Trash cans:** Release, letting go, and the removal of negative energies

47. **Umbrellas:** Protection, shielding, and warding against negative influences

48. **Vases:** Containment of energy or intentions in a vessel, also symbolize growth and life force in flowers

49. **Wall decorations:** Personal symbols, wards, or sigils for protection and intention setting

50. **Wine or water glasses:** Communion, celebration, and raising energy; they can be used for rituals, toasting intentions, or channeling energies during ceremonies.

RECOMMENDED READING

Blackthorn's Protection Magic: A Witch's Guide to Mental and Physical Self-Defense by Amy Blackthorn

Cottage Witchery: Natural Magick for Hearth and Home by Ellen Dugan

Easy Organic Gardening and Moon Planting by Lyn Bagnall

The Element Encyclopedia of 20,000 Dreams: The Ultimate A–Z to Interpret the Secrets of Your Dreams by Theresa Cheung

Everyday Magic: Spells & Rituals for Modern Living by Dorothy Morrison

Garden Witchery: Magick from the Ground Up by Ellen Dugan

The Magical Household: Empower Your Home with Love, Protection, Health and Happiness by Scott Cunningham and David Harrington

The Magick of Food: Rituals, Offerings & Why We Eat Together by Gwion Raven

Sacred Smoke: Clear Away Negative Energies and Purify Body, Mind, and Spirit by Amy Blackthorn

Sigil Witchery: A Witch's Guide to Crafting Magick Symbols by Laura Tempest Zakroff

Soapmaking: A Magickal Guide by Alicia Grosso

A Treasury of American Indian Herbs: Their Lore and Their Use for Food, Drugs, and Medicine by Virginia Scully

BIBLIOGRAPHY

Ashkenazi, Michael. *Handbook of Japanese Mythology*. Santa Barbara, CA: ABC-CLIO, 2003.

Auset, Priestess Brandi. *The Goddess Guide: Exploring the Attributes and Correspondences of the Divine Feminine.* Woodbury, MN: Llewellyn Publications, 2009.

Cassidy, Cody. "Who Discovered Soap? What to Know about the Origins of the Life-Saving Substance." Time. May 5, 2020. https://time.com/5831828/soap-origins/.

Cunningham, Scott, and David Harrington. *The Magical Household: Spells & Rituals for the Home*. Woodbury, MN: Llewellyn Publications, 1983.

Donmoyer, Patrick J. "Hex Signs: Sacred and Celestial Symbolism in Pennsylvania Dutch Barn Stars." Glencairn Museum. March 22, 2019. https://www.glencairnmuseum.org/newsletter/2019/3/19/hex-signs-sacred-and-celestial-symbolism-in-pennsylvania-dutch-barn-stars.

"Eternal Fire." Indo-European Connection. November 16, 2020. https://www.indo-european-connection.com/religion/customs/eternal-fire.

Faye. "The Pantheon: Korean Gods and Goddesses." Korea By Me. https://koreabyme.com/the-pantheon-korean-gods-and -goddesses/.

Hunter, MaryCarol R., Brenda W. Gillespie, and Sophie Yu-Pu Chen. "Urban Nature Experiences Reduce Stress in the Context of Daily Life Based on Salivary Biomarkers." *Frontiers in Psychology* 10 (April 2019). https://doi.org/10.3389/fpsyg .2019.00722.

Jordan, Kyle. "Bes: Ancient Egyptian God, Fighter, Dancer, Companion." Ashmolean Museum. Accessed December 18, 2023. https://www.ashmolean.org/article/bes-ancient -egyptian-god-fighter-dancer-companion.

King, Charles. "The Organization of Roman Religious Beliefs." *Classical Antiquity* 22, no. 2 (October 2003): 275–312. https://doi.org/10.1525/ca.2003.22.2.275.

Leafar, Elhoim. *The Magical Art of Crafting Charm Bags: 100 Mystical Formulas for Success, Love, Wealth, and Wellbeing.* Newburyport, MA: Weiser Books, 2017.

Meier, Allison C. "Is There a Witch Bottle in Your House?" JSTOR Daily. May 13, 2019. https://daily.jstor.org/is -there-a-witch-bottle-in-your-house/.

Monaghan, Patricia. *Encyclopedia of Goddesses & Heroines.* Novato, CA: New World Library, 2014. Kindle.

"Native Land." Native Land Digital. Accessed November 25, 2023. https://native-land.ca/.

Ó Crualaoich, Gearóid. "Continuity and Adaptation in Legends of Cailleach Bhéarra." *Béaloideas* 56 (1988): 153–78. https://doi .org/10.2307/20522313.

Ogden, Daniel. *Magic, Witchcraft, and Ghosts in the Greek and Roman Worlds*. New York: Oxford University Press, 2002.

Pamita, Madame. *Baba Yaga's Book of Witchcraft: Slavic Magic from the Witch of the Woods*. Woodbury, MN: Llewellyn Publications, 2022.

Parks, Shoshi. "What the Color 'Haint Blue' Means to the Descendants of Enslaved Africans." Atlas Obscura. January 14, 2020. https://www.atlasobscura.com/articles/what-haint-blue -means-to-descendants-enslaved-africans.

"Soaps & Detergents History." The American Cleaning Institute (ACI). Accessed November 11, 2023. https://www .cleaninginstitute.org/understanding-products/why -clean/soaps-detergents-history.

Tennyson, Alfred. "The Lady of Shalott (1832)." Poetry Foundation. https://www.poetryfoundation.org/poems /45359/the-lady-of-shalott-1832.

Thrope, Samuel. "Magic Bowls of Antiquity." Aeon. May 24, 2016. https://aeon.co/essays/what-should-be-done-with -the-magic-bowls-of-jewish-babylonia.

Tuite, Kevin. "'Antimarriage' in Ancient Georgian Society." *Anthropological Linguistics* 42, no. 1 (2000): 37–60. http://www.jstor.org/stable/30028744.

Weatherstone, Lunaea. *Tending Brigid's Flame: Awaken to the Celtic Goddess of Hearth, Temple, and Forge.* Woodbury, MN: Llewellyn Publications, 2015.

Yoshimura, Ayako. "To Believe *and* Not to Believe: A Native Ethnography of Kanashibari in Japan." *Journal of American Folklore* 128, no. 508 (Spring 2015): 146–48. https://doi.org/10.5406/jamerfolk.128.508.0146.

INDEX

B